SPARKNOTES™

5 Practice Tests for the SAT II Math IIC

2003 Edition

Editorial Director Justin Kestler

Executive Editor Ben Florman

Managing Editor Vince Janoski

Technical Director Tammy Hepps

Series Editor John Crowther

Editor Anthony Keene

Contributing Editor Jen Chu

This edition published by Spark Publishing.

Spark Publishing
A Division of SparkNotes LLC
120 Fifth Avenue, 8th Floor
New York, NY 10011

Please submit all comments and questions or report errors to www.sparknotes.com/errors

Library of Congress information available upon request

Printed and bound in Canada

ISBN 1-58663-869-6

SparkNotes is neither affiliated with nor endorsed by Harvard University.

Welcome to SparkNotes Test Preparation

IF YOU WANT TO SCORE HIGH ON THE SAT II MATH IIC, YOU NEED TO KNOW more than just the material—you need to know how to take the test. Practice tests are the most effective method for learning the ins and outs of the test. But practice tests that accurately reflect the actual SAT II Math IIC have been hard to find—until now. *5 More Practice Tests for the SAT II Math IIC* is the first book anywhere dedicated to giving you accurate practice tests so you can perfect your test-taking skills. This book contains:

- **Five full-length SAT II Math IIC tests.** The practice tests in this book are the most accurate, true-to-life tests available. Our experts, who've been teaching the SAT II Math IIC for years, researched the exam extensively so they could give you tests that reflect exactly what you'll see at the test center. Our tests replicate the format and content of the actual test so closely that nothing will catch you off guard on test day.

- **Clear, helpful explanations for every question—so you can study smarter.** Our explanations do more than tell you the right answer—they identify flaws in your thinking and show you exactly what topics you need to work on. We help you pinpoint your weaknesses, so you can make your studying more efficient by going straight to the stuff you need to review.

- **Specific, proven strategies for the SAT II Math IIC.** We give you smart, easy strategies on the best ways to guess, pace yourself, and find shortcuts to answers. These strategies help you maximize your score by showing you how to avoid the test's traps and turn the test's format to your own advantage.

Contents

Orientation

Practice Tests

Orientation

Introduction to the SAT II Tests

T HE SAT II SUBJECT TESTS ARE CREATED and administered by the College Board and the Educational Testing Service (ETS), the two organizations responsible for producing the dreaded SAT I (usually referrred to simply as the SAT). The SAT II Subject Tests were created to serve as complements to the SAT I. Whereas the three-hour-long SAT I seeks to test your critical thinking skills through math and verbal questions, the one-hour SAT II tests examine your knowledge about particular subjects, such as math, writing, and biology.

In our opinion, the SAT II Subject Tests are better tests than the SAT I because they cover clearly defined topics rather than an ambiguous set of critical thinking skills. However, just because the SAT II Subject Tests do a better job of testing your knowledge than the SAT I does, they are not necessarily easier. A "better" test is not always "better for you" in terms of how easy it will be or how much you have to study.

In comparison to the SAT I, there are good and bad things about the SAT II Subject Tests.

The Good

- Because SAT II Subject Tests cover actual topics like math, biology, and writing, you can effectively study for them. If you don't know a topic in mathematics, such as how to interpret the graph of a parabola, you can easily look it up and learn it. For this reason, the SAT II tests are straightforward tests: if you know your stuff, you will do well.

- Often, the classes you've taken in school have already prepared you well for the test. If you've taken two years of algebra, a year of geometry, and a trigonometry or precalculus course, you will have studied most of the topics on the SAT II Math IIC.

- In preparing for the Math, History, and Chemistry SAT II tests, you really are learning math, history, and chemistry. In other words, you are gaining valuable, even interesting knowledge. You might actually find the process of studying for an SAT II test to be worthwhile and gratifying. Few can say the same about studying for the SAT I.

The Bad

- Because SAT II Subject Tests quiz you on specific knowledge, it is much harder to "beat" or "outsmart" them than it is to outsmart the SAT I. On the SAT I, you can use all sorts of tricks or strategies to figure out an answer. There are far fewer strategies to help you on the SAT II. Don't get us wrong: having test-taking skills will help you on an SAT II, but knowing the subject will help you much more. To do well on the SAT II, you can't just rely on your natural smarts and wits. You need to study.

Colleges and the SAT II Subject Tests

Why would you take an SAT II Subject Test? There's only one reason: colleges want you to, and sometimes require you to.

Colleges care about SAT II Subject Tests for two related reasons. First, the tests demonstrate your interest, knowledge, and skill in specific topics. Second, because SAT II tests are standardized, they show how your skills in math (or biology or writing) measure up to the skills of high school students nationwide. The grades you get in high school don't offer such a measurement to colleges: some high schools are more difficult than others, meaning that students of equal ability might receive different grades from different schools. SAT II tests provide colleges with a yardstick against which colleges can measure your, and every other applicant's, knowledge and skills.

When it comes down to it, colleges like the SAT II tests because the tests make the colleges' job easier. The tests are the colleges' tool. But because you know how colleges use the SAT II, you can make the tests your tool as well. SAT II tests allow colleges to easily compare you to other applicants. This means that the SAT II tests provide you with an excellent chance to shine. If you got a 93 in a math class, and some kid in another high school across the country got a 91, colleges won't know how to evaluate the scores. They don't know whose class was harder or whose teacher was a tough grader or whose high school inflates grades. But if you get a 720 on the SAT II Math IIC, and that other kid gets a 650, colleges will recognize the difference in your scores.

The Importance of SAT II Tests in College Applications

Time for some perspective: SAT II tests are *not* the primary tools that colleges use to decide whether to admit an applicant. High school grades, extracurricular activities, and SAT or ACT scores are all more important to colleges than your scores on SAT II tests. If you take AP tests, those scores will also be more important to colleges than your SAT II scores. But because SAT II tests provide colleges with such a convenient measurement tool, they are an important *part* of your application to college. Good SAT II scores can give your application the boost that moves you from the maybe pile into the accepted pile.

College Placement

Occasionally, colleges use SAT II tests to determine placement. For example, if you do very well on the SAT II Math IIC, you might be exempted from a basic math class. Though colleges do not often use SAT II tests for placement purposes, it's worth finding out whether the colleges to which you are applying do.

Scoring the SAT II Subject Tests

There are three different interpretations of your SAT II Math IIC score. The "raw score" is a simple score of how you did on the test, like the grade you might receive on a normal test in school. The "percentile score" takes your raw score and compares it to the rest of the raw scores in the country for the same test. Percentile scores let you know how you did on the test in comparison to your peers. The "scaled score," which ranges from 200–800, compares your score to the scores received by all students who have ever taken that particular SAT II.

The Raw Score

You will never see your SAT II raw score because the raw score is not included in the SAT II score report. But you should understand how it is calculated, since this knowledge can affect your strategy on the test.

A student's raw score is based entirely on the number of questions that student answered correctly, answered incorrectly, or left blank. You earn one point for every correct answer; you lose a quarter of a point for every incorrect answer; you get no points for questions left blank.

Calculating the raw score is easy. Simply add up the number of questions you answered correctly and the number of questions answered incorrectly. Then multiply the number of wrong answers by $\frac{1}{4}$, and subtract this value from the number of right answers.

$$\text{raw score} = (\text{correct answers}) - \frac{1}{4}(\text{wrong answers})$$

In the chapter called "Strategies for the SAT II Math IIC," we'll discuss how the rules for calculating a raw score affect strategies for guessing and leaving questions blank.

Percentiles

A student's percentile is based on the percentage of the total test-takers who received a lower raw score than he or she did. Say, for example, you had a friend named Evariste Gaulois who received a score that placed him in the 79th percentile. His percentile score tells him that he scored better on the Math IIC than 78% of the other students who took the same test. It also means that 21% of the students taking that test scored as well or better.

The Scaled Score

The scaled score takes the raw score and uses a formula to place it onto the standard SAT II scale of 200–800. The curve to convert raw scores to scaled scores differs from test to test. For example, a raw score of 33 on the Math IC will scale to a 600 while the same raw score of 33 on the Math IIC will scale to a 700. In fact, the scaled score can even vary on different editions of the *same* test. A raw score of 33 on the February 2003 Math IIC might scale to a 710, while a 33 in June 2003 might scale to a 690. These differences in scaled scores exist to accommodate differences in difficultly level and student performance. The difference in the curve for various versions of the same test will not vary by more than 20 points or so.

Which SAT II Subject Tests to Take

There are three types of SAT II tests: those you *must* take, those you *should* take, and those you *shouldn't* take.

- The SAT II tests you must take are those that are required by the colleges you are interested in.

- The SAT II tests you should take are tests that aren't required, but which you'll do well on, thereby impressing the colleges looking at your application.

- You shouldn't take the SAT II tests that aren't required and which cover subjects you don't feel confident about.

Determining Which SAT II Tests are Required

To find out if the colleges to which you are applying require that you take a particular SAT II test, you'll need to do a bit of research. Call the schools you're interested in, look at college web pages, or talk to your guidance counselor. Often, colleges request that you take the following SAT II tests:

- The Writing SAT II test

- One of the two Math SAT II tests (either Math IC or Math IIC)

- Another SAT II in some other subject of your choice

Not all colleges follow these guidelines, however, so you should take the time to research which tests you need to take in order to apply to the colleges that interest you.

Deciding Which Math SAT II to Take

Some students take both Math SAT II tests, but there really isn't a good reason for it. Instead, you should choose to take one test over the other. You should make this choice based on several factors.

1. **Test content.** The two tests cover similar topics, but the Math IIC covers more material than the Math IC does. Level IC covers three years of college-preparatory math: two years of algebra and one year of geometry. Level IIC assumes that in addition to those three years you've also taken a year of trigonometry and/or precalculus.

   Math IC

   Algebra

   Plane geometry (lines and angles, triangles, polygons, circles)

   Solid geometry (cubes, cylinders, cones, spheres, etc.)

   Coordinate geometry (in two dimensions)

   Trigonometry (properties and graphs of sine, cosine, and tangent functions, identities)

   Algebraic functions

   Statistics and sets (distributions, probability, permutations and combinations, groups and sets)

Math IC

Miscellaneous topics (logic, series, limits, complex and imaginary numbers)

Math IIC (covers all areas in Math IC with some additional concepts)

Algebra

Plane geometry

Solid geometry

Coordinate geometry (in two and three dimensions, vectors, polar coordinates, parametric equations)

Trigonometry (cosecant, secant, cotangent functions, inverse functions in non-right triangles)

Statistics and Sets

Miscellaneous topics

2. **Question Difficulty.** Not only does the Math IIC cover additional topics, it also covers the basic topics in more difficult ways than the Math IC does.

3. **College Choice.** As you choose between the two tests, keep in mind the specific colleges you're applying to. Colleges with a strong focus on math, such as MIT and Cal Tech, require the Math IIC test. Most other colleges have no such requirement, but some schools may prefer that you take the IIC.

4. **Battle of the Test Curves.** The two tests are scored by very different curves. The Level IIC test is scored on a much more liberal curve: you can miss six or seven questions at the IIC level and still achieve a score of 800. On the IC test, however, you would probably need to answer all the questions correctly to get a perfect score. In another example, if you wanted to get a 600 on either test, you would need around 20 correct answers on the IIC test, and 33 on the IC test. Some students who have a strong enough math background to take the Math IIC see that the IC is a less difficult test and think that they can get a marvelous score on the IC while their score on the IIC will only be average. But if these students get tripped up by just one or two questions on the Math IC, their scores will not be the impressive showstoppers that they might have expected.

All in all, if you have the math background to take the Level IIC test, you should go for it. Some students decide to take the Math IC because it's easier, even though they have taken a precalculus course. We don't recommend this plan. True, those students will probably do well on the Math IC test, but colleges will most certainly be more impressed by a student who does pretty well on the Math IIC than one who does very well on the Math IC. Also, the friendly curve on the Math IIC means that students who know enough math to take the IIC might very well get a better score on the IIC than they would on the IC.

If you still can't decide which of the two Math SAT IIs to take, try a practice test of each.

Deciding If You Should Take an SAT II that Isn't Required

To decide whether you should take a test that isn't required, you have to know two things:

1. What a good score on that SAT II test is

2. Whether you can get that score or higher

Below, we have included a list of the most commonly taken SAT II tests and the average scaled score on each. If you feel confident that you can get a score that is significantly above the average (50 points is significant) taking the test will probably strengthen your college application. Please note that if you are hoping to attend an elite school, you might have to score significantly more than 50 points higher than the national average. The following list is just a general guideline. It's a good idea to call the schools that interest you or talk to a guidance counselor to get a more precise idea of what score you should be shooting for.

Test	Average Score
Writing	590–600
Literature	590–600
American History	580–590
World History	570–580
Math IC	580–590
Math IIC	655–665
Biology E/M	590–600
Chemistry	605–615
Physics	635–645

Introduction

As you decide which tests to take, be realistic with yourself. Don't just assume you're going to do well without at least taking a practice test and seeing where you stand.

It's a good idea to take three SAT II tests that cover a range of subjects, such as one math SAT II, one humanities SAT II (history or writing), and one science SAT II. But there's no real reason to take *more* than three SAT II tests. Once you've taken the SAT II tests you need to take, the best way to set yourself apart from other students is to take AP courses and tests. AP tests are harder than the SAT II tests, and as a result they carry quite a bit more distinction. SAT II tests give you the opportunity to show colleges that you can learn and do well when you need to. Taking AP tests shows colleges that you *want* to learn as much as you can.

When to Take an SAT II Subject Test

The best time to take an SAT II Subject Test is right after you've finished a year-long course in that subject. If, for example, you've finished extensive courses on algebra and geometry by the eleventh grade, then you should take the Math IC test near the end of that year when the subject is still fresh in your mind. (This rule does not apply for the writing, literature, and foreign language SAT II tests; it's best to take those after you've had as much study in the area as possible.)

Unless the colleges to which you are applying use the SAT II for placement purposes, there is no point in taking any SAT II tests after November of your senior year, since you won't get your scores back from ETS until after college application deadlines have passed.

ETS usually sets testing dates for SAT II Subject Tests in October, November, December, January, May, and June. However, not every subject test is administered in each of these months. To check when the test you want to take is being offered, visit the College Board website at www.collegeboard.com or do some research in your school's guidance office.

Registering for SAT II Tests

To register for the SAT II test(s) of your choice, you have to fill out some forms and pay a registration fee. We know, we know—it's ridiculous that *you* have to pay for a test that colleges require you to take in order to make *their* jobs easier. But, sadly, there isn't anything we, or you, can do about it. It is acceptable for you to grumble here about the unfairness of the world.

After grumbling, of course, you still have to register. There are two ways to register: online or by mail. To register online, go to www.collegeboard.com. To register by mail, fill out and send in the forms enclosed in the *Registration Bulletin*, which should be available in your high school's guidance office. You can also request a copy of the *Bulletin* by calling the College Board at (609) 771-7600, or writing to:

College Board SAT Program
P.O. Box 6200
Princeton, NJ 08541-6200

You can register to take up to three SAT II tests for any given testing day. Unfortunately, even if you decide to take three tests in one day, you'll still have to pay a separate registration fee for each.

Introduction

Introduction to the SAT II Math IIC

IMAGINE TWO PEOPLE TREKKING THROUGH a jungle toward a magical and therapeutic waterfall. Now, who will reach the soothing waters first, the native to the area, who never stumbles because she knows the placement of every tree and all the twists and turns, or the tourist who keeps falling down and losing his way because he doesn't pay any attention to the terrain? The answer is obvious. Even if the tourist is a little faster, the native will still win, because she knows how to navigate the terrain and turn it to her advantage.

There are no waterfalls or gorgeous jungle scenery on the SAT IIs, but this example illustrates an important point. The structure of the SAT II Math IIC is the jungle; taking the test is the challenging trek. Your score is the waterfall.

In this chapter we're going to describe the "terrain" of the Math IIC test. In the next chapter on strategy, we will show you how to navigate and use the terrain to get the best score possible.

13

Content of the SAT II Math IIC

The Math IIC test covers a variety of mathematical topics. ETS, the company that writes the SAT II Math IIC, provides the following breakdown of the topics covered on the test:

Topic	Percent of Test	Usual Number of Questions
Algebra	18%	9
Plane Geometry	—	—
Solid Geometry	8%	4
Coordinate Geometry	12%	6
Trigonometry	20%	10
Functions	24%	12
Statistics and Sets	6%	3
Miscellaneous	12%	6

While accurate, this breakdown is too broad to really help you direct your studying for the test. We've created the following detailed breakdown based on careful examination of the test:

Topic	Percent of Test	Usual Number of Questions
Algebra	18%	9
Arithmetic	2%	1
Equation solving	5%	2.5
Binomials, polynomials, quadratics	14%	7
Solid Geometry	8%	4
Solids (cubes, cylinders, cones, etc.)	4%	2
Inscribed solids, solids by rotation	1%	0.5
Coordinate Geometry	12%	6
Lines and distance	6%	3
Conic sections (parabolas, circles)	5%	2.5
Coordinate space	2%	1

Topic	Percent of Test	Usual Number of Questions
Graphing	2%	1
Vectors	1%	0.5
Trigonometry	20%	10
Basic functions (sine, cosine, tangent)	12%	6
Trigonometric identities	4%	2
Inverse trigonometric functions	2%	1
Trigonometry in non-right triangles	1%	0.5
Graphing trigonometric functions	1%	0.5
Functions	24%	12
Basic, compound, inverse functions	8%	4
Graphing functions	6%	3
Domain and range of functions	8%	4
Statistics and Sets	6%	3
Mean, median, mode	2%	1
Probability	2%	1
Permutations and combinations	4%	2
Group questions, sets	1%	0.5
Miscellaneous	12%	6
Arithmetic and geometric series	4%	2
Logic	1%	0.5
Limits	1%	0.5
Imaginary numbers	1%	0.5

Each question in the practice tests has been categorized according to these topics, so that when you study your practice tests, you can very precisely identify your weaknesses.

Format of the SAT II Math IIC

The SAT II Math IIC is a one-hour long test made up of 50 multiple-choice questions. The instructions for the test are straightforward. You should memorize them so you don't waste time reading them on the day of the test.

> For each of the following problems, decide which is the BEST of the choices given. If the exact numerical value is not one of the choices, select the choice that best approximates this value. Then fill in the corresponding oval on the answer sheet.

Simple, right? Unfortunately, the instructions don't cover many important aspects about the format and rules of the test:

- The 50 questions progress in order of difficulty, from the easiest to the hardest.

- You can skip to different questions during the test. While you don't want to skip around randomly, the ability to skip the occasional question is helpful, as we will explain in the next chapter.

- All questions are worth the same number of points, regardless of the level of difficulty.

These facts can greatly affect your approach to taking the test, as we will show in the next chapter, which deals with strategy.

The Calculator

Unlike the SAT I, in which a calculator is permitted but not essential to the test, the Math IIC demands the use of a calculator. In fact, that's what the "C" in IIC signifies. What's more, some questions are specifically designed to test your calculator skills.

It is therefore wise to learn certain calculator essentials before taking the SAT II Math IIC. First off, make sure you have the right type of calculator. Virtually every type of calculator is allowed on the test, including the programmable and graphing kinds. Laptops, minicomputers, or any machine that prints, makes noise, or needs to be plugged in are not allowed.

Whatever calculator you use should have all the following functions:

- Exponential powers

- Base-10 logarithms

- Sine, cosine, tangent

Make sure you practice performing these functions well before the day of the test. More about how to use calculators on the test follows in the next chapter.

Scoring the SAT II Math IIC

Scoring on the SAT II Math IIC is very similar to the scoring for all other SAT II tests. For every right answer, you earn 1 point. For every wrong answer, you lose $\frac{1}{4}$ of a point. For every question you leave blank, you earn 0 points. Add these points up, and you get your raw score. ETS then converts your raw score to a scaled score according to a special curve. We have included a generalized version of that curve in the table below. Note that the curve changes slightly for each edition of the test, so the table shown will be close to, but not exactly the same as, the table used by the ETS for the particular test you take. You should use this chart to convert your raw scores on practice tests into a scaled score.

Scaled Score	Average Raw Score	Scaled Score	Average Raw Score
800	50	570	18
800	49	560	17
800	48	550	16
800	47	540	15
800	46	530	14
800	45	520	13
800	44	510	12
800	43	500	11
790	42	490	10
780	41	480	9
770	40	470	8
760	39	450	7
750	38	440	6
740	37	430	5
730	36	420	4
720	35	410	3
710	34	400	2
700	33	390	1
690	32	380	0
680	31	370	−1
680	30	360	−2
670	29	350	−3
660	28	340	−4
650	27	330	−5
640	26	320	−6
630	25	310	−7
630	24	300	−8
620	23	300	−9
610	22	290	−10
600	21	290	−11
590	20	280	−12
580	19	280	−13

In addition to its function as a conversion table, this chart contains crucial information: it tells you that you can do very well on the SAT II Math IIC without answering every question correctly. In fact, you could skip some questions and get some other questions wrong and still earn a perfect score of 800.

For example, in a test of 50 questions, you could score:

- 800 if you answered 44 right, 4 wrong, and left 2 blank

- 750 if you answered 40 right, 8 wrong, and left 2 blank

- 700 if you answered 35 right, 8 wrong, and left 7 blank

- 650 if you answered 30 right, 12 wrong, and left 8 blank

- 600 if you answered 25 right, 16 wrong, and left 9 blank

This chart should prove to you that when you're taking the test you should not imagine your score plummeting with every question you can't confidently answer. You can do very well on this test without knowing or answering everything. So don't get unnecessarily wound up if you run into a difficult question. The key to doing well on the SAT II Math IIC is to take the whole test well, and to follow a strategy that ensures you will answer all the questions you can, while intelligently guessing on the questions you feel less certain about. We will talk about such strategies in the next chapter.

The SAT II Math IIC

Strategies for the SAT II Math IIC

A MACHINE, NOT A PERSON, WILL SCORE your SAT II Math IIC test. The tabulating machine sees only the filled-in ovals on your answer sheet. It does not care how you came to these answers; it cares only whether your answers are correct. So whether you knew the right answer or just took a lucky guess, the machine will award you one point. Think of this scoring system as a message to you from the ETS: "We care only about your answers, and not about any of the thought behind them."

It's obvious that the SAT II Math IIC test allows you to show off your knowledge of math; but the test gives you the same opportunity to show off your fox-like cunning by figuring out what strategies will allow you to best display that knowledge. Remember, the SAT II test is your tool to get into college, so treat it as your tool. It wants right answers? Give it right answers, using whatever strategies you can.

Basic Rules of SAT II Test-Taking

There are some rules that apply to all SAT II tests. These rules are so obvious that we hesitate to call them "strategies." Some of these rules will seem more like common sense to you than anything else. We don't disagree. However, given the cruel ways a timed test can warp and mangle common sense, we offer this list.

Avoid Carelessness

There are two types of carelessness, both of which will cost you points. The first type of carelessness results from moving too fast on the test, whether that speed is caused by overconfidence or frantic fear. In speeding through the test, you make yourself vulnerable to misinterpreting the question, overlooking one of the answer choices, or making a logical or mathematical mistake. As you take the test, make a conscious effort to approach the test calmly, and not to move so quickly that you become prone to making mistakes.

Whereas the first type of carelessness can be caused by overconfidence, the second type of carelessness results from frustration or lack of confidence. Some students take a defeatist attitude toward tests, assuming they won't be able to answer many of the questions. Such an attitude is a form of carelessness, because it causes the student to ignore reality. Just as the overconfident student assumes she can't be tricked and therefore gets tricked, the student without confidence assumes he can't answer questions and therefore at the first sign of difficulty gives up.

Both kinds of carelessness steal points from you. Avoid them.

Be Careful Gridding In Your Answers

The computer that scores SAT II tests is unmerciful. If you answered a question correctly, but somehow made a mistake in marking your answer grid, the computer will mark that question as wrong. If you skipped question 5, but put the answer to question 6 in row 5, and the answer to question 7 in row 6, etc., thereby throwing off your answers for an entire section . . . it gets ugly.

Some test prep books advise you to fill in your answer sheet five questions at a time rather than one at a time. Some suggest that you do one question and then fill in the corresponding bubble. We think you should fill out the answer sheet whatever way feels most natural to you; just make sure you're careful while doing it. In our opinion, the best way to ensure that you're being careful is to talk silently to yourself. As you figure out an answer in the test booklet and transfer it over to the answer sheet, say to yourself: "Number 23, B. Number 24, E. Number 25, A."

Know What's in the Reference Area

At the beginning of the SAT II Math IIC there is a reference area that provides you with basic geometric formulas and information.

THE FOLLOWING INFORMATION IS FOR YOUR REFERENCE IN ANSWERING
SOME OF THE QUESTIONS IN THIS TEST.

Volume of a right circular cone with radius r and height h: $V = \frac{1}{3}\pi r^2 h$

Lateral area of a right circular cone with circumference of the base c and slant height l: $S = \frac{1}{2}cl$

Volume of a sphere with radius r: $V = \frac{4}{3}\pi r^3$

Surface area of a sphere with radius r: $S = 4\pi r^2$

Volume of a pyramid with base area B and height h: $V = \frac{1}{3}Bh$

You should know all of these formulas without the reference; don't neglect to memorize and understand the formulas just because you have the reference area as a crutch. Instead, view the reference area as a guide to the formulas that will likely be on the test. If you know those formulas without having to flip back to the reference area, you'll save time, which puts you one step ahead.

Write All Over Your Test Booklet . . .

Draw diagrams or write out equations to help you think. Mark up graphs or charts as necessary. Cross out answers that can't be right. The test booklet is yours to write on, and writing can often help clarify your thoughts so that you can work more quickly with fewer mistakes.

. . . But Remember That the SAT Rewards Answers, Not Work

Having told you to write in your test book, we're going to qualify that advice. Doing math scratchwork can definitely help you avoid careless errors, but doing pristine work, or more work than necessary, can be more time consuming than it's worth. You must find a balance between speed and accuracy. You need to be able to follow and understand your work, but others don't. Nobody will see your work, so don't write it out as if you're being judged.

The Importance of the Order of Difficulty

Imagine that you are taking a test that consists of two questions. After your teacher hands out the test, and before you set to work, a helpful little gnome whispers, "The first problem is very simple, the second is much harder." Would the gnome's statement affect the way you approach the two problems? The answer, of course, is yes. For a "very simple" question, it seems likely that you should be able to answer it quickly and without much, or any, agonized second-guessing. On a "much harder" question, you will probably have to spend much more time, both to come up with an answer and to check your work to make sure you didn't make an error somewhere along the way.

What about all the other students who didn't hear the gnome? They might labor over the first, easy question, exhaustively checking their work, and wasting time that they'll need for the tricky second problem. Then, when those other students do get to the second problem, they might not check their work or be wary of traps, since they have no idea that the problem is so difficult.

Because Math IIC questions are ordered by difficulty, it's as if you have that helpful little gnome sitting next to you for the entire test.

Knowing When to Be Wary

Most students answer the easy Math IIC questions correctly. Only some students get moderate questions right. Very few students get difficult questions right. What does this mean to you? It means that when you are going through the test, you can often trust your first instincts on an easy question. With difficult questions, however, you should be more cautious. There is a reason most people get these questions wrong: not only are they more difficult, containing more sophisticated vocabulary or mathematical concepts, they are also often tricky, full of enticing wrong answers that seem correct. But because the Math IIC orders its questions by difficulty, the test tells when to take a few extra seconds to make sure you haven't been fooled by an answer that only *seems* right.

The tricky answers seem right because they are actually the answers you would get if you were to make a mathematical or logical mistake while working on the problem. For example, let's say you're flying through the test and have to multiply $6 \times 8 \times 3$. So you quickly multiply 6 and 8 to get 42 and then multiply by 3 to get 126. You look down at the answers and there's 126! That's the answer you came to, and there it is among the answer choices like a little stamp of approval, so you mark it down as your answer and get the question wrong: $6 \times 8 = 48$, not 42, making the correct answer 144.

From this example, you should learn that just because the answer you got is among the answer choices, your answer is not necessarily the right one. The Math IIC is designed to punish those who make careless errors. Don't be one of them. After you get an answer, quickly check your work again.

Math Questions and Time

There are often several ways to answer a Math IIC question. You can use trial and error, you can set up and solve an equation, and, for some questions, you might be able to answer the question quickly, intuitively, and elegantly, if you can just spot how. These different approaches to answering questions vary in the amount of time they take. Trial and error generally takes the longest, while the elegant method of relying on an intuitive understanding of conceptual knowledge takes the least amount of time.

Take, for example, the following problem:

> Which has a greater area, a square with sides measuring 4 cm, or a circle with a radius of the same length?

Math IIC Strategies

The most obvious way to solve this problem is simply to plug 4 into the formulas for the area of a square and the area of a circle. Let's do it: Area of a square = s^2, so the area of this square = $4^2 = 16$. Area of a circle = πr^2, so the area of this circle must therefore be $\pi 4^2 = 16\pi$. 16π is obviously bigger than 16, so the circle must be bigger. That worked nicely. But a faster approach would have been to draw a quick to-scale diagram with the square and circle superimposed.

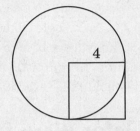

An even quicker way would have been to understand the equations of area for a square and circle so well that it was just *obvious* that the circle was bigger, since the equation for the circle will square the 4 and multiply it by π whereas the equation for the square will only square the 4.

While you may not be able to become a math whiz and just *know* the answer, you can learn to look for a quicker route, such as choosing to draw a diagram instead of working out the equation. And, as with the example above, a quicker route is not necessarily a less accurate one. Making such choices comes down to practice, being aware that those other routes are out there, and basic mathematical ability.

The value of time-saving strategies is obvious: less time spent on some questions allows you to devote more time to difficult problems. It is this issue of time that separates the students who do terrifically on the test and those who merely do well. Whether or not the ability to find accurate shortcuts is an actual measure of mathematical prowess is not for us to say, but the ability to find those shortcuts absolutely matters on this test.

Shortcuts Are Really Math Intuition

Now that you know all about shortcuts, you should use them wisely. Don't go into every question searching for a shortcut; it might end up taking longer than the normal route. Instead of seeking out math shortcuts, you should simply be mindful of the possibility that one might exist. If you go into each question knowing there could be a shortcut and keep your mind open as you think about the question, you will find the shortcuts you need.

To some extent, with practice you can teach yourself to recognize when a question might contain a shortcut. For example, simply from the problem above, you know that there will probably be a shortcut for questions that give you the dimensions of two shapes and ask you to compare them: you can just draw a diagram. A frantic test taker might see the information given and then seize on the simplest route and work out the equations. But with some calm and perspective you can see that drawing a diagram is the best idea.

The fact that we advocate using shortcuts doesn't mean you shouldn't focus on learning how to work a problem out. In fact, we can guarantee that you're not going to find a shortcut for a problem *unless* you know how to work it out the long way. After all, a shortcut just uses your knowledge to find a faster way to answer the question. To put it another way, we could just as easily use the term math intuition instead of the word shortcut. You have to have a knowledge base to work from in order to have anything on which to base your intuition. In contrast, you might be able to figure out an answer by trial and error even if you don't see exactly how to answer the problem.

Making Your Calculator Work for You

As we've already mentioned, the calculator is a very important part of the Math IIC test. You need to have the right kind of calculator, be familiar with its operations, and above all, know how to use it intelligently.

There are four types of questions on the test: calculator-friendly, calculator-neutral, calculator-unfriendly, and calculator-useless. According to the ETS, about 60 percent of the test falls under the calculator-neutral and -friendly categories. That is, calculators are useful or necessary on 30 out of the 50 questions on the SAT II Math IIC. The other 20 questions are calculator-unfriendly and -useless. The trick is to be able to identify the different types of questions on the test. Here's a breakdown of each of the four types, with examples.

Calculator-Friendly Questions

A calculator is extremely helpful and often necessary to solve calculator-friendly questions. Problems demanding exact values for exponents, logarithms, or trigonometric functions will most likely need a calculator. Computations that you wouldn't be able to do easily in your head are prime suspects for a calculator. Here's an example:

If $f(x) = \sqrt{x} - 2x^2 + 5$, then what is $f(3.4)$?

(A)   −18.73
(B)   −16.55
(C)   −16.28
(D)   −13.32
(E)   −8.42

This is a simple function question in which you are asked to evaluate $f(x)$ at the value 3.4. All you have to do to solve this problem is plug in 3.4 for the variable x and carry out the operations in the function. But unless you know the square root and square of 3.4 off the top of your head, which most test-takers probably wouldn't (and shouldn't), then this problem is extremely difficult to answer without a calculator.

But with a calculator, all you need to do is take the square root of 3.4, subtract twice the square of 3.4, and then add 5. You get answer choice (C), –16.28.

Calculator-Neutral Questions

You have two different choices when faced with a calculator-neutral question. A calculator is useful for these types of problems, but it's probably just as quick and easy to work the problem out by hand.

If $8x = 4^3 \times 2^3$, what is the value of x?

(A) 2
(B) 3
(C) 5
(D) 7
(E) 8

When you see the variable x as a power, you should think logarithms. A logarithm is the power to which you must raise a given number to equal another number, so in this case, we need to find the exponent x, such that $8^x = 4^3 \times 2^3$. From the definition of logarithms, we know that given an equation of the form $a^x = b$, $\log_a b = x$. So you could type in $\log_8 (4^3 \times 2^3)$ on your trusty calculator and find that $x = 3$.

Or, you could recognize that 2 and 4 are both factors of 8, and thinking a step further, that $2^3 = 8$ and $4^3 = 64 = 82$. Put together, $4^3 \times 2^3 = 8^2 \times 8 = 8^3$. We come to the same answer that $x = 3$, and that (B) is the right answer.

These two processes take about the same amount of time, so choosing one over the other is more a matter of personal preference than one of strategy. If you feel quite comfortable with your calculator, then you might not want to risk the possibility of making a mental math mistake and should choose the first method. But if you're more prone to error when working with a calculator, then you should choose the second method.

Calculator-Unfriendly Questions

It is possible to answer calculator-unfriendly questions by using a calculator. But while it's possible, it isn't a good idea. These types of problems often have built-in short-cuts—if you know and understand the principle being tested, you can bypass potentially tedious computation with a few simple calculations. Here's a problem that you could solve much more quickly and effectively without the use of a calculator:

$$\frac{\left(\cos^2(3 \times 63°) + \sin^2(3 \times 63°)\right)^4}{2} =$$

(A) .3261
(B) .5
(C) .6467
(D) .7598
(E) .9238

If you didn't take a moment to think about this problem, you might just rush into it wielding your calculator, calculating the cosine and sine functions, squaring them each and then adding them together, etc. But if you take a closer look, you'll see that $\cos^2(3 \times 63°) + \sin^2(3 \times 63°)$ is a trigonometric identity. More specifically, it is a Pythagorean Identity: $\sin^2 q + \cos^2 q = 1$ for any angle q. So, the expression $\{\cos^2(3 \times 63°) + \sin^2(3 \times 63°)\}^4 / 2$ simplifies down to $1^4/2 = 1/2 = .5$. Answer choice (B) is correct.

Calculator-Useless Questions

Even if you wanted to, you wouldn't be able to use your calculator on calculator-useless problems. For the most part, problems involving algebraic manipulation or problems lacking actual numerical values would fall under this category. You should easily be able to identify problems that can't be solved with a calculator. Quite often, the answers for these questions will be variables rather than numbers. Take a look at the following example:

$(x + y - 1)(x + y + 1) =$

(A) $(x + y)^2$
(B) $(x + y)^2 - 1$
(C) $x^2 - y^2$
(D) $x^2 + x - y + y^2 + 1$
(E) $x^2 + y^2 + 1$

This question tests you on an algebraic topic—that is, how to find the product of two polynomials—and requires knowledge of algebraic principles rather than calculator acumen. You're asked to manipulate variables, not produce a specific value. A calculator would be of no use here.

To solve this problem, you would have to notice that the two polynomials are in the format of a Difference of Two Squares: $(a + b)(a - b) = a^2 - b^2$. In our case, $a = x + y$ and $b = 1$. As a result, $(x + y - 1)(x + y + 1) = (x + y)^2 - 1$. Answer choice (B) is correct.

Don't Immediately Use Your Calculator

The fact that the test contains all four of these question types means that you shouldn't get trigger-happy with your calculator. Just because you've got an awesome shiny hammer doesn't mean you should try to use it to pound in thumbtacks. Using your calculator to try to answer every question on the test would be just as unhelpful.

Instead of reaching instinctively for your calculator, you should come up with a problem-solving plan for each question. Take a brief look at each question so that you understand what it's asking you to do, and then decide whether you should use a calculator to solve the problem at all. That brief instant of time invested in making such decisions will save you a great deal of time later on. For example, what if you came upon the question:

> If $(3, y)$ is a point on the graph of $f(x) = \dfrac{x^2 - 5x + 4}{11x - 44}$, then what is y?
>
> (A)   −3
> (B)   −1.45
> (C)   0
> (D)   .182
> (E)   4.87

A trigger-happy calculator user might immediately plug in 3 for x. But the student who takes a moment to think about the problem will probably see that the calculation would be much simpler if the function were simplified first. To start, factor 11 out of the denominator:

$$f(x) = \frac{x^2 - 5x + 4}{11x - 44} = \frac{x^2 - 5x + 4}{11(x - 4)}$$

Then, factor the numerator to its simplest form:

$$f(x) = \frac{x^2 - 5x + 4}{11(x - 4)} = \frac{(x - 4)(x - 1)}{11(x - 4)}$$

The $(x - 4)$ cancels out, and the function becomes $f(x) = (x - 1)/11$. At this point you could shift to the calculator and calculate $f(x) = {}^{(3 - 1)}\!/11 = {}^2\!/11 = .182$, which is answer (D). If you were very comfortable with math, however, you would see that you don't even have to work out this final calculation. ${}^2\!/11$ can't work out to any answer other than (D), since you know that ${}^2\!/11$ isn't a negative number, won't be equal to zero, and also won't be greater than 1.

Approaching Math IIC Questions

Though there are four different types of questions on the Math IIC, there is a standard procedure that you should use to approach all of them.

Math IIC Strategies

1. Read the question without looking at the answers. Determine what the question is asking and come to some conclusion about how to solve it. Do not look at the answers unless you decide that using the process of elimination is the best way to go (we describe how to use the process of elimination below).

2. If you think you can solve the problem, go ahead. Once you've derived an answer, only then see if your answer matches one of the choices.

3. Once you've decided on an answer, test it quickly to make sure it's correct, and move on.

Working Backward: The Process of Elimination

If you run into difficulty while trying to solve a regular multiple-choice problem, you might want to try the process of elimination. On every question the answer is right in front of you, hidden among those five answer choices. So if you can't solve the problem directly, you might be able to plug each answer into the question to see which one works.

Not only can this process help you when you can't figure out a question, there are times when it can actually be faster than setting up an equation, especially if you work strategically. Take the following example:

A classroom contains 31 chairs, some of which have arms and some of which do not. If the room contains 5 more armchairs than chairs without arms, how many armchairs does it contain?

(A)   10
(B)   13
(C)   16
(D)   18
(E)   21

Given this question, you could build the equations:

$$\text{total chairs } (31) = \text{armchairs } (x) + \text{normal chairs } (y)$$
$$\text{normal chairs } (y) = \text{armchairs } (x) - 5$$

Then, since $y = (x - 5)$, you can make the equation:

$$31 = x + (x - 5)$$
$$31 = 2x - 5$$
$$36 = 2x$$
$$x = 18$$

This approach of building and working out the equations will produce the right answer, but it takes a long time! What if you strategically plugged in the answers instead? Since the numbers ascend in value, let's choose the one in the middle: (C) 16. This is a smart strategic move because if we plug in 16 and discover that it is too small a number to satisfy the equation, we can eliminate (A) and (B) along with (C). Alternatively, if 16 is too big, we can eliminate (D) and (E) along with (C).

So our strategy is in place. Now let's work it out. If you have 16 armchairs, then you would have 11 normal chairs and the room would contain 27 total chairs. We needed the total numbers of chairs to equal 31, so clearly (C) is not the right answer. But because the total number of chairs was too few, you can also eliminate (A) and (B), the answer choices with smaller numbers of armchairs. If you then plug in (D) 18, you have 13 normal chairs and 31 total chairs. There's your answer. In this instance, plugging in the answers takes less time, and, in general, just seems easier.

Notice that the last sentence began with the words "in this instance." Working backward and plugging in is not always the best method. For some questions it won't be possible to work backward at all. For the test, you will need to build up a sense of when working backward can most help you. A good rule of thumb for deciding whether to work backward is:

- Work backward when the question describes an equation of some sort and the answer choices are all simple numbers.

If the answer choices contain variables, working backward will often be quite difficult —more difficult than working out the problem would be. If the answer choices are complicated, with hard fractions or radicals, plugging in might prove so complex that it's a waste of time.

Substituting Numbers

Substituting numbers is a lot like working backward, except the numbers you plug into the equation *aren't* in the answer choices. Instead, you have to strategically decide on numbers to substitute into the question to take the place of variables.

For example, take the question:

Math IIC Strategies

If p and q are odd integers, then which of the following must be odd?

(A) $p + q$
(B) $p - q$
(C) $p^2 + q^2$
(D) $p^2 \times q^2$
(E) $p^2 + q$

It might be hard to conceptualize how the two variables in this problem interact. But what if you chose two odd numbers, let's say 5 and 3, to represent the two variables? Once you begin this substitution it quickly becomes clear that

(A) $p + q = 5 + 3 = 8$
(B) $p - q = 5 - 3 = 2$
(C) $p^2 + q^2 = 25 + 9 = 34$
(D) $p^2 \times q^2 = 25 \times 9 = 225$
(E) $p + q^2 = 5 + 9 = 14$

By picking two numbers that fit the definition of the variables provided by the question, it becomes clear that the answer has to be (D) $p^2 \times q^2$ since it multiplies to 225. By the way, you could have answered this question without doing the multiplication to 225 since two odd numbers, such as 9 and 25, when multiplied, will always result in an odd number.

Substituting numbers can help you transform problems from the abstract into the concrete. However, you have to remember to keep the substitution consistent. If you're using a 5 to represent p, don't suddenly start using 3. Also, when picking numbers to use as substitutes, pick wisely. Choose numbers that are easy to work with and that fit the definitions provided by the question.

Guessing and the Math IIC

Should you guess on the SAT II Math IIC? We'll begin to answer this question by posing a question of our own:

> G. O. Metry is holding five cards, numbered 1-5. Without telling you, he has selected one of the numbers as the "correct" card. If you pick a single card, what is the probability that you will choose the "correct" card?

The answer, of course, is $\frac{1}{5}$. But just as important, you should recognize that the question precisely describes the situation you're in when you blindly guess the answer to any SAT II Math IIC question: you have a $\frac{1}{5}$ chance of getting the question right. If you were to guess on ten questions, you would, according to probability, get two questions right and eight questions wrong.

- 2 right answers gets you 2 raw points

- 8 wrong answers gets you 8 × −¼ points = −2 raw points

Those ten answers, therefore, net you a total of *zero* points. Your guessing was a complete waste of time, which is precisely what the ETS wants. They designed the scoring system so that blind guessing is pointless.

Educated Guessing

But what if your guessing isn't blind? Consider the following question:

$x + 2x = 6$, what is the value of x?

(A) −2
(B) 2
(C) 3
(D) 0
(E) 1

Let's say you had no idea how to solve this problem, but you did realize that 0 multiplied by any number equals 0, and that $0 + 2 × 0$ cannot add up to 6. This means that you can eliminate "0" as a possible answer, and now have four choices from which to choose. Is it now worth it to guess? Probability states that if you are guessing between four choices you will get one question right for every three you get wrong. For that one correct answer you'll get 1 point, and for the three incorrect answers you'll lose a total of ¾ of a point. $1 − ¾ = ¼$, meaning that if you can eliminate even one answer, the odds of guessing turn in your favor: you become more likely to gain points than to lose points.

Therefore, the rule for guessing on the Math IIC test is simple: *if you can eliminate even one answer-choice on a question, you should definitely guess*. And if you follow the critical thinking methods we described above about how to eliminate answer choices, you should be able to eliminate at least one answer from almost every question.

Guessing As Partial Credit

Some students feel that guessing is similar to cheating, that in guessing correctly credit is given where none is due. But instead of looking at guessing as an attempt to gain undeserved points, you should look at it as a form of partial credit. Take the example of the question above. Most people taking the test will see that adding two zeroes will never equal six, and will only be able to throw out that choice as a possible answer. But let's say that you also knew that negative numbers added together cannot equal a positive number 6. Don't you deserve something for that extra knowledge? Well, you do get something: when you look at this question, you can throw out both "0" and "−2" as answer choices, leaving you with a $\frac{1}{3}$ chance of getting the question right if you guess. Your extra knowledge gives you better odds of getting this question right, exactly as extra knowledge should.

Pacing

As we said earlier, the questions on the SAT II Math IIC are organized from least to most difficult: the basic material appears near the beginning, and the advanced topics show up at the end. You can always have a sense of what is awaiting you later on in the test. Use this information. Part of your job is to make sure you don't spend too much time on the easiest questions. Don't put yourself in the position of having to leave blank those questions near the end of the test that you could have answered *if only you had more time*.

True, answering 50 math questions in 60 minutes is not the easiest of tasks, but if you learn how to pace yourself, you should be able to look at every single question on the test. Note that we said "look at" every question on the test. We didn't say "answer" every question on the test. There is a very big difference between the two.

It is unlikely that you will be able to answer every question on the test. Some questions will stump you, completely resisting your efforts to eliminate even one possible answer choice. Others might demand so much of your time that answering them becomes more trouble than it's worth. While taking five minutes to solve a particularly difficult question might strike you as a moral victory when you're taking the test, it's quite possible that you could have used that same time to answer six other questions that would have vastly increased your score. Instead of getting bogged down in individual questions, you will do better if you learn to skip, and leave for later, the very difficult questions that you either can't answer or that will take an extremely long time to answer.

By perfecting your pacing on practice tests, you can make sure that you will see every question on the test. And this way, you can select which questions you will and won't answer, rather than running out of time before reaching the end of the test. You're no longer allowing the test to decide, by default, which questions you won't answer.

There are a few simple rules that, if followed, will make pacing yourself much easier.

- Make sure not to get bogged down in any one question.

- Answer every question to which you know the answer, and make an educated guess for every question in which you can quickly eliminate at least one answer choice.

- Skip questions that refer to concepts completely foreign to you. If you look at the question and answers and have no idea what topics they cover, you have little chance of even coming up with an educated guess. Mark the question in some way to indicate that it is very difficult. Return to it only if you have answered everything else. Remember to skip that line on your answer sheet!

Setting a Target Score

You can make the job of pacing yourself much easier if you go into the test knowing how many questions you have to answer correctly in order to earn the score that you want. So, what score do you want to get? Obviously, you should strive for the best score possible, but be realistic: consider how much you know about math and how well you do in general on SAT-type tests. You should also consider what exactly defines a good score at the colleges to which you're applying: is it a 680? A 740? Talk to the admissions offices of the colleges you might want to attend, do a little research in college guidebooks, or talk to your guidance counselor. No matter how you do it, you should find out what the average score is of students going to the schools you want to attend. Take that number and set your target score above it (you want to be above average, right?). Then take a look at the chart we showed you before:

You will get:

- 800 if you answered 44 right, 4 wrong, and left 2 blank

- 750 if you answered 40 right, 8 wrong, and left 2 blank

- 700 if you answered 35 right, 8 wrong, and left 7 blank

- 650 if you answered 30 right, 12 wrong, and left 8 blank

- 600 if you answered 25 right, 16 wrong, and left 9 blank

So let's say the average score for the SAT II Math IIC for the school you want to attend is a 700. You should set your target at about 750. Looking at this chart, you can see that in order to get that score, you need to get 40 questions right, and you can get 8 wrong and leave 2 blank.

If you know all these numbers going into the test, you can pace yourself accordingly. You should use practice tests to teach yourself the proper pace, increasing your speed if you find that you aren't getting to answer all the questions you need to, or decreasing your pace if you find that you're rushing and making careless mistakes. If you reach your target score during preparation, give yourself a cookie and take a break for the day. But just because you hit your target score doesn't mean you should stop working altogether. In fact, you should view reaching your target score as a clue that you can do *better* than that score: set a new target 50-100 points above your original, and work to pick up your pace a little bit and skip fewer questions.

By working to improve in manageable increments, you can slowly work up to your top speed, integrating your new knowledge about how to take the test and the subjects it covers without overwhelming yourself by trying to take on too much too soon. If you can handle working just a little faster without becoming careless and losing points, your score will certainly go up. If you meet your new target score again, repeat the process.

Practice Tests

Practice Tests Are Your Best Friends

IN THIS CRAZY WORLD OF OURS, THERE IS one thing that you can always take for granted: the SAT II Math IIC will stay the same. From year to year and test to test, of the 50 Math IIC questions, seven or eight questions will cover equation solving, four to five will cover graphing functions, two to three will cover conic sections, etc. Obviously, different versions of the SAT II Math IIC aren't *exactly* the same. Individual questions will never repeat from test to test. But the subjects that the questions test, and the way in which the questions test those subjects, *will* stay constant.

This constancy can be a great benefit to you as you study for the test. To show how you can use the similarity between different versions of the SAT II Math IIC test to your advantage, we provide a case study.

Using the Similarity of the SAT II Math IIC for Personal Gain

One day, an eleventh grader named Molly Bloom sits down at the desk in her room and takes a practice test for the SAT II Math IIC. Because it makes this example much simpler, let's say she takes the entire test and gets only one question wrong. Molly checks her answers and then jumps from her chair and does a little dance, shimmying to the tune of her own success. After her euphoria passes, she begins to wonder which question she got wrong and returns to her chair. She discovers that the question dealt with parabolas. Looking over the question, Molly at first thinks the test writers made a mistake and that she was right. But at second glance, she realizes that she had misidentified the vertex of the parabola. Molly saw she didn't have a good grasp on how to graph a parabola given its equation and studies up on her coordinate geometry. She learns the basics of conic sections and *what* causes a parabola's vertex to shift from the origin. All this takes her about ten minutes, after which she vows never to make a mistake on a question involving parabolas.

Analyzing Molly Bloom

Molly's actions seem minor. All she did was study a question she got wrong until she understood why she got it wrong and what she should have done to get it right. But the implications loom large. Molly answered the question incorrectly because she didn't understand the topic it was testing, and the practice test pointed out her shortcoming in the most noticeable way possible: she got the question wrong. After doing her goofy little dance, Molly wasn't content to simply see what the correct answer was and get on with her day. She wanted to see *how* and *why* she got the question wrong and what she should have done or needed to know to get it right. So, with a look of determination and a self-given pep talk, she spent time studying the question, discovered her misunderstanding of parabola graphs, and nailed down the ideas behind the material. If Molly were to take that same test again, she definitely would not get that question wrong.

"But she never will take that same test again, so she's never going to see that particular question again," some poor sap who hasn't read this guide might exclaim. "She wasted her time. Wow, Molly Bloom is dumb!"

Why That Poor Sap Really Is a Poor Sap

In some sense, that poor sap is correct: Molly never will take that exact practice test again. But the poor sap is wrong to call Molly derogatory names, because, as we know, the SAT II Math IIC is remarkably similar from year to year—both in the topics it covers and in the way it poses questions about those topics. Therefore, when Molly taught herself about conic sections and their graphs, she learned how to answer the similar questions dealing with parabolas and circles that will *undoubtedly* appear on every future practice test and on the real Math IIC.

By studying the results of her practice test and figuring out why she got her one question wrong and what she should have known and done to get it right, Molly has targeted a weakness and overcome it.

Molly and You

Molly has it easy. She took a practice test and got only one question wrong. Less than one percent of all people who take the SAT II Math IIC will be so lucky. Of course, the only reason Molly got that many right was so that we could use her as an easy example.

So, what if you take a practice test and get 15 questions wrong, and your errors span a number of different math topics? You should do exactly what Molly did. Take your test and *study it*. Identify every question you got wrong, figure out why you got it wrong, and then teach yourself what you should have done to get the question right. If you can't figure out your error, find someone who can.

Think about it. What does an incorrect answer mean? That wrong answer identifies a weakness in your test-taking, whether that weakness is an unfamiliarity with a particular math topic or a tendency to be careless. If you got 15 questions wrong on a practice test, then each of those 15 questions identifies a weakness in your ability to take the SAT II Math IIC or your knowledge about the topics tested by the SAT II Math IIC. But as you study each question and figure out why you got that question wrong, you are learning how to answer the questions that will appear on the real test. You are discovering your exact math weaknesses and addressing them, and you are learning to understand not just the knowledge behind the question, but the way that ETS asks its questions as well.

If you got 15 questions wrong, it will take a bit more time to study your mistakes. But if you invest that time and study your practice test properly, you will be avoiding future mistakes. Each successive practice test you take should have fewer errors, meaning less time spent studying those errors. More important, you'll be pinpointing what you need to study for the real SAT II Math IIC, identifying and overcoming your weaknesses, and learning to answer an increasing variety of questions on the specific topics covered by the test. Taking practice tests and studying them will allow you to teach yourself how to recognize and handle whatever the SAT II Math IIC throws at you.

Taking a Practice Test

The example of Miss Molly Bloom shows why studying practice tests can be an extremely powerful study tool. Now we're going to explain how to use that tool.

Controlling Your Environment

Although no one but you ever needs to see your practice-test scores, you should do everything in your power to make the practice test feel like the real SAT II Math IIC. The more your practice resembles the real thing, the more helpful it will be. When taking a practice test, follow these rules:

Take the tests timed. Don't give yourself any extra time. Be stricter with yourself than the meanest proctor you can think of. Also, don't give yourself time off for bathroom breaks. If you have to go to the bathroom, let the clock keep running; that's what'll happen on the real Math IIC.

Take the test in a single sitting. Training yourself to endure an hour of test-taking is part of your preparation.

Find a place to take the test without distractions. Don't take the practice test in a room with lots of people walking through it. Go to a library, your bedroom, an empty classroom—anywhere quiet.

By following these guidelines, you will be more focused while taking the practice test and you will achieve your target score more quickly. However, don't be too discouraged if you find these rules too strict; you can always bend them a little. Preparing for the SAT II Math IIC should not be so torturous that you don't study! Do whatever you have to do to make yourself study.

Ultimately, if you can follow all of the above rules to the letter, you will probably be better off. But if following those rules makes studying excruciating, find little ways to bend them so they don't interfere too much with your concentration.

Practice Test Strategy

You should take the test as if it were the real deal: go for the highest score you can get. This does not mean that you should be more daring than you would be on the actual test, guessing blindly even when you can't eliminate an answer. It doesn't mean that you should carelessly speed through the test. Follow the rules for guessing and for skipping questions that we outlined earlier. The more closely your attitude and strategies during the practice test reflect those you'll employ during the actual test, the more the practice test will accurately predict your strengths and weaknesses. You'll learn what areas you should study and how to pace yourself during the test.

Scoring Your Practice Test

After you take your practice test, you'll want to score it and see how you did. However, when you do your scoring, don't just tally up your raw score. As part of your scoring, you should also keep a list of every question you got wrong and every question you skipped. This list will be your guide when you study your test.

Studying Your . . . No, Wait, Go Take a Break

You know how to have fun. Go do that for a while. Come back when you're refreshed.

Studying Your Practice Test

After grading your test, you should have a list of the questions you answered incorrectly or skipped. Studying your test involves using this list and examining each question you answered incorrectly, figuring out why you got the question wrong and understanding what you could have done to get the question right.

Why did you get the question wrong?

There are three reasons why you might have gotten an individual question wrong.

1. You thought you solved the answer correctly, but you actually didn't.

2. You managed to eliminate some answer choices and then guessed among the remaining answers; unfortunately, you guessed wrong.

3. You knew the answer but somehow made a careless mistake.

You should know which of these reasons applies to each question you got wrong.

What could you have done to get the question right?

The reasons you got a question wrong affect how you should think about it while studying your test.

If You Got a Question Wrong for Reason 1–Lack of Knowledge

A question answered incorrectly for Reason 1 identifies a weakness in your knowledge of the math tested on the Math IIC test. Discovering this wrong answer gives you an opportunity to target your weakness.

For example, if the question you got wrong refers to factoring quadratics, don't just memorize the roots of certain equations. Learn the fundamental techniques that make different quadratics result in different roots. Remember, you will *not* see a question exactly like the question you got wrong. But you probably *will* see a question that covers the same topic as the practice question. For that reason, when you get a question wrong, don't just figure out the right answer to the question. Study the broader topic that the question tests.

If You Got a Question Wrong for Reason 2–Guessing Wrong

If you guessed wrong, review your guessing strategy. Did you guess intelligently? Could you have eliminated more answers? If yes, why didn't you? By thinking in this critical way about the decisions you made while taking the practice test, you can train yourself to make quicker, more decisive, and better decisions.

If you took a guess and chose the incorrect answer, don't let that sour you on guessing. Even as you go over the question and figure out if there were any ways for you to have answered the question without having to guess, remind yourself that if you eliminated at least one answer, you followed the right strategy even if you got the question wrong.

If You Got a Question Wrong for Reason 3–Carelessness

If you discover you got a question wrong because you were careless, it might be tempting to say to yourself, "Oh, I made a careless error," and assure yourself you won't do that again. That is not enough. You made that careless mistake for a reason, and you should try to figure out why. Whereas getting a question wrong because you didn't know the answer constitutes a weakness in your knowledge about the test, making a careless mistake represents a weakness in your *method of taking the test*.

To overcome this weakness, you need to approach it in the same critical way you would approach a lack of knowledge. Study your mistake. Reenact your thought process on the problem and see where and how your carelessness came about: were you rushing? Did you jump at the first answer that seemed right instead of reading all the answers? Know your error and look it in the eye. If you learn precisely what your mistake was, you are much less likely to make that mistake again.

If You Left the Question Blank

It is also a good idea to study the questions you left blank on the test, since those questions constitute a reservoir of lost points. A blank answer is a result either of:

1. A total inability to answer a question

2. A lack of time

In the case of the first possibility, you should see if there was some way you might have been able to eliminate an answer choice or two and put yourself in a better position to guess. In the second case, look over the question and see whether you think you could have answered it. If you could have, then you know that you are throwing away points and probably working too slowly. If you couldn't, then carry out the steps above: study the relevant material and review your guessing strategy.

The Secret Weapon: Talking to Yourself

Yeah, it's embarrassing. Yeah, you'll look silly. But other than physical violence, talking to yourself is perhaps the best way to pound something into your brain. As you go through the steps of studying a question, you should talk them out. When you verbalize something to yourself, it makes it much harder to delude yourself into thinking that you're working if you're really not.

SAT II Math IIC
Practice Test 1

MATH IIC TEST 1 ANSWER SHEET

1.	Ⓐ Ⓑ Ⓒ Ⓓ Ⓔ		18.	Ⓐ Ⓑ Ⓒ Ⓓ Ⓔ		35.	Ⓐ Ⓑ Ⓒ Ⓓ Ⓔ
2.	Ⓐ Ⓑ Ⓒ Ⓓ Ⓔ		19.	Ⓐ Ⓑ Ⓒ Ⓓ Ⓔ		36.	Ⓐ Ⓑ Ⓒ Ⓓ Ⓔ
3.	Ⓐ Ⓑ Ⓒ Ⓓ Ⓔ		20.	Ⓐ Ⓑ Ⓒ Ⓓ Ⓔ		37.	Ⓐ Ⓑ Ⓒ Ⓓ Ⓔ
4.	Ⓐ Ⓑ Ⓒ Ⓓ Ⓔ		21.	Ⓐ Ⓑ Ⓒ Ⓓ Ⓔ		38.	Ⓐ Ⓑ Ⓒ Ⓓ Ⓔ
5.	Ⓐ Ⓑ Ⓒ Ⓓ Ⓔ		22.	Ⓐ Ⓑ Ⓒ Ⓓ Ⓔ		39.	Ⓐ Ⓑ Ⓒ Ⓓ Ⓔ
6.	Ⓐ Ⓑ Ⓒ Ⓓ Ⓔ		23.	Ⓐ Ⓑ Ⓒ Ⓓ Ⓔ		40.	Ⓐ Ⓑ Ⓒ Ⓓ Ⓔ
7.	Ⓐ Ⓑ Ⓒ Ⓓ Ⓔ		24.	Ⓐ Ⓑ Ⓒ Ⓓ Ⓔ		41.	Ⓐ Ⓑ Ⓒ Ⓓ Ⓔ
8.	Ⓐ Ⓑ Ⓒ Ⓓ Ⓔ		25.	Ⓐ Ⓑ Ⓒ Ⓓ Ⓔ		42.	Ⓐ Ⓑ Ⓒ Ⓓ Ⓔ
9.	Ⓐ Ⓑ Ⓒ Ⓓ Ⓔ		26.	Ⓐ Ⓑ Ⓒ Ⓓ Ⓔ		43.	Ⓐ Ⓑ Ⓒ Ⓓ Ⓔ
10.	Ⓐ Ⓑ Ⓒ Ⓓ Ⓔ		27.	Ⓐ Ⓑ Ⓒ Ⓓ Ⓔ		44.	Ⓐ Ⓑ Ⓒ Ⓓ Ⓔ
11.	Ⓐ Ⓑ Ⓒ Ⓓ Ⓔ		28.	Ⓐ Ⓑ Ⓒ Ⓓ Ⓔ		45.	Ⓐ Ⓑ Ⓒ Ⓓ Ⓔ
12.	Ⓐ Ⓑ Ⓒ Ⓓ Ⓔ		29.	Ⓐ Ⓑ Ⓒ Ⓓ Ⓔ		46.	Ⓐ Ⓑ Ⓒ Ⓓ Ⓔ
13.	Ⓐ Ⓑ Ⓒ Ⓓ Ⓔ		30.	Ⓐ Ⓑ Ⓒ Ⓓ Ⓔ		47.	Ⓐ Ⓑ Ⓒ Ⓓ Ⓔ
14.	Ⓐ Ⓑ Ⓒ Ⓓ Ⓔ		31.	Ⓐ Ⓑ Ⓒ Ⓓ Ⓔ		48.	Ⓐ Ⓑ Ⓒ Ⓓ Ⓔ
15.	Ⓐ Ⓑ Ⓒ Ⓓ Ⓔ		32.	Ⓐ Ⓑ Ⓒ Ⓓ Ⓔ		49.	Ⓐ Ⓑ Ⓒ Ⓓ Ⓔ
16.	Ⓐ Ⓑ Ⓒ Ⓓ Ⓔ		33.	Ⓐ Ⓑ Ⓒ Ⓓ Ⓔ		50.	Ⓐ Ⓑ Ⓒ Ⓓ Ⓔ
17.	Ⓐ Ⓑ Ⓒ Ⓓ Ⓔ		34.	Ⓐ Ⓑ Ⓒ Ⓓ Ⓔ			

REFERENCE INFORMATION

THE FOLLOWING INFORMATION IS FOR YOUR REFERENCE IN ANSWERING SOME OF THE QUESTIONS IN THIS TEST:

Volume of a right circular cone with radius r and height h: $V = \frac{1}{3}\pi r^2 h$

Lateral area of a right circular cone with circumference of the base c and slaight height ℓ: $S = \frac{1}{2}c\ell$

Volume of a sphere with radius r: $V = \frac{4}{3}\pi r^3$

Surface area of a sphere with radius r: $S = 4\pi r^2$

Volume of a pyramid with base area B and height h: $V = \frac{1}{3}Bh$

MATHEMATICS LEVEL IIC TEST

For each of the following problems, decide which is the BEST of the choices given. If the exact numerical value is not one of the choices, select the choice that best approximates this value. Then fill in the corresponding oval on the answer sheet.

Notes: (1) A calculator will be necessary for answering some (but not all) of the questions in this test. For each question you will have to decide whether or not you should use a calcuator. The calculator you use must be at least a scientific calculator; programmable calculators and calculators that can display graphs are permitted.

(2) For some questions in this test you may need to decide whether your calculator should be in radian or degree mode.

(3) Figures that accompany problems in this test are intended to provide information useful in solving the problems. They are drawn as accurately as possible EXCEPT when it is stated in a specific problem that its figure is not drawn to scale. All figures lie in a plane unless otherwise indicated.

(4) Unless otherwise specified, the domain of any function f is assumed to be the set of all real numbers x for which $f(x)$ is a real number.

(5) Reference information that may be useful in answering the questions in this test can be found on the page preceding Question 1.

USE THIS SPACE FOR SCRATCHWORK.

. If $\dfrac{1}{\sqrt[3]{x^2 - 2}} = 5$, then x could be

(A) −1.42
(B) 0
(C) 1.38
(D) 1.52
(E) 2.01

. $\dfrac{10!}{2!8!} =$

(A) 50
(B) 45
(C) 40
(D) 35
(E) 30

GO ON TO THE NEXT PAGE

USE THIS SPACE FOR SCRATCHWORK.

3. If a function G is defined on triplets of positive numbers as $G(a, b, c) = \sqrt[3]{a \cdot b \cdot c}$, then which of the following is equal to $G(1, 2, 3)$?

(A) $G\left(\frac{1}{7}, 6, 12\right)$

(B) $G\left(\frac{1}{3}, 6, 4\right)$

(C) $G\left(\frac{7}{2}, 5, 8\right)$

(D) $G\left(\frac{7}{2}, \frac{1}{14}, 24\right)$

(E) $G\left(\frac{7}{2}, \frac{1}{7}, 11\right)$

4. In Figure 1, if AB contains the center of the circle, C is any point on the circle distinct from A or B, and $\sin s = \frac{5}{13}$, then $\sin z =$

(A) $\frac{7}{13}$

(B) $\frac{8}{13}$

(C) $\frac{12}{13}$

(D) $\frac{13}{12}$

(E) $\frac{4}{3}$

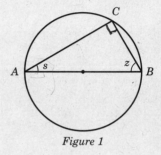

Figure 1

5. If $g(x) = \dfrac{1}{1 + \sqrt{x}}$, then what is the value of $g(g(2))$?

(A) 2.4

(B) 1.2

(C) 0.61

(D) 0.58

(E) 0.42

6. $|3 - 4i| =$

(A) 2.5

(B) 5

(C) $5i$

(D) $\sqrt{7}i$

(E) 25

GO ON TO THE NEXT PAGE

7. The graph of which of the following is perpendicular to the graph of $y = -\frac{x}{5} + \frac{2}{5}$?

(A) $y = \frac{x}{5} + 3$

(B) $y = 5x + .1$

(C) $y = -5x + \frac{2}{5}$

(D) $y = \frac{5}{2}x - \frac{1}{5}$

(E) $y = \frac{2}{5}x + 5$

8. If $x \neq 0$ or $x \neq 1$, then $\dfrac{1}{1 - \dfrac{1}{1 - x}} =$

(A) $1 - \frac{1}{x}$

(B) $\frac{1}{x} - 1$

(C) $\frac{1 - x}{x}$

(D) $2 + \frac{1}{x}$

(E) $\frac{x + 1}{-x}$

9. The graph of $y = ax^2 + bx + c$ <u>cannot</u> have points in the third or fourth quadrants if

(A) $b^2 - 4ac > 0$ and $b > a$
(B) $b^2 - 4ac > 0$ and $b < 0$
(C) $b^2 - 4ac = 0$ and $a < 0$
(D) $b^2 - 4ac < 0$ and $a < 0$
(E) $b^2 - 4ac < 0$ and $a > 0$

10. If $\sec\theta = 7$, then $\tan^2\theta + 1 =$

(A) 49
(B) 48
(C) $\cos^2\theta$
(D) 7
(E) $\sin^2\theta$

GO ON TO THE NEXT PAGE

11. $\dfrac{\dfrac{1}{a} - \dfrac{1}{b}}{\dfrac{1}{a^2} - \dfrac{1}{b^2}} =$

   (A) $\dfrac{a-b}{ab}$

   (B) $\dfrac{a+b}{ab}$

   (C) $\dfrac{ab}{b-a}$

   (D) $\dfrac{ab}{b+a}$

   (E) $\dfrac{1}{a} - \dfrac{1}{b}$

12. In a bag containing 6 oranges and 5 apples, what is the probability of withdrawing, without replacement, 1 orange and then 2 apples?

   (A) $\dfrac{4}{33}$

   (B) $\dfrac{5}{33}$

   (C) $\dfrac{1}{8}$

   (D) $\dfrac{100}{1331}$

   (E) $\dfrac{16}{1331}$

13. What is the sum of the roots of the equation $x^4 - 1 = 0$?

   (A) $-2i$
   (B) -1
   (C) 0
   (D) $4i$
   (E) $6i$

14. In Figure 2, if $\theta = 89°$, what is the value of z?

   (A) 0.03
   (B) 2
   (C) 100
   (D) 114.58
   (E) 114.60

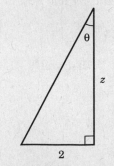

Note: Figure not drawn to scale.
Figure 2

15. If Mary makes $25 per hour for the first 30 hours she works, $30 per hour for each additional hour of work up to 40 hours, and $40 per hour for each hour of work over 40 hours, then how many hours must she work in order to make $1330?

(A) 38
(B) 42
(C) 45
(D) 47
(E) 50

16. An operation is defined on two pairs of real numbers by

$(x, y) \oplus (w, t) = \dfrac{x - y}{w + t}$, where $w + t \neq 0$. If

$(2, 1) \oplus (3, t) = (3, 1) \oplus (3, -t)$, then $t =$

(A) −2
(B) −1
(C) 0
(D) 1
(E) 2

7. The probability of event A occurring is $\dfrac{1}{3}$. The probability of event B occurring is $\dfrac{1}{2}$, and the probability of both event A and B occurring simultaneously is $\dfrac{1}{5}$. What is the probability of event A or B occurring?

(A) $\dfrac{19}{30}$

(B) $\dfrac{5}{6}$

(C) $\dfrac{1}{2}$

(D) $\dfrac{3}{4}$

(E) $\dfrac{1}{30}$

GO ON TO THE NEXT PAGE

18. The Golden Mean is defined using the zeros of the function $f(x) = x^2 + x - 1$. Which of the following is the larger of the two zeros?

(A) −1.618
(B) 0.618
(C) 1.618
(D) 3.241
(E) 5.011

19. In Figure 3, square *ABCD* is inscribed within a sphere of radius 2. The center of the sphere, point *O*, is contained in the square *ABCD*. What is the area of the square?

(A) $3\sqrt{2}$
(B) 4
(C) $4\sqrt{2}$
(D) 8
(E) $8\sqrt{2}$

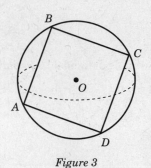

Figure 3

20. If $\log_7(\log_5(\log_3(x))) = 0$, then $x =$

(A) 243
(B) 125
(C) 49
(D) 25
(E) 1.4

21. Which of the following are the coordinates of the points at which the hyperbola $\frac{x^2}{4} - \frac{y^2}{3} = 1$ intersects the graph of the line $y = 1$?

(A) (−2.31, 0) and (2.31, 0)
(B) (−2.31, 1) and (2.31, 1)
(C) (−1.44, 1) and (1.44, 1)
(D) (−1, 1) and (1, 1)
(E) (−2.25, 1) and (2.25, 1)

22. The remainder when $3x^5 - 4x^3 + x - 1$ is divided by $x - 2$ is

(A) 73
(B) 65
(C) 31
(D) 0
(E) −15

GO ON TO THE NEXT PAGE

23. In Figure 4, $\tan\theta =$

(A) $\dfrac{y}{r}$

(B) $\dfrac{x}{r}$

(C) $\dfrac{y}{x}$

(D) $\dfrac{x}{y}$

(E) $\dfrac{r}{x+y}$

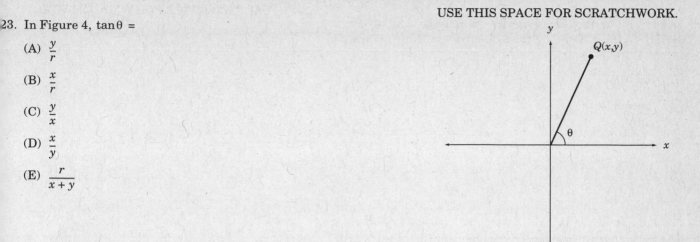

Figure 4

24. The distance between the points $(1, 2, 4)$ and $(-3, 7, 5)$ is approximately

(A) 1.11
(B) 4.47
(C) 5.48
(D) 6.48
(E) 10.10

25. What is the area of a parallelogram that has vertices at $(1, 1)$, $(3, 8)$, $(8, 1)$, and $(10, 8)$?

(A) 64
(B) 49
(C) 36
(D) 25
(E) 16

26. What is the minimum value of the function $f(x) = 2x^2 - 4x + 7$?

(A) 5
(B) 4.8
(C) 2.4
(D) 0
(E) -2

27. A population of birds grows at a rate of 7% per year. If there were 1200 birds in 1980, how many will there be in 2003?

(A) 4643
(B) 4968
(C) 5316
(D) 5688
(E) 5690

GO ON TO THE NEXT PAGE

28. If $m = (z-1)^3$ and $n = \dfrac{1}{z}$, what is m in terms of n?

    (A) $\left(\dfrac{1-n}{n}\right)^3$

    (B) $\left(\dfrac{n-1}{n}\right)^3$

    (C) $\left(\dfrac{1+n}{n^2}\right)^3$

    (D) $(1-n)^2$

    (E) $(n-1)^3$

29. The second term of a <u>geometric</u> sequence is 12 and the fourth term is 192. Which of the following could be the sum of the first 6 terms?

    (A) 882
    (B) 1023
    (C) 4095
    (D) 5000
    (E) 6400

30. What is the value of $\tan(\sin^{-1}(0.8))$?

    (A) $\dfrac{3}{4}$

    (B) 1

    (C) $\dfrac{4}{3}$

    (D) $\dfrac{5}{3}$

    (E) 2

31. An ellipse centered at $(1, 3)$ has a major axis of length 12 and a minor axis of length 8. Which of the following could be the equation of such an ellipse?

    (A) $\dfrac{(x+1)^2}{144} + \dfrac{(y+3)^2}{64} = 1$

    (B) $\dfrac{(x-1)^2}{144} + \dfrac{(y-3)^2}{64} = 1$

    (C) $\dfrac{(x+1)^2}{36} + \dfrac{(y+3)^2}{16} = 1$

    (D) $\dfrac{(x-1)^2}{36} + \dfrac{(y-3)^2}{16} = 1$

    (E) $\dfrac{(x-1)^2}{36} - \dfrac{(y-3)^2}{16} = 1$

GO ON TO THE NEXT PAGE

32. If $\cos\theta = a\sin\theta$ and $\tan\theta = 4$, then $a =$

(A) 4
(B) 0.50
(C) 0.45
(D) 0.33
(E) 0.25

33. A right, circular cone has a slant height of 10 and a base diameter of 12. What is its volume?

(A) 96π
(B) 144π
(C) 384π
(D) 500π
(E) 625π

34. If $2\cos^2\theta - 5\cos\theta + 2 = 0$, then θ could be which of the following?

(A) $\dfrac{\pi}{6}$

(B) $\dfrac{\pi}{4}$

(C) $\dfrac{\pi}{3}$

(D) $\dfrac{5\pi}{6}$

(E) π

35. If Figure 5 represents a portion of the graph of $h(x) = ax^3 + bx^2 + cx + d$, then which of the following <u>must</u> be true?

I. $a > 0$
II. $d = 0$
III. $b = 0$

(A) I only
(B) II only
(C) I and II only
(D) II and III only
(E) I, II, and III

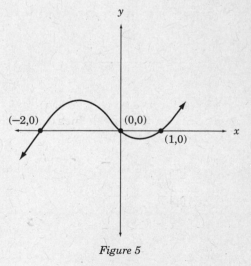

Figure 5

GO ON TO THE NEXT PAGE

36. The circle $x^2 + y^2 = 4$ is tangent to the circle
$(x - 2\sqrt{2})^2 + (y + 2\sqrt{2})^2 = 4$. What are the coordinates of the
point of tangency?

   (A) $(\sqrt{2}, -\sqrt{2})$
   (B) $(\sqrt{2}, \sqrt{2})$
   (C) $(-\sqrt{2}, -\sqrt{2})$
   (D) $(2, -2)$
   (E) $(2, 2)$

37. Which of the following could be the graph of $g(x) = 2^x - 2^{-x}$
over the interval $[-2, 2]$?

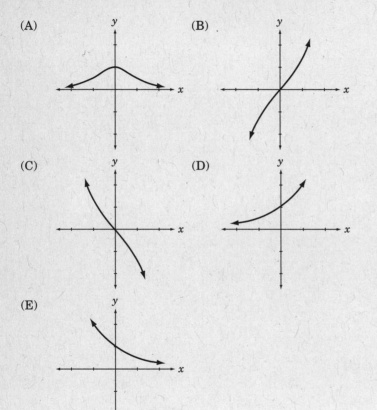

(A)

(B)

(C)

(D)

(E)

38. If $\dfrac{n}{m}$ is a positive odd integer, which of the following <u>must</u> also be a positive odd integer?

(A) $\dfrac{m}{n}$

(B) $\dfrac{n+2}{m}$

(C) $\dfrac{m}{n+1}$

(D) $\left(\dfrac{m}{n}\right)^2$

(E) $\left(\dfrac{n}{m}\right)^2$

39. A function f has the property that $f(x+2) = f(x)$ for all x in the domain. Which could be a portion of the graph of f?

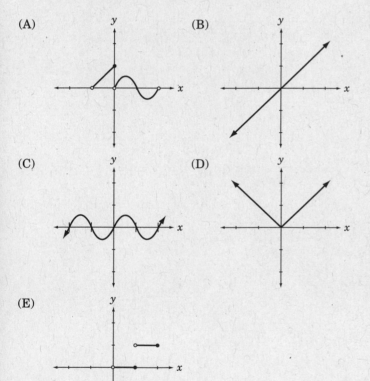

(A)

(B)

(C)

(D)

(E)

GO ON TO THE NEXT PAGE

40. What is $\lim\limits_{x \to 1} \dfrac{x^3 + x^2 - 2x}{x^2 - 3x + 2}$?

    (A) −4
    (B) −3
    (C) −2.5
    (D) 2
    (E) The limit does not exist

41. $\triangle ABC$ has side $a = 5$, side $b = 6$, and side $c = 10$. What is the measure of $\angle C$?

    (A) 135.21°
    (B) 130.54°
    (C) 120°
    (D) 65.27°
    (E) 60°

42. The circle $x^2 + y^2 = 10$ is symmetric across

    I. the x-axis
    II. the y-axis
    III. any line that passes through the origin

    (A) I only
    (B) II only
    (C) I and II only
    (D) I, II, and III
    (E) None of the above

GO ON TO THE NEXT PAGE

43. The solution to $\begin{cases} x + y \geq 4 \\ x \leq 4 \\ y \leq 4 \end{cases}$ is represented graphically by

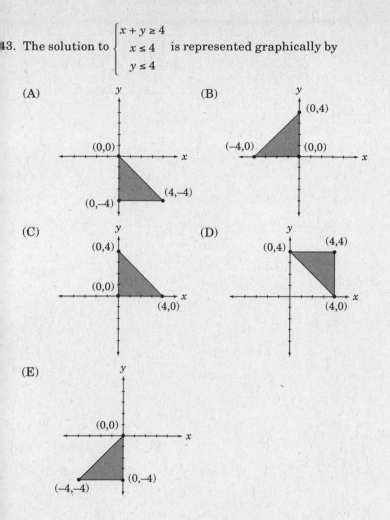

(A)

(B)

(C)

(D)

(E)

44. Let $\partial f(x)$ be defined as the slope of the graph of $y = f(x)$. For example, if $f(x) = 2x + 1$, then $\partial f(x) = 2$ for all x. Suppose that the graphs of $f(x)$ and $g(x)$ are distinct lines, and that $\partial f(x) = \partial g(x)$, then which of the following must be true?

   I. $f(x) = g(x)$
  II. The graph of $f(x)$ is parallel to the graph of $g(x)$
 III. $f(x) - g(x) = k$, where k is a constant

   (A) I only
   (B) II only
   (C) I and II only
   (D) II and III only
   (E) I, II, and III

GO ON TO THE NEXT PAGE

USE THIS SPACE FOR SCRATCHWORK.

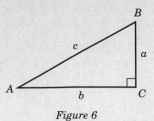

Figure 6

45. In Figure 6, $\sin(B - A)$ is equal to which of the following?

(A) $\dfrac{a^2 - b^2}{c^2}$

(B) $\dfrac{a^2 - b^2}{a^2 + b^2}$

(C) $\dfrac{b^2 - a^2}{b^2 + a^2}$

(D) $\dfrac{c^2}{b^2 - a^2}$

(E) $\dfrac{c^2}{a^2 - b^2}$

46. What is the least positive integer n for which 2^n has 16 digits?

(A) 48
(B) 49
(C) 50
(D) 51
(E) 55

47. A regular pentagon is inscribed within a circle of radius 1. What is the area of the pentagon?

(A) 1
(B) 1.55
(C) 1.71
(D) 2.20
(E) 2.38

48. If $f(x) = \dfrac{1}{\pi}\log_3(x^5 + 1)$ for $x > -1$, then $f^{-1}(x) =$

(A) $\sqrt[3]{5^{\pi x} - 1}$

(B) $\sqrt[5]{3^{\pi x} - 1}$

(C) $\sqrt[5]{3^{\pi x - 1}}$

(D) $\sqrt[5]{3^{\pi x + 1}}$

(E) $\sqrt[5]{3^{\pi x}} - 1$

GO ON TO THE NEXT PAGE

49. What is the radius of a sphere that has a surface area numerically 20% larger than its volume?

    (A) 4
    (B) 3.33
    (C) 2.67
    (D) 2.5
    (E) 0.40

50. A scientific committee must be chosen so that it consists of 2 physicists, 1 mathematician, and 3 biologists. If the pool of candidates is comprised of 15 physicists, 10 mathematicians, and 25 biologists, then how many different committees are possible?

    (A) 4,830,000
    (B) 2,415,000
    (C) 1,610,000
    (D) 805,000
    (E) 500,000

S T O P

IF YOU FINISH BEFORE TIME IS CALLED, YOU MAY CHECK YOUR WORK ON THIS TEST ONLY.
DO NOT TURN TO ANY OTHER TEST IN THIS BOOK.

SAT II Math IIC
Practice Test 1
Explanations

Calculating Your Score

Question Number	Correct Answer	Right	Wrong	Question Number	Correct Answer	Right	Wrong	Question Number	Correct Answer	Right	Wrong
1.	A	——	——	18.	B	——	——	35.	C	——	——
2.	B	——	——	19.	D	——	——	36.	A	——	——
3.	D	——	——	20.	A	——	——	37.	B	——	——
4.	C	——	——	21.	B	——	——	38.	E	——	——
5.	C	——	——	22.	B	——	——	39.	C	——	——
6.	B	——	——	23.	C	——	——	40.	B	——	——
7.	B	——	——	24.	D	——	——	41.	B	——	——
8.	A	——	——	25.	B	——	——	42.	D	——	——
9.	E	——	——	26.	A	——	——	43.	D	——	——
10.	A	——	——	27.	D	——	——	44.	D	——	——
11.	D	——	——	28.	A	——	——	45.	B	——	——
12.	A	——	——	29.	C	——	——	46.	C	——	——
13.	C	——	——	30.	C	——	——	47.	E	——	——
14.	A	——	——	31.	D	——	——	48.	B	——	——
15.	D	——	——	32.	E	——	——	49.	D	——	——
16.	B	——	——	33.	A	——	——	50.	B	——	——
17.	A	——	——	34.	C	——	——				

Your raw score for the SAT II Math IIC test is calculated from the number of questions you answer correctly and incorrectly. Once you have determined your composite score, use the conversion table on page 18 of this book to calculate your scaled score. To calculate your raw score, count the number of questions you answered correctly: _____
                                                                                                A

Count the number of questions you answered incorrectly, and multiply that number by $\frac{1}{4}$:

_____ × $\frac{1}{4}$ = _____
       B   C

Subtract the value in field C from value in field A: _____
                                                      D

Round the number in field D to the nearest whole number. This is your raw score: _____
                                                                                    E

Math IIC Test 1 Explanations

1. **(A)** *Algebra: Equation Solving*

This is a straightforward test of your algebraic manipulation skills.

$$\frac{1}{\sqrt[3]{x^2-2}} = 5$$

$$\frac{1}{x^2-2} = 125$$

$$\frac{1}{125} = x^2-2$$

$$\frac{1}{125} + 2 = x^2$$

$$2.008 = x^2$$

$$x = \pm 1.42$$

2. **(B)** *Statistics: Permutations and Combinations*

This question asks you to do a basic calculation with factorials. You should memorize the following formula for calculating a factorial: $n! = n(n-1)(n-2)...(3)(2)(1)$.

$$\frac{10!}{2!8!} = \frac{10 \cdot 9 \cdot 8 \cdot 7 \cdot 6 \cdot 5 \cdot 4 \cdot 3 \cdot 2 \cdot 1}{2 \cdot 1 \cdot 8 \cdot 7 \cdot 6 \cdot 5 \cdot 4 \cdot 3 \cdot 2 \cdot 1}$$

$$= \frac{10 \cdot 9}{2 \cdot 1}$$

$$= 45$$

3. **(D)** *Functions: Evaluating Functions*

The key to this problem is realizing that since $G(a, b, c) = G(1, 2, 3)$, you need to find a triplet of positive numbers such that $a \cdot b \cdot c = 1 \cdot 2 \cdot 3 = 6$. The cube root is not important for finding the correct answer.

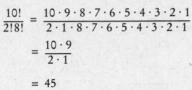

$$G\left(\frac{7}{2}, \frac{1}{14}, 24\right) = \sqrt[3]{\frac{7}{2} \cdot \frac{1}{14} \cdot 24}$$

$$= \sqrt[3]{6}$$

$$= G(1, 2, 3)$$

4.   **(C)**   *Plane Geometry: Triangles, Circles; Trigonometry: Basic Functions*

In this question, you have a triangle inscribed within a circle such that the circle's diameter forms one of the triangle's sides. No matter where you draw the two other sides of the triangle along the circle's circumference, the sides will form a right angle. The circle's diameter will form the hypotenuse of the right triangle. Since $\angle ACB = 90°$, you can use basic trig to answer this problem.

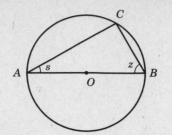

If $\sin s = \dfrac{5}{13}$, you know that, for the angle s, the opposite side (BC) is 5 and the hypotenuse (AB) is 13. Using the Pythagorean Theorem, you can determine that $AC = 12$ and $\sin z = \dfrac{12}{13}$.

5.   **(C)**   *Functions: Evaluating Functions*

When you come across a compound expression such as $g(g(2))$, you first need to determine the value of $g(2)$ and then plug that value back into the function $g(x)$.

$$g(2) = \frac{1}{1 + \sqrt{2}}$$

$$g(g(2)) = \frac{1}{1 + \sqrt{\dfrac{1}{1 + \sqrt{2}}}}$$

$$= \frac{1}{1 + 0.6436}$$

$$= 0.61$$

6.   **(B)**   *Miscellaneous Math: Complex Numbers*

Most graphing calculators can handle complex number expressions, but you can easily calculate the answer to this question by hand. The absolute value of a complex number of the form $a + bi$ is defined as $|a + bi| = \sqrt{(a + bi)(a - bi)}$.

$$\begin{aligned}
|3 - 4i| &= \sqrt{(3 - 4i)(3 + 4i)} \\
&= \sqrt{9 - 12i + 12i - 16i^2} \\
&= \sqrt{9 + 16} \text{, since } i^2 = -1 \\
&= \sqrt{25} \\
&= 5
\end{aligned}$$

7.   **(B)**   *Coordinate Geometry: Lines*

The line $y = mx + b$ is perpendicular to the line $y = Mx + b$ if and only if their slopes have the following relationship: $m = \dfrac{-1}{M}$. You can see that the graph of the line perpendicular to $y = -\dfrac{x}{5} + \dfrac{2}{5}$ must have a slope $m = -\dfrac{1}{-\frac{1}{5}}$ or $m = 5$. Answer choice (B) is correct since it is the only line with a slope of 5.

8. **(A)** *Algebra: Algebraic Manipulation*

Although the math needed for solving this question is straightforward, you need to be meticulous when manipulating a complex algebraic expression like this one. A careless error could easily get you the wrong answer.

$$\frac{1}{1 - \dfrac{1}{1-x}} = \frac{1}{\dfrac{1-x}{1-x} - \dfrac{1}{1-x}}$$

$$= \frac{1}{\dfrac{1-x-1}{1-x}}$$

$$= \frac{1}{\dfrac{-x}{1-x}}$$

$$= \frac{1-x}{-x}$$

$$= \frac{-x}{-x} + \frac{1}{-x}$$

$$= 1 - \frac{1}{x}$$

9. **(E)** *Functions: Graphing Functions*

You can always calculate the roots of a quadratic equation by plugging its coefficients into the quadratic formula. But if you don't need to know the actual values of the roots, you can use the coefficients of the equation to calculate the discriminant, which tells you the type and number of roots the equation has. Given a quadratic of the form $y = ax^2 + bx + c$, the discriminant D is defined as $D = b^2 - 4ac$. If $D > 0$, the quadratic has 2 distinct real roots and 2 x-intercepts. If $D = 0$, the equation has 1 rational repeated root and touches the x-axis at one point only (think of a parabola with its vertex on the x-axis). If $D < 0$, the equation has no real roots (but 2 complex conjugate ones) and, therefore, never crosses the x-axis.

The question states that the graph of the quadratic cannot have points in the third or fourth quadrants, the two quadrants below the x-axis. This means the graph cannot cross below the x-axis, although it can be tangent to the x-axis (the axes are not considered to be part of the quadrants); thus the discriminant must be less than or equal to zero. Since the function can't cross below the x-axis, the coefficient a must be positive so that the graph opens upward. Only answer choice (E) completely satisfies these conditions.

10. **(A)** *Trigonometry: Pythagorean Identities*

You should be prepared to use any of the Pythagorean Identities on this test. The solution to this problem depends on the identity, $\tan^2\theta + 1 = \sec^2\theta$. If $\sec\theta = 7$, then $\sec^2\theta = 7^2 = 49$. When you substitute for $\sec^2\theta$, you get $\tan^2\theta + 1 = 49$.

11. **(D)** *Algebra: Algebraic Manipulation*

Again, you need to pay close attention as you simplify the expression.

$$\frac{\frac{1}{a} - \frac{1}{b}}{\frac{1}{a^2} - \frac{1}{b^2}} = \frac{\frac{b-a}{ab}}{\frac{b^2 - a^2}{a^2 b^2}}$$

$$= \frac{\frac{b-a}{ab}}{\frac{(b-a) \cdot (b+a)}{a^2 b^2}}$$

$$= \frac{\frac{1}{ab}}{\frac{1 \cdot (b+a)}{a^2 b^2}}$$

$$= \frac{ab}{b+a}$$

12. **(A)** *Statistics: Probability*

"Without replacement" means that the number of fruit in the bag diminishes by 1 each time a piece of fruit is withdrawn. The probability of pulling out an orange first is $\frac{6}{11}$, since initially there are 6 oranges among the 11 pieces of fruit (6 oranges plus 5 apples). Since only 10 pieces of fruit remain after the removal of the orange, the probability of the second fruit being an apple is $\frac{5}{10}$. Finally, the probability of the last piece of fruit also being an apple is $\frac{4}{9}$. Multiply the three probabilities together to find the probability of withdrawing an orange and then 2 apples consecutively; $\frac{6}{11} \cdot \frac{5}{10} \cdot \frac{4}{9} = \frac{4}{33}$.

13. **(C)** *Algebra: Polynomials*

There are two approaches to this problem. The first is to factor this quartic equation and then add together its roots:

$$x^4 - 1 = (x^2 - 1)(x^2 + 1)$$
$$= (x - 1)(x + 1)(x - i)(x + i) = 0$$

The roots are $1, -1, i, -i$. You can add them together to find the answer:

$$1 + (-1) + i + (-i) = 0$$

The second approach is to recall that for an equation in the form $0 = ax^4 + bx^3 + cx^2 + dx + e$, the sum of the roots must equal $-\frac{b}{a}$. In the equation $x^4 - 1 = 0$, the coefficient b is equal to 0, so the sum of the roots is equal to $-\frac{0}{1}$, or 0.

14. **(A)** *Trigonometry: Basic Functions*

Since the triangle is a right triangle, you know $\tan\theta = \frac{2}{z}$, where 2 is opposite the angle θ and z is adjacent. Plug in $\theta = 89°$, and solve for z.

$$\tan 89° = \frac{2}{z}$$

$$57.29 \approx \frac{2}{z}$$

$$z \approx \frac{2}{57.29}$$

$$z \approx 0.03$$

15. **(D)** *Fundamentals: Word Problems*

If Mary works 30 hours, she will make $25 \cdot 30 = 750$ dollars, so you know she must work overtime to make a total of \$1330. If she works 40 hours in total, then she would make $25 \cdot 30 + 10 \cdot 30 = 1050$ dollars. In order to make \$280 dollars more, she has to work an extra 7 hours at \$40/hour. The total amount of time she must work is $30 + 10 + 7 = 47$ hours.

16. **(B)** *Functions: Evaluating Functions*

The difficult part of solving an arbitrary operation problem is simply unwinding the new definition. If $(x, y) \oplus (w, t) = \frac{x - y}{w + t}$, then $(2, 1) \oplus (3, t) = \frac{2 - 1}{3 + t}$ and $(3, 1) \oplus (3, -t) = \frac{3 - 1}{3 + (-t)}$. You can solve for t by setting these two equations equal to each other.

$$\frac{2 - 1}{3 + t} = \frac{3 - 1}{3 - t}$$

$$\frac{1}{3 + t} = \frac{2}{3 - t}$$

$$3 - t = 2(3 + t)$$

$$3 - t = 6 + 2t$$

$$-3 = 3t$$

$$t = -1$$

17. **(A)** *Statistics: Probability*

You are expected to know the following formula for determining probability. Given the probability of A (denoted $P(A)$), the probability of B (denoted $P(B)$), and the probability of A and B (denoted $P(A \cap B)$), then the probability of A or B (denoted $P(A \cup B)$) can be calculated by $P(A \cup B) = P(A) + P(B) - P(A \cap B)$. Since $P(A)$, $P(B)$, and $P(A \cap B)$ are given in the question, all you need to do is plug them into the formula:

$$P(A \cup B) = \frac{1}{3} + \frac{1}{2} - \frac{1}{5}$$

$$= \frac{19}{30}$$

18. **(B)** *Algebra: Polynomials*

This problem asks you to find the larger of the two zeros of the function $f(x) = x^2 + x - 1$. You should use the quadratic formula to find the solutions to $0 = x^2 + x - 1$, where $a = 1$, $b = 1$ and $c = -1$.

$$\frac{-b \pm \sqrt{b^2 - 4ac}}{2a} = \frac{-1 \pm \sqrt{1 - (4 \cdot 1 \cdot (-1))}}{2}$$
$$= \frac{-1 \pm \sqrt{5}}{2}$$
$$= \frac{-1 \pm 2.236}{2}, \text{ which is approximately } -1.618 \text{ or } 0.618.$$

19. **(D)** *Solid Geometry: Solids that Aren't Prisms; Plane Geometry: Polygons*

If the center of the sphere is also the center of the square, then you know that the radius of the sphere is half the length of the diagonal of the square (and that the diagonal of the square is equal to the sphere's diameter).

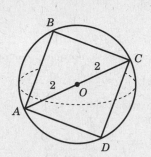

The area of a square can be written as $Area = s^2$, where s is the length of a side, or equivalently as $Area = \frac{1}{2}d^2$, where d is the diagonal of the square. You know $d = 2r$ and $r = 2$, so $d = 4$. Thus $Area = \frac{1}{2} \cdot 4^2 = 8$.

If you didn't memorize this formula for the test, you can always find the length of the square's sides by seeing that the diagonal forms two 45-45-90 triangles. If the hypotenuse of those triangles (the diagonal of the square) is 4, then the lengths of the square's sides are equal to $2\sqrt{2}$, and $(2\sqrt{2})^2 = 8$.

20. **(A)** *Algebra: Equation Solving, Logarithms*

A logarithm expresses an exponential relationship. The definition of a logarithm shows that $\log_b y = x$ is equivalent to the expression $b^x = y$. Applying this definition three times to the given equation will allow you to find x by "unwrapping" the logarithms.

$$\log_7(\log_5(\log_3(x))) = 0$$
$$\log_5(\log_3(x)) = 7^0 \text{ and } 7^0 = 1$$
$$\log_3(x) = 5^1$$
$$x = 3^5$$
$$= 243$$

21. **(B)** *Solid Geometry: Hyperbolas*

This problem is actually simpler than it appears at first glance. To find the points of intersection between a given hyperbola and the line $y = 1$, you just plug in the value 1 for y and then solve for x.

$$\frac{x^2}{4} - \frac{1^2}{3} = 1$$

$$\frac{x^2}{4} = \frac{4}{3}$$

$$x^2 = \frac{16}{3}$$

$$x = \pm\frac{4}{\sqrt{3}}$$

$$= \pm 2.31$$

Since $y = 1$, you can see that answer choice (B) is correct.

22. **(B)** *Algebra: Polynomials*

According to the polynomial version of long division, any polynomial $p(x)$ can be written as $p(x) = (x - a) \cdot q(x) + R$, where $p(x)$ is the original polynomial, $(x - a)$ is the divisor, $q(x)$ is the quotient, and R is the remainder. The most efficient way to find the remainder is to plug a into $p(x)$, since $p(a) = (a - a) \cdot (q(a) + R)$, or $p(a) = R$. Since the divisor is $x - 2$, you know that $a = 2$. You can calculate the remainder R by plugging 2 into $p(x)$:

$$R = 3 \cdot (2)^5 - 4(2)^3 + 2 - 1$$
$$= 96 - 32 + 2 - 1$$
$$= 65$$

23. **(C)** *Trigonometry: Basic Functions; Coordinate Geometry: Coordinate Plane*

The best way to answer this question is to make a right triangle by drawing a line down from point Q to the x-axis.

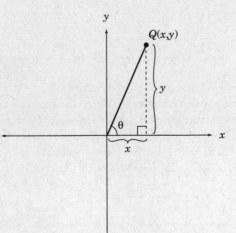

The coordinates of point Q will give you the lengths of two sides of the triangle—the sides opposite and adjacent to the angle θ. Once you have determined the opposite and adjacent sides, you can use simple trig to calculate the value of θ. The side opposite θ has a length equal to the value of the y-coordinate of Q and the adjacent side has a length equal to that of the x-coordinate.

$$\tan\theta = \frac{opposite}{adjacent}$$
$$= \frac{y}{x}$$

24. **(D)** *Coordinate Geometry: Lines and Distance*

This is a straightforward check to see whether you know the formula for the distance between points in 3-dimensional space. When you have two points in space (x_1, y_1, z_1) and (x_2, y_2, z_2), then the distance between them is given by $d = \sqrt{(x_1 - x_2)^2 + (y_1 - y_2)^2 + (z_1 - z_2)^2}$.

$$
\begin{aligned}
d &= \sqrt{(1-(-3))^2 + (2-7)^2 + (4-5)^2} \\
&= \sqrt{4^2 + (-5)^2 + (-1)^2} \\
&= \sqrt{16 + 25 + 1} \\
&= \sqrt{42} \\
&= 6.48
\end{aligned}
$$

25. **(B)** *Plane Geometry: Polygons; Coordinate Geometry: Coordinate Plane*

This question tells you that the four coordinates form a parallelogram. You should draw a picture of this parallelogram to help you solve this problem.

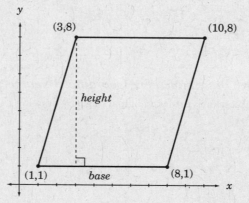

In this picture, you can see that the base of the parallelogram is equal to the distance between points $(1, 1)$ and $(8, 1)$. You can find this distance by finding the difference between the x-coordinates of the points: $8 - 1 = 7$. (The y-coordinates of these points are the same, so you don't need to worry about them.) Because the sides in a parallelogram are parallel, you can find the height by finding the difference between the y-coordinates of points $(3, 8)$ and $(1, 1)$: $8 - 1 = 7$. Since the area of a parallelogram is given by $Area = Base \cdot Height$, for this parallelogram the $Area = 7 \cdot 7 = 49$.

26. **(A)** *Functions: Graphing Functions*

You can use your graphing calculator to solve this question, or you can do the calculation by hand. Since the graph of this quadratic equation is an upward-opening parabola, the y-coordinate of the vertex must be the minimum value of the function. Your first step should be to calculate the vertex of this function. You can do this by rewriting the equation as $y = a(x-h)^2 + k$, where (h, k) is the vertex of the parabola:

$$y = 2x^2 - 4x + 7$$
$$= 2(x^2 - 2x) + 7$$

Now you need to change $(x^2 - 2x)$ so that it factors into the form $(x-h)^2$. You can do this by "completing the square"—adding a constant to both sides of the equation. In this case, add 2 to each side to complete the square:

$$y + 2 = 2(x^2 - 2x + 1) + 7$$
$$y = 2(x - 1)^2 + 5$$

So the vertex is the point $(1, 5)$, and the minimum value must be 5.

27. **(D)** *Algebra: Equation Solving, Exponential Growth and Decay*

The formulas for growth and decay are fair game on the Math IIC test. Given an original population P, a percentage rate of growth or decay r (written as a decimal) and a length of time t, you can use the following formula to calculate the population after an amount of time, t.

$$P(t) = P(1 \pm r)^t$$

Since the length of time is $2003 - 1980 = 23$ years, plug in 23 for t:

$$P(23) = 1200(1 + 0.07)^{23}$$
$$= 1200(1.07)^{23}$$
$$= 1200 \cdot 4.74053$$
$$\approx 5688$$

28. **(A)** *Algebra: Systems of Equations*

The question asks you to rewrite m in terms of n. Since both m and n are given in terms of z, you should first solve for z in terms of n. If $n = \frac{1}{z}$, then $z = \frac{1}{n}$. Now you can substitute the expression for z in the equation $m = (z-1)^3$.

$$m = (z - 1)^3$$
$$= \left(\frac{1}{n} - 1\right)^3$$
$$= \left(\frac{1 - n}{n}\right)^3$$

29. **(C)** *Miscellaneous Math: Sequences and Series*

The Math IIC will probably include a question on sequences, so you should memorize the sequence formulas. The formula for a general term of a geometric sequence $\{a, ar, ar^2, \ldots\}$ is given by $a \cdot r^{n-1} = a_n$, where a is the first term in the sequence, a_n is the n-th term, and the ratio r is a constant. The sum of the first n terms in a geometric series is given by $S = \frac{a(1 - r^n)}{1 - r}$. In order to determine the sum of the first 6 terms in this geometric series, you will need to find the values of a and r first. Using the formula for a general term in the sequence, you have:

$$12 = a \cdot r^1, \text{ since 12 is the second term.}$$
$$192 = a \cdot r^3, \text{ since 192 is the fourth term.}$$

Dividing the bottom equation by the top equation, you get:

$$\frac{192}{12} = \frac{ar^3}{ar^1}$$
$$16 = r^2$$
$$r = \pm 4$$

If $r = -4$, then $a = -3$. And if $r = 4$, then $a = 3$.

Plug the sets of numbers into the formula for S. When you try the positive pair of numbers, you'll see that:

$$S = \frac{3(1 - 4^6)}{1 - 4}$$
$$S = 4095, \text{ which is answer choice (C).}$$

30. **(C)** *Trigonometry: Inverse Trigonometric Functions*

The fastest way to solve this question is to use a calculator. First find $\sin^{-1}(0.8)$, and then plug the result into $\tan x$.

$$\sin^{-1}(0.8) \approx 53.130°$$
$$\tan(53.130°) \approx 1.333$$
$$= \frac{4}{3}$$

31. **(D)** *Coordinate Geometry: Ellipses*

You should arrange the information given in the question as an equation for an ellipse. The general equation for an ellipse centered at the point (h, k) is given by $\frac{(x - h)^2}{a^2} + \frac{(y - k)^2}{b^2} = 1$, where the length of the major axis is either $2a$ or $2b$ and the length of the minor axis is accordingly either $2b$ or $2a$. Assume for the moment that the major axis is $2a$ (in other words, that the major axis is horizontal), and see whether you can fit the given data to one of the answer choices. If $2a = 12$, then $a = 6$ and $a^2 = 36$. Similarly, if $2b = 8$, then $b = 4$ and $b^2 = 16$. (h, k), the center of the ellipse, is given in the question as $(1, 3)$. Thus the equation could be:

$$\frac{(x - 1)^2}{36} + \frac{(y - 3)^2}{16} = 1, \text{ which is answer choice (D).}$$

32. **(E)** *Trigonometry: Basic Functions*

A trigonometric equation of this sort always requires some form of manipulation. You want to see if you can rewrite $\cos\theta = a \cdot \sin\theta$ in a simpler form. Since you're solving for a, isolate a on one side of the equation. Divide both sides by $\cos\theta$ and then divide by a to obtain:

$$\frac{1}{a} = \frac{\sin\theta}{\cos\theta}$$
$$\frac{1}{a} = \tan\theta$$

You're told that $\tan\theta = 4$, so you can write the following equation:

$$\frac{1}{a} = 4$$
$$a = \frac{1}{4} \text{ or } 0.25$$

33. **(A)** *Solid Geometry: Prisms*

The formula for the volume of a cone requires the cone's radius and height. The question tells you that the base diameter of the cone is 12, so you know that the radius is 6. To find the height of the cone, draw a picture, including the radius and slant height.

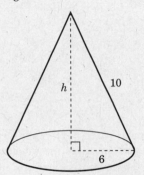

A right triangle is formed by the radius of the cone's base, the slant height of the cone, and the height of the cone. You can solve for the height of the cone using the Pythagorean Theorem, where the slant height of the cone is the hypotenuse of the triangle and the radius of the cone is one of the triangle's legs.

$$h = \sqrt{10^2 - 6^2}$$
$$= \sqrt{100 - 36}$$
$$= \sqrt{64} \text{ or } 8$$

Now that you have the cone's height, you can find its volume:

$$V = \frac{1}{3}\pi r^2 h$$
$$= \frac{1}{3}\pi \cdot 36 \cdot 8$$
$$= 96\pi$$

34. **(C)** *Algebra: Equation Solving; Trigonometry: Inverse Trigonometric Functions*

This problem may seem daunting until you realize that the expression involving $\cos\theta$ is really only a quadratic equation in which $\cos\theta$ takes the place of x. You should factor the equation because factoring often reveals solutions to seemingly complicated problems on the Math IIC.

$$2\cos^2\theta - 5\cos\theta + 2 = 0$$
$$(2\cos\theta - 1)(\cos\theta - 2) = 0$$

If $\cos\theta - 2 = 0$, then $\cos\theta = 2$, which has no real solutions. If $2\cos\theta - 1 = 0$, then $\cos\theta = \frac{1}{2}$ and $\theta = \frac{\pi}{3}, \frac{5\pi}{3}$. Choice (C), which is $\frac{\pi}{3}$, is correct.

35. **(C)** *Algebra: Polynomials*

This question asks you for information on the coefficients of the function and provides you with the function and a portion of its graph. From the graph, you can determine that the roots of this cubic polynomial are $r_1 = -2$, $r_2 = 0$, and $r_3 = 1$.

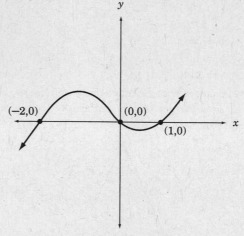

Figure 5

You can rewrite the polynomial as $h(x) = a(x - r_1)(x - r_2)(x - r_3)$, which becomes $h(x) = a(x + 2)(x - 0)(x - 1)$ when you substitute the values of the roots. Multiply this out to get $h(x) = a(x^3 + x^2 - 2x)$. Since, as you can see from the graph, overall the function increases as x increases, $a > 0$. Also, d must be equal to zero since there is no constant term in the function, and b is *not* equal to zero since there is an x^2 term.

36. **(A)** *Coordinate Geometry: Circles*

You are looking for the point where these two circles are tangent—in other words, where their (x, y) coordinates are equal. Since the equations of the two circles both equal 4 ($x^2 + y^2 = 4$ and $(x - 2\sqrt{2})^2 + (y + 2\sqrt{2})^2 = 4$), you can simply set these expressions equal to each other to solve for x and y.

$$x^2 + y^2 = (x - 2\sqrt{2})^2 + (y + 2\sqrt{2})^2$$
$$x^2 + y^2 = x^2 - 4\sqrt{2}x + 8 + y^2 + 4\sqrt{2}y + 8$$

When you rearrange and cancel terms, you get:

$$x = 2\sqrt{2} + y$$

Plug this expression for x back into $x^2 + y^2 = 4$ in order to solve for y.

$$(2\sqrt{2} + y)^2 + y^2 = 4$$

$$8 + 4\sqrt{2}y + 2y^2 = 4$$
$$2y^2 + 4\sqrt{2}y + 4 = 0 \text{, which is a perfect square}$$

$$2(y + \sqrt{2})^2 = 0$$

Now you know $y = -\sqrt{2}$. Plug this value for y into $x = 2\sqrt{2} + y$ to get $x = \sqrt{2}$. The point of tangency is $(\sqrt{2}, -\sqrt{2})$.

37. **(B)** *Functions: Graphing Functions*

You can graph the function $g(x) = 2^x - 2^{-x}$ on your calculator to find the correct answer. You can also answer this question without a calculator. Since $g(0) = 1 - 1 = 0$, you know the graph must pass through $(0, 0)$, ruling out answer choices (A), (D), and (E). Additionally, $g(1) = 2 - \frac{1}{2}$ means the graph must pass through $\left(1, \frac{3}{2}\right)$, so you can eliminate (C), leaving you with the correct answer choice, (B).

38. **(E)** *Fundamentals: Integers*

The result of an odd number multiplied by another odd number must be odd; thus an odd number raised to any positive integer power must remain odd (for example, $3^3 = 27$ and $3^4 = 81$). The only answer choice that must be odd is (E) because it is the square of a positive odd integer (an odd number multiplied by itself).

    You can rule out the other answer choices. Choice (A) is a fraction, not an integer; n will always be larger than m if $\frac{n}{m}$ is an integer, because the reverse, $\frac{m}{n}$, will always be a fraction. If, for example, $n = 6$ and $m = 2$, then $\frac{n}{m} = 3$, but $\frac{m}{n} = \frac{1}{3}$. Choice (C) is a fraction because it simply increases the denominator of $\frac{m}{n+1}$. Choice (D) squares choice (A); thus it is also a fraction. Choice (B) can be either odd or even. If $\frac{n}{m} = \frac{6}{2} = 3$, then $\frac{n+2}{m} = \frac{8}{2} = 4$.

39. **(C)** *Functions: Graphing Functions*

When you see something like $f(x + 2) = f(x)$, you should instantly realize you're dealing with a periodic function, where the value of y repeats at a regular interval. The period of this function is 2 because the value of $f(x)$ repeats itself when x increases by 2. You need to find a graph with a period of 2 (in other words, a graph which repeats itself over every interval of length 2). Algebraically you can see that $f(-2 + 2) = f(-2)$, so $f(0) = f(-2)$, and $f(0 + 2) = f(0)$, so $f(2) = f(0)$. The only answer choice that satisfies these conditions is (C).

40. **(B)** *Miscellaneous Math: Limits*

There will almost certainly be a limit question on the Math IIC. To answer this question, you must reduce the function into its most basic form; otherwise, the function will appear to be undefined at the point it approaches (try plugging 1 into the original version, and you'll end up with the undefined quantity $\frac{0}{0}$). Remember to factor and to cancel like terms before plugging in 1.

$$\lim_{x \to 1} \frac{x^3 + x^2 - 2x}{x^2 - 3x + 2} = \lim_{x \to 1} \frac{x(x+2)(x-1)}{(x-2)(x-1)}$$

$$= \lim_{x \to 1} \frac{x(x+2)}{(x-2)}$$

Now you can plug in $x = 1$:

$$= \frac{1(1+2)}{1-2}$$

$$= -3$$

41. **(B)** *Trigonometry: Solving Non-Right Triangles*

You can use either the law of sines or the law of cosines to solve non-right triangles. This problem requires the law of cosines because you are given only the three sides of the triangle and no angles.

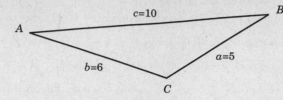

The law of cosines states that $c^2 = a^2 + b^2 - 2ab\cos C$. You can use this to find $\angle C$.

$$10^2 = 5^2 + 6^2 - (2 \cdot 5 \cdot 6 \cdot \cos C)$$

$$100 = 25 + 36 - 60\cos C$$

$$-\frac{39}{60} = \cos C$$

$$\cos^{-1}\left(\frac{-39}{60}\right) = C$$

$$130.54° = C$$

42. **(D)** *Functions: Transformations and Symmetry*

The given equation describes a circle of radius $\sqrt{10}$ centered at the origin of the coordinate plane. Looking at the figure below you can see that any line that passes through the origin will divide the circle symmetrically in half. Since both the x- and y-axes are specific lines through the origin you can see that I, II, and III must be true.

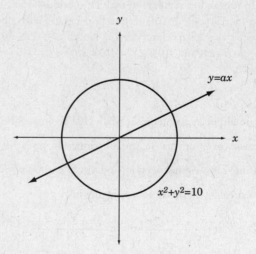

43. **(D)** *Coordinate Geometry: Linear Inequalities, Graphing*

To find the graph of the set of equations, you first need to graph the equations individually; then you can find the intersection of the three graphs. The graph of $x + y \geq 4$ is equivalent to the graph of $y \geq 4 - x$, which is shown below.

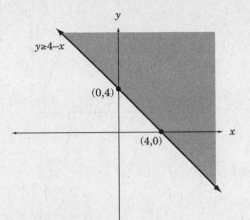

The graphs of $x \leq 4$ and $y \leq 4$ look like this:

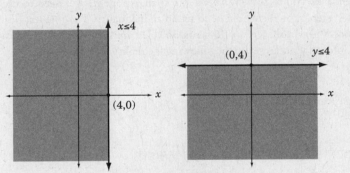

The intersection of all these graphs is given by answer choice (D).

44. **(D)** *Coordinate Geometry: Lines and Distance*

If the graph of $f(x)$ is a line, then $f(x)$ must be in the form of $f(x) = m_1 x + b_1$. Similarly, $g(x)$ must be of the form $g(x) = m_2 x + b_2$. The question states that $\partial f(x) = m_1$ and $\partial g(x) = m_2$. If $\partial f(x) = \partial g(x)$, then $m_1 = m_2$. The lines must be parallel because their slopes are equal. Additionally, if $m_1 = m_2$, then:

$$\begin{aligned} f(x) - g(x) &= m_1 x + b_1 - (m_2 x + b_2) \\ &= (m_1 - m_2)x + b_1 - b_2 \\ &= 0x + b_1 - b_2 \\ &= b_1 - b_2, \text{ which is a constant.} \end{aligned}$$

Statement I is not necessarily true because the lines can have different y-intercepts. But II and III are always true, and the correct answer is (D).

45. **(B)** *Trigonometry: Sum and Difference Formulas*

This question tests you on angle addition/subtraction. You should definitely memorize the sum and difference formulas for both sine and cosine. To answer this question, recall that $\sin(A - B) = \sin A \cos B - \cos A \sin B$. Apply this formula to the triangle in the figure below:

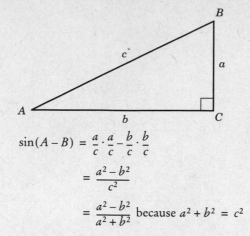

$$\sin(A - B) = \frac{a}{c} \cdot \frac{a}{c} - \frac{b}{c} \cdot \frac{b}{c}$$

$$= \frac{a^2 - b^2}{c^2}$$

$$= \frac{a^2 - b^2}{a^2 + b^2} \text{ because } a^2 + b^2 = c^2$$

46. **(C)** *Fundamentals: Logarithms, Inequalities*

Since this problem asks you to solve for n when n is an exponent, you need to use logarithms in your solution. Your first step, though, should be to set up an inequality. The smallest positive integer with 16 digits is 10^{15}, since it is a 1 followed by 15 zeros. Since 2^n must be equal to or greater than the smallest positive 16-digit integer, you can set up the following inequality:

$$2^n \geq 10^{15}$$

Now take the logarithm of each side:

$$\log 2^n \geq \log 10^{15}$$

Apply the power rule of logarithms to the inequality to get:

$$n \cdot \log 2 \geq \log 10^{15}$$

$$n \geq \frac{\log 10^{15}}{\log 2}$$

$$n \geq 49.83$$

Thus the least positive integer n is 50.

47. **(E)** *Plane Geometry: Polygons*

The figure below shows a regular pentagon inscribed within a circle of radius 1.

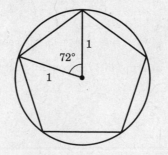

The easiest way to calculate the area of the pentagon is to see that the pentagon consists of 5 triangles whose central angle θ is $\frac{360}{5} = 72°$. The area of one of these triangles is given by $A = \frac{1}{2}ab\sin\theta = \frac{1}{2} \cdot 1 \cdot 1 \cdot \sin 72°$, where a and b are two sides of the triangle and θ is the angle they make. Multiply the area of this triangle by 5 to get the area of the pentagon.

$$Area = 5 \cdot \frac{1}{2} \cdot 1 \cdot 1 \cdot \sin 72°$$
$$= 2.38$$

48. **(B)** *Functions: Inverse Functions*

Solving for the inverse function of $f(x)$ requires three steps. First, replace $f(x)$ with y. Second, switch x and y. Third, solve for y. The expression you get for y is the inverse function of f.

$$f(x) = \frac{1}{\pi}\log_3(x^5 + 1)$$
$$y = \frac{1}{\pi}\log_3(x^5 + 1)$$
$$x = \frac{1}{\pi}\log_3(y^5 + 1)$$
$$\pi x = \log_3(y^5 + 1)$$
$$3^{\pi x} = y^5 + 1 \text{, since } 3^x \text{ is the inverse of } \log_3 x$$
$$3^{\pi x} - 1 = y^5$$
$$\sqrt[5]{3^{\pi x} - 1} = y$$
$$\sqrt[5]{3^{\pi x} - 1} = f^{-1}(x)$$

49. **(D)** *Solid Geometry: Solids that Aren't Prisms*

Given a sphere of radius r, the volume and surface area of the sphere are calculated by the formulas $V = \frac{4}{3}\pi r^3$ and $SA = 4\pi r^2$ respectively. The question states that the surface area is numerically 20% larger than the volume; this relationship can be expressed as $SA = 1.2V$, where 120% is the decimal 1.2.

$$4\pi r^2 = 1.2 \cdot \frac{4}{3}\pi r^3$$
$$\frac{5}{2} = r$$

50. **(B)** *Statistics: Permutations and Combinations*

The Math IIC writers expect you to know the formulas for permutations and combinations. In this problem, the order of selection is not important, since you are choosing undifferentiated committees. When you choose r objects out of a total of n objects, the formula for the number of possible choices is $\binom{n}{r} = \frac{n!}{r!(n-r)!}$. (In many textbooks and on many calculators $\binom{n}{r}$ is denoted nCr.) Since you are choosing 2 physicists out of 15, 1 mathematician out of 10, and 3 biologists out of 25, you can write the following:

$$\binom{15}{2} \cdot \binom{10}{1} \cdot \binom{25}{3} = \frac{15!}{2!13!} \cdot \frac{10!}{1!9!} \cdot \frac{25!}{3!22!}$$

$$= \frac{15 \cdot 14}{2 \cdot 1} \cdot \frac{10}{1} \cdot \frac{25 \cdot 24 \cdot 23}{3 \cdot 2 \cdot 1}$$

$$= \frac{28980000}{12}$$

$$= 2415000$$

SAT II Math IIC
Practice Test 2

MATH IIC TEST 2 ANSWER SHEET

1. Ⓐ Ⓑ Ⓒ Ⓓ Ⓔ	18. Ⓐ Ⓑ Ⓒ Ⓓ Ⓔ	35. Ⓐ Ⓑ Ⓒ Ⓓ Ⓔ
2. Ⓐ Ⓑ Ⓒ Ⓓ Ⓔ	19. Ⓐ Ⓑ Ⓒ Ⓓ Ⓔ	36. Ⓐ Ⓑ Ⓒ Ⓓ Ⓔ
3. Ⓐ Ⓑ Ⓒ Ⓓ Ⓔ	20. Ⓐ Ⓑ Ⓒ Ⓓ Ⓔ	37. Ⓐ Ⓑ Ⓒ Ⓓ Ⓔ
4. Ⓐ Ⓑ Ⓒ Ⓓ Ⓔ	21. Ⓐ Ⓑ Ⓒ Ⓓ Ⓔ	38. Ⓐ Ⓑ Ⓒ Ⓓ Ⓔ
5. Ⓐ Ⓑ Ⓒ Ⓓ Ⓔ	22. Ⓐ Ⓑ Ⓒ Ⓓ Ⓔ	39. Ⓐ Ⓑ Ⓒ Ⓓ Ⓔ
6. Ⓐ Ⓑ Ⓒ Ⓓ Ⓔ	23. Ⓐ Ⓑ Ⓒ Ⓓ Ⓔ	40. Ⓐ Ⓑ Ⓒ Ⓓ Ⓔ
7. Ⓐ Ⓑ Ⓒ Ⓓ Ⓔ	24. Ⓐ Ⓑ Ⓒ Ⓓ Ⓔ	41. Ⓐ Ⓑ Ⓒ Ⓓ Ⓔ
8. Ⓐ Ⓑ Ⓒ Ⓓ Ⓔ	25. Ⓐ Ⓑ Ⓒ Ⓓ Ⓔ	42. Ⓐ Ⓑ Ⓒ Ⓓ Ⓔ
9. Ⓐ Ⓑ Ⓒ Ⓓ Ⓔ	26. Ⓐ Ⓑ Ⓒ Ⓓ Ⓔ	43. Ⓐ Ⓑ Ⓒ Ⓓ Ⓔ
10. Ⓐ Ⓑ Ⓒ Ⓓ Ⓔ	27. Ⓐ Ⓑ Ⓒ Ⓓ Ⓔ	44. Ⓐ Ⓑ Ⓒ Ⓓ Ⓔ
11. Ⓐ Ⓑ Ⓒ Ⓓ Ⓔ	28. Ⓐ Ⓑ Ⓒ Ⓓ Ⓔ	45. Ⓐ Ⓑ Ⓒ Ⓓ Ⓔ
12. Ⓐ Ⓑ Ⓒ Ⓓ Ⓔ	29. Ⓐ Ⓑ Ⓒ Ⓓ Ⓔ	46. Ⓐ Ⓑ Ⓒ Ⓓ Ⓔ
13. Ⓐ Ⓑ Ⓒ Ⓓ Ⓔ	30. Ⓐ Ⓑ Ⓒ Ⓓ Ⓔ	47. Ⓐ Ⓑ Ⓒ Ⓓ Ⓔ
14. Ⓐ Ⓑ Ⓒ Ⓓ Ⓔ	31. Ⓐ Ⓑ Ⓒ Ⓓ Ⓔ	48. Ⓐ Ⓑ Ⓒ Ⓓ Ⓔ
15. Ⓐ Ⓑ Ⓒ Ⓓ Ⓔ	32. Ⓐ Ⓑ Ⓒ Ⓓ Ⓔ	49. Ⓐ Ⓑ Ⓒ Ⓓ Ⓔ
16. Ⓐ Ⓑ Ⓒ Ⓓ Ⓔ	33. Ⓐ Ⓑ Ⓒ Ⓓ Ⓔ	50. Ⓐ Ⓑ Ⓒ Ⓓ Ⓔ
17. Ⓐ Ⓑ Ⓒ Ⓓ Ⓔ	34. Ⓐ Ⓑ Ⓒ Ⓓ Ⓔ	

REFERENCE INFORMATION

THE FOLLOWING INFORMATION IS FOR YOUR REFERENCE IN ANSWERING SOME OF THE QUESTIONS IN THIS TEST:

Volume of a right circular cone with radius r and height h: $V = \frac{1}{3}\pi r^2 h$

Lateral area of a right circular cone with circumference of the base c and slaight height ℓ: $S = \frac{1}{2}c\ell$

Volume of a sphere with radius r: $V = \frac{4}{3}\pi r^3$

Surface area of a sphere with radius r: $S = 4\pi r^2$

Volume of a pyramid with base area B and height h: $V = \frac{1}{3}Bh$

MATHEMATICS LEVEL IIC TEST

For each of the following problems, decide which is the BEST of the choices given. If the exact numerical value is not one of the choices, select the choice that best approximates this value. Then fill in the corresponding oval on the answer sheet.

<u>Notes:</u> (1) A calculator will be necessary for answering some (but not all) of the questions in this test. For each question you will have to decide whether or not you should use a calcuator. The calculator you use must be at least a scientific calculator; programmable calculators and calculators that can display graphs are permitted.

(2) For some questions in this test you may need to decide whether your calculator should be in radian or degree mode.

(3) Figures that accompany problems in this test are intended to provide information useful in solving the problems. They are drawn as accurately as possible EXCEPT when it is stated in a specific problem that its figure is not drawn to scale. All figures lie in a plane unless otherwise indicated.

(4) Unless otherwise specified, the domain of any function f is assumed to be the set of all real numbers x for which $f(x)$ is a real number.

(5) Reference information that may be useful in answering the questions in this test can be found on the page preceding Question 1.

USE THIS SPACE FOR SCRATCHWORK.

1. If $f(x) = \dfrac{1}{\sqrt[3]{2 + x^2}}$, what is the value of $f(-3)$?

    (A) -0.52
    (B) -0.45
    (C) 0.45
    (D) 0.95
    (E) 1.16

2. $\dfrac{1}{p}\left(\dfrac{p}{a} - \dfrac{c}{p}\right) =$

    (A) $\dfrac{1}{a} - \dfrac{c}{p^2}$

    (B) $\dfrac{1}{a} - \dfrac{c}{p}$

    (C) $\dfrac{1}{ap} - \dfrac{c}{p^2}$

    (D) $\dfrac{1}{ap} - \dfrac{c}{p}$

    (E) $\dfrac{p - ac}{p}$

GO ON TO THE NEXT PAGE

USE THIS SPACE FOR SCRATCHWORK.

3. What is the area of a right triangle with an angle of 34° and with shorter leg of 7?

   (A) 12.2
   (B) 16.5
   (C) 33.1
   (D) 36.3
   (E) 37

4. If $\sqrt[4]{3x} = 2.8$, then $x =$

   (A) 0.43
   (B) 1.8
   (C) 7.2
   (D) 19.8
   (E) 20.5

5. Figure 1 shows a portion of the graph of the function $y = f(x)$. Which of the following is the period of $f(x)$?

   (A) $\dfrac{\pi}{2}$

   (B) π

   (C) $\dfrac{3\pi}{2}$

   (D) 2π

   (E) 7

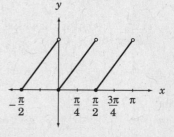

Figure 1

6. Given a point P in the plane, the set of all points in the plane that are the same distance d from P is described by:

   (A) A square with a center P
   (B) A circle with a radius d, centered at P
   (C) A circle with a radius d^2, centered at P
   (D) An ellipse with center P
   (E) None of the above

GO ON TO THE NEXT PAGE

7. If $x + 3$ is a factor of $x^3 - 3x^2 + kx + 5$, then $k =$

(A) $7\frac{1}{3}$

(B) $15\frac{2}{3}$

(C) 16

(D) $16\frac{1}{3}$

(E) 17

8. In Figure 2, which of the following is equal to $h \cdot \sin\theta$?

(A) $\dfrac{d}{c}$

(B) $\dfrac{d}{a}$

(C) a

(D) b

(E) c

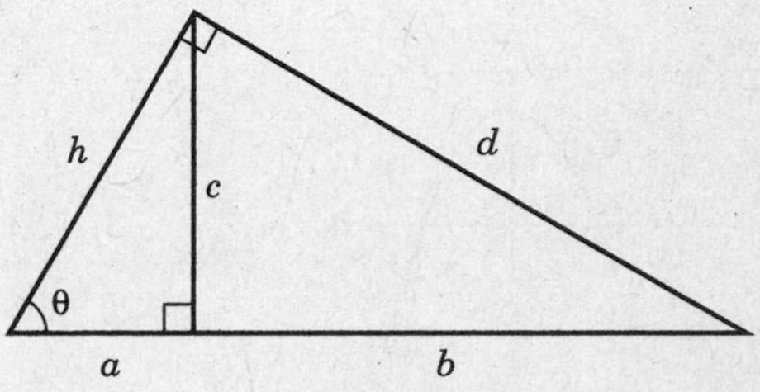

Figure 2

9. If $\dfrac{\frac{3}{2}}{\frac{x}{8}} = x$, then x could equal which of the following?

(A) $\sqrt{2}$
(B) $\sqrt{3}$
(C) $2\sqrt{3}$
(D) $3\sqrt{2}$
(E) $4\sqrt{3}$

GO ON TO THE NEXT PAGE

10. If z varies directly with w, then which of the following graphs could represent the relationship between z and w?

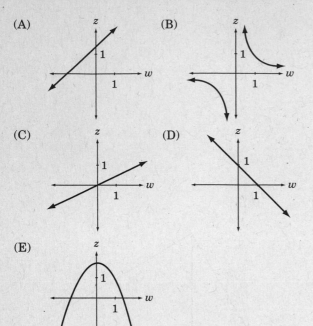

(A)

(B)

(C)

(D)

(E)

11. If $\sec\theta \cdot \sin\theta = 2$, what is the value of $\cot\theta$?

(A) -3

(B) $-\dfrac{1}{2}$

(C) 0

(D) $\dfrac{1}{2}$

(E) 4

12. If $f(x) = \sqrt{1 + 3x^3}$ and $g(x) = \dfrac{x+1}{2x+1}$, then $f(g(5)) =$

(A) 1.02

(B) 1.22

(C) 2.17

(D) 2.39

(E) 5.40

GO ON TO THE NEXT PAGE

13. A tension wire is attached to an antenna that stands perpendicular to the ground. The wire is 120 feet long and makes an angle of 39° with respect to the ground. What is the height of the antenna?

 (A) 118.7 ft
 (B) 101.6 ft
 (C) 100 ft
 (D) 93.3 ft
 (E) 75.5 ft

4. The graph of $y = |f(x)|$ is shown in Figure 3. Which of the following could not be the graph of $y = f(x)$?

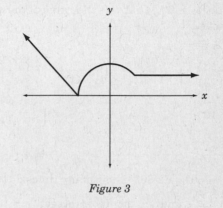

Figure 3

(A)

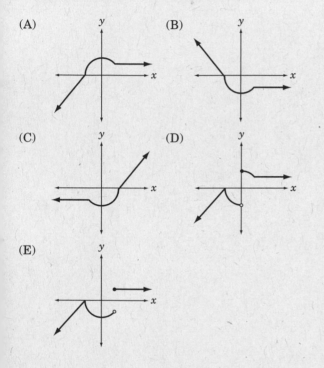

(B)

(C)

(D)

(E)

5. Line l is defined by the equation $Ax + By = C$. Which of the following lines is perpendicular to the line l?

 (A) $Dx + By = A$
 (B) $Cx - Ay = B$
 (C) $Ax - By = C$
 (D) $Bx + Ay = C$
 (E) $Bx - Ay = D$

GO ON TO THE NEXT PAGE

USE THIS SPACE FOR SCRATCHWORK.

16. What is the area of a square inscribed within a sphere of radius 6 such that the center of the sphere is contained in the square?

(A) 81
(B) 72
(C) 64
(D) 60.1
(E) 49

17. The average, or arithmetic mean, of 5 numbers is 75. When one of the numbers is removed, the average of the remaining numbers is 60. What was the value of the number that was removed?

(A) 140
(B) 135
(C) 131
(D) 130
(E) 100

18. For $-360° \le x \le 360°$, how many times do the graphs of $y = \dfrac{1}{100}x$ and $y = \sin(x)$ intersect?

(A) 0
(B) 1
(C) 2
(D) 3
(E) 4

19. If $\dfrac{n!}{(n-1)!} = \dfrac{n!}{(n-2)!}$, then n could be which of the following?

(A) 2
(B) 3
(C) 4
(D) 5
(E) 7.1

GO ON TO THE NEXT PAGE

20. If a six-sided die is rolled 3 times, what is the probability of rolling <u>at least</u> one odd number?

(A) $\dfrac{1}{2}$

(B) $\dfrac{2}{3}$

(C) $\dfrac{7}{8}$

(D) $\dfrac{8}{9}$

(E) 1

21. In a class of 120 students, 75 take biology, 60 take chemistry, and 40 take neither biology nor chemistry. What percentage of the class takes both biology and chemistry?

(A) 40.9%
(B) 45.8%
(C) 50%
(D) 55%
(E) Not enough information to tell

22. A geometric sequence has a first term equal to 2 and a fourth term equal to $\dfrac{1}{4}$. What is the sixth term in the sequence?

(A) $\dfrac{3}{8}$

(B) $\dfrac{1}{8}$

(C) $\dfrac{1}{16}$

(D) $\dfrac{1}{32}$

(E) $\dfrac{1}{64}$

23. The domain of $f(x) = \sqrt{9 - x^2}$ is given by which of the following?

(A) $-3 \le x \le 3$
(B) $-3 < x < 3$
(C) $x \le -3$ or $x \ge 3$
(D) $x < -3$ or $x > 3$
(E) $-9 \le x \le 9$

GO ON TO THE NEXT PAGE

24. If the lengths of the sides of a triangle are in a ratio of 2: 3: 4, what is the degree measure of the smallest angle?

   (A) 76°
   (B) 66°
   (C) 37°
   (D) 31°
   (E) 29°

25. If $0 = 2x^2 + kx + 1$ has no real roots, then which of the following must be true of k ?

   (A) $k = 0$
   (B) $-1 < k < 1$
   (C) $-2 < k < 2$
   (D) $-2\sqrt{2} < k < 2\sqrt{2}$
   (E) $-2\sqrt{2} \le k \le 2\sqrt{2}$

26. In Figure 4, what is the area of the shaded region?

   (A) 15
   (B) 14
   (C) 12
   (D) 10
   (E) 9

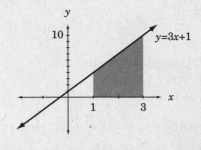

Figure 4

27. What is the range of the function $f(x) = \dfrac{7}{x} - 3$?

   (A) All real numbers except -7
   (B) All real numbers except -3
   (C) All real numbers except 7
   (D) All real numbers except 0
   (E) All real numbers

28. The radius and height of a right circular cone are equal. If the volume of the cone is 10, what is the diameter of the cone's base?

   (A) 6.28
   (B) 5.12
   (C) 4.24
   (D) 2.12
   (E) 2.00

 GO ON TO THE NEXT PAGE

29. If $f(x) = 2x + 1$ and $f(g(x)) = -x$, then $g(x) =$

(A) $-(x + 1)$

(B) $\frac{1}{2}(x + 1)$

(C) $-\frac{1}{2}(x + 1)$

(D) $2(x - 1)$

(E) $2(x + 1)$

30. A line has parametric equations $x = 2t + 1$ and $y = t - 3$, where t is the parameter. What is the slope of the line?

(A) 0

(B) $\frac{1}{2}$

(C) $\frac{2}{3}$

(D) 2

(E) 3

1. At 12:00 noon the population of bacteria in a petri dish was 1000. For any later time t, the population in the dish can be calculated using the function $P(t) = 1,000(1.45)^t$, with t given in hours. How many bacteria will be present at 3:20 P.M.?

(A) 1786
(B) 2801
(C) 2999
(D) 3405
(E) 3450

2. If $2x - 5y = -10$ and $x^2 = y$ for $x \le 0$, then $x =$

(A) 1.63
(B) 1.28
(C) 0
(D) −1.01
(E) −1.23

GO ON TO THE NEXT PAGE

USE THIS SPACE FOR SCRATCHWORK.

33. Which of the following could be the equation of an ellipse centered at $(3, 2)$ and tangent to both the x-axis and the y-axis?

(A) $\dfrac{(x-3)^2}{9} + \dfrac{(x-2)^2}{4} = 1$

(B) $\dfrac{(x-3)^2}{9} - \dfrac{(x-2)^2}{4} = 1$

(C) $\dfrac{(x+3)^2}{9} + \dfrac{(x+2)^2}{4} = 1$

(D) $\dfrac{(x-3)^2}{3} + \dfrac{(y-2)^2}{2} = 1$

(E) $\dfrac{(x-3)^2}{3} + \dfrac{(y-2)^2}{2} = 1$

34. If $f(x) = 2^{x-1}$, then $f^{-1}(x) =$

(A) $\ln x + 1$
(B) $\log_2(x-1)$
(C) $\log_2 x - 1$
(D) $\log_2 x + 1$
(E) $\log_2(x+1)$

35. In Figure 5, what is the area of $\triangle ABC$ in terms of θ ?

(A) $8\sin^2\theta$
(B) $16\sin\theta\cos\theta$
(C) $8\sin\theta\cos\theta$
(D) $4\sin\theta\cos\theta$
(E) $8\cos^2\theta$

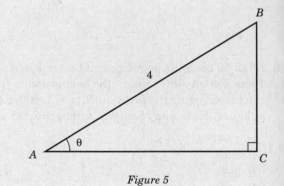

Figure 5

36. If $x_1 = 1$ and $x_{n+1} = \dfrac{x_n}{x_n + 1}$, then $x_4 =$

(A) $-\dfrac{1}{2}$

(B) $-\dfrac{1}{8}$

(C) 0

(D) $\dfrac{1}{4}$

(E) $\dfrac{1}{2}$

GO ON TO THE NEXT PAGE

37. $a + bi$ and $c + di$ are two complex numbers. If
$(a + bi)(c + di) = 1$, then which of the following must be true?

(A) $ac + bd = 0$
(B) $ab + cd = 0$
(C) $ac - bd = 1$
(D) $ad - bc = 1$
(E) $ad - bc = i$

38. If a card is drawn at random from a standard deck of 52 cards, what is the probability that it is a red card <u>or</u> a Queen?

(A) $\dfrac{1}{26}$

(B) $\dfrac{7}{13}$

(C) $\dfrac{8}{13}$

(D) $\dfrac{14}{52}$

(E) $\dfrac{15}{26}$

39. If $4^n = 2^{n^2 + n - 6}$, then n could be which of the following?

(A) -1.2
(B) 0
(C) 1.3
(D) 2
(E) 3

40. If vector $\vec{v} = (1, 3)$ and vector $\vec{w} = (2, -7)$, then which of the following is equal to $2\vec{v} - 3\vec{w}$?

(A) $(-8, -18)$
(B) $(8, -18)$
(C) $(2, 27)$
(D) $(-4, 27)$
(E) $(-4, -27)$

GO ON TO THE NEXT PAGE

41. If $\sin^{-1}(\cos\theta) = \dfrac{\pi}{6}$ for $0 \le \theta \le \dfrac{\pi}{2}$, then θ could equal:

    (A) $\dfrac{\pi}{3}$

    (B) $\dfrac{\pi}{2}$

    (C) $\dfrac{3\pi}{2}$

    (D) $\dfrac{4\pi}{3}$

    (E) $\dfrac{5\pi}{6}$

42. $3x$, $2x + 1$, and $4x - 3$ (where x is a real number) form the first three terms of a geometric sequence. Which of the following could be the value of x ?

    (A) 2.12
    (B) 1.70
    (C) 1.01
    (D) 0.07
    (E) −1.2

43. Which of the following could <u>not</u> be formed by the intersection of a cube and a cone?

    (A) A point
    (B) A line segment
    (C) A circle
    (D) A rectangle
    (E) A cylinder

44. What is the value of $\displaystyle\lim_{x \to \infty} \dfrac{2x^2 + 3x + 1}{5x^2 - 2x + 3}$?

    (A) $-\infty$

    (B) $-\dfrac{2}{5}$

    (C) 0

    (D) $\dfrac{2}{5}$

    (E) $+\infty$

GO ON TO THE NEXT PAGE

45. If $2\sin^2\theta - \cos\theta + 1 = 0$ for $0 \le \theta \le \frac{\pi}{2}$, then θ is:

(A) −0.07
(B) 0
(C) 0.12
(D) 0.13
(E) 0.17

46. In how many different ways can 5 people sit in a row of 10 chairs?

(A) 1500
(B) 15000
(C) 15120
(D) 30240
(E) 60480

7. The contrapositive of the statement "If the trees are green, then it is <u>not</u> December" is:

(A) If it is December, then the trees are green.
(B) If it is December, then the trees are not green.
(C) If it is not December, then the trees are not green.
(D) If it is not December, then the trees are green.
(E) If the trees are not green, then it is December.

8. If $f(x) = \sqrt[7]{5x^3 - 3}$ what is the value of $f^{-1}(1)$?

(A) 0.75
(B) 0.8
(C) 0.93
(D) 1.03
(E) 1.11

9. What is the solution set to $\dfrac{1}{x^2 + x - 6} < 0$?

(A) $-2 < x < 3$
(B) $-2 \le x \le 3$
(C) $-3 < x < 2$
(D) $-3 \le x \le 2$
(E) $1 < x < 2$

GO ON TO THE NEXT PAGE

50. Which of the following is the center of the conic section defined by the equation $9x^2 - y^2 - 18x + 4y - 31 = 0$?

    (A) $(1, 2)$
    (B) $(3, 2)$
    (C) $(1, -2)$
    (D) $(-1, -2)$
    (E) $(-1, 2)$

S T O P

IF YOU FINISH BEFORE TIME IS CALLED, YOU MAY CHECK YOUR WORK ON THIS TEST ONLY.
DO NOT TURN TO ANY OTHER TEST IN THIS BOOK.

SAT II Math IIC
Practice Test 2
Explanations

Calculating Your Score

Question Number	Correct Answer	Right	Wrong	Question Number	Correct Answer	Right	Wrong	Question Number	Correct Answer	Right	Wrong
1.	C	—	—	18.	D	—	—	35.	C	—	—
2.	A	—	—	19.	A	—	—	36.	D	—	—
3.	D	—	—	20.	C	—	—	37.	C	—	—
4.	E	—	—	21.	B	—	—	38.	B	—	—
5.	A	—	—	22.	C	—	—	39.	E	—	—
6.	B	—	—	23.	A	—	—	40.	D	—	—
7.	D	—	—	24.	E	—	—	41.	A	—	—
8.	E	—	—	25.	D	—	—	42.	B	—	—
9.	C	—	—	26.	B	—	—	43.	E	—	—
10.	C	—	—	27.	B	—	—	44.	D	—	—
11.	D	—	—	28.	C	—	—	45.	B	—	—
12.	B	—	—	29.	C	—	—	46.	D	—	—
13.	E	—	—	30.	B	—	—	47.	B	—	—
14.	C	—	—	31.	E	—	—	48.	C	—	—
15.	E	—	—	32.	E	—	—	49.	C	—	—
16.	B	—	—	33.	A	—	—	50.	A	—	—
17.	B	—	—	34.	D	—	—				

Your raw score for the SAT II Math IIC test is calculated from the number of questions you answer correctly and incorrectly. Once you have determined your composite score, use the conversion table on page 18 of this book to calculate your scaled score. To calculate your raw score, count the number of questions you answered correctly: _____
A

Count the number of questions you answered incorrectly, and multiply that number by $\frac{1}{4}$:

$$ \underline{\hspace{3cm}} \times \frac{1}{4} = \underline{\hspace{3cm}} $$
B   C

Subtract the value in field C from value in field A: _____
D

Round the number in field D to the nearest whole number. This is your raw score: _____
E

Math IIC Test 2 Explanations

1. **(C)** *Functions: Evaluating Functions*

To answer this question, all you need to do is plug -3 in for x.

$$f(x) = \frac{1}{\sqrt[3]{2 + x^2}}$$

$$f(-3) = \frac{1}{\sqrt[3]{2 + (-3)^2}}$$

$$= \frac{1}{\sqrt[3]{2 + 9}}$$

$$= \frac{1}{\sqrt[3]{11}}$$

$$\approx 0.45$$

2. **(A)** *Algebra: Algebraic Manipulation*

This question asks you to distribute an algebraic expression:

$$\frac{1}{p}\left(\frac{p}{a} - \frac{c}{p}\right) = \frac{p}{pa} - \frac{c}{p \cdot p}$$

$$= \frac{1}{a} - \frac{c}{p \cdot p}$$

$$= \frac{1}{a} - \frac{c}{p^2}$$

3. **(D)** *Plane Geometry: Triangles; Trigonometry: Basic Functions*

You know three pieces of information about the triangle: it has a right ($90°$) angle, a $34°$ angle, and a shorter leg of length 7. Since you know two of the triangle's three angles, you can determine the third: $180 - 90 - 34 = 56°$. Because the shorter of the two legs in a right triangle faces the smallest angle in the triangle, you can tell that the leg of length 7 is opposite the $34°$ angle. Now you know enough to draw a picture of the triangle:

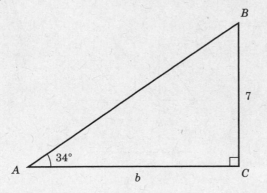

The area of $\triangle ABC$ is $\frac{1}{2}bh = \frac{1}{2}b(7)$. Use right triangle trigonometry to find the base of the triangle.

$$\tan 34° = \frac{\text{opposite}}{\text{adjacent}}$$

$$\tan 34° = \frac{7}{b}$$

$$b = \frac{7}{\tan 34°}$$

$$\approx 10.38$$

Plug this value for the base into the area formula:

$$\text{Area} = \frac{1}{2}(10.38)(7)$$

$$\approx 36.32$$

4. **(E)** *Algebra: Equation Solving*

Solving for x requires isolating it on one side of the equation. Get rid of the fourth root over x by raising both sides of the equation to the fourth power.

$$\sqrt[4]{3x} = 2.8$$

$$3x = (2.8)^4$$

$$x = \frac{(2.8)^4}{3}$$

$$= 20.5$$

5. **(A)** *Functions: Graphing Functions*

A periodic function is a function that repeats itself at regular intervals over a given domain. A function $f(x)$ has a period of c if $f(x + c) = f(x)$, for all x in the domain. The graph shown in the question repeats itself every interval of $\frac{\pi}{2}$, so $\frac{\pi}{2}$ is the period of the function.

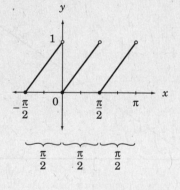

6. **(B)** *Plane Geometry: Circles*

This question tests you on the definition of a circle. A circle is a set of points that are the same distance from a given point called the center. The distance from the center is called the radius. In this case, the set of all points that are the same distance d from a given point P is a circle of radius d and center P.

7. **(D)** *Algebra: Polynomials*

There are two unknown variables in this question: x and k. The question tells you that $(x + 3)$ is a factor of a polynomial, practically crying out for you to use polynomial long division to solve the problem. The polynomial version of long division says that any polynomial $p(x)$ can be written $p(x) = (x - a) \cdot Q(x) + R$, where $(x - a)$ is the divisor, $Q(x)$ is the quotient, and R is the remainder. The remainder R can be found by plugging a into $p(x)$, since $P(a) = (a - a) \cdot Q(a) + R = R$.

Since you want to solve for k, you need to make it the only unknown in an equation. You can do this by plugging in a value for x that will give you a value you've already determined for $p(x)$. In this question, $(x + 3)$ is the divisor $(x - a)$, where $a = -3$. Because $(x + 3)$ is a factor of $p(x)$, it divides $p(x)$ evenly, leaving no remainder. Since $R = 0$, you know $p(a) = 0$. You can solve for k by setting $p(a) = 0$, where $a = -3$:

$$0 = (-3)^3 - 3(-3)^2 - 3k + 5$$
$$= -27 - 27 - 3k + 5$$
$$= -49 - 3k$$
$$16\frac{1}{3} = k$$

8. **(E)** *Trigonometry: Basic Functions*

Most of the figure is irrelevant to the solution. The part that matters is the small triangle with sides h, c, and a on the left side of the big triangle:

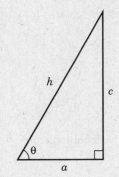

Since this a right triangle, $\sin\theta = \dfrac{c}{h}$ and $h \cdot \sin\theta = c$.

9. **(C)** *Algebra: Equation Solving, Fractions*

Dividing one fraction by a second one is the same as multiplying the first fraction by the reciprocal of the second:

$$\frac{\frac{3}{2}}{\frac{x}{8}} = \frac{3}{2} \cdot \frac{8}{x}$$
$$= \frac{12}{x}$$

According to the question, you should set this new fraction equal to x.

$$x = \frac{12}{x}$$

$$x^2 = 12$$

$$x = \pm\sqrt{12}$$

$$= \pm 2\sqrt{3}$$

Choice (C) is $2\sqrt{3}$, so it's the right answer.

10. **(C)** *Algebra: Writing Equations, Variation*

The question says that z varies directly with w. Direct variation means that w increases as z increases and that w decreases as z decreases. You can write this relationship as the $z = kw$, where k is a constant number. The constant k tells you that z and w are not necessarily equal but that they are related to each other.

If you graph this equation in the (w, z) plane, you'll get a straight line passing through the origin. Only answer choice (C) fits this description.

11. **(D)** *Trigonometry: Basic Functions*

When you're manipulating trigonometric expressions like this one, you should try to rewrite the equation in terms of sine, cosine, and tangent. For this question, you need to remember the definition of secant: $\sec\theta = \frac{1}{\cos\theta}$.

$$\sec\theta\sin\theta = 2$$

$$\frac{1}{\cos\theta}\sin\theta = 2$$

$$\frac{\sin\theta}{\cos\theta} = 2$$

$$\tan\theta = 2$$

You can now find the cotangent by using the definition: $\cot\theta = \frac{1}{\tan\theta}$.

$$\cot\theta = \frac{1}{2}$$

12. **(B)** *Functions: Compound Functions*

To evaluate the compound function $f(g(5))$, you should first find $g(5)$. Then you can plug the value of $g(5)$ into $f(x)$.

$$g(5) = \frac{5+1}{2\cdot 5+1}$$

$$= \frac{6}{11}$$

$$f\left(\frac{6}{11}\right) = \sqrt{1 + 3\left(\frac{6}{11}\right)^3}$$

$$= 1.22$$

13. **(E)** *Trigonometry: Basic Functions*

When you have a word problem involving trigonometry, you should try to illustrate the problem first. This problem tells you a 120-foot tension wire reaches from the ground to the top of an antenna, which forms a right angle with the ground. The ground and the antenna are the two legs of a right triangle. The wire is the hypotenuse of the right triangle, and it forms an angle of 39° with the ground. You can illustrate these facts like this:

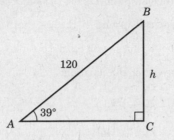

Since $\triangle ABC$ is a right triangle, you can use trig to find the height of the antenna:

$$\sin(39°) = \frac{h}{120}$$

$$120 \cdot \sin(39°) = h$$

$$75.5 = h$$

14. **(C)** *Functions: Graphing Functions*

$y = |f(x)|$ means that y is always positive. Even if $f(x)$ is a negative number, y is positive because it's equal to the absolute value of $f(x)$. When graphing $y = |f(x)|$, you reflect all the negative values of $f(x)$ across the x-axis to make them positive. For example:

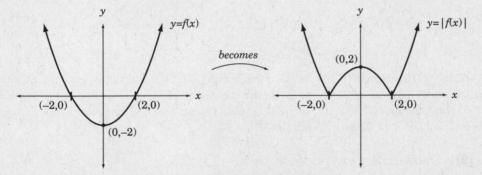

For each answer choice, reflect the negative values of $f(x)$ across the x-axis. Only the graph in choice (C) will not transform into the graph shown in the question.

15. **(E)** *Coordinate Geometry: Lines and Distance*

If a line l has a slope of m, then a line perpendicular to l has a slope equal to $-\frac{1}{m}$. Your first step should be to rearrange the equation for line l to find its slope.

$$Ax + By = C$$

$$By = -Ax + C$$

$$y = -\frac{A}{B}x + \frac{C}{B}$$

From this equation, you know that the slope of l is equal to $-\dfrac{A}{B}$. You can now see that when the equation for l is written as $Ax + By = C$, you can find the slope by taking the negative of the x-coefficient divided by the y-coefficient.

A line perpendicular to l must have a slope equal to $\dfrac{B}{A}$, so you're looking for an equation that has B as its x-coefficient and A as its y-coefficient. Both (D) and (E) have these coefficients, but when you divide and negate the coefficients in (D), you end up with $-\dfrac{B}{A}$ because both of the coefficients are positive. (E), on the other hand, has one negative coefficient, so you get the positive slope $\dfrac{B}{A}$, so (E) is the correct answer. You can check that (E) is right by rewriting the equation:

$$Bx - Ay = D$$
$$-Ay = -Bx + D$$
$$y = \frac{B}{A}x - \frac{D}{A}$$

16. **(B)** *Solid Geometry: Solids that Aren't Prisms*

First sketch the square and the sphere described in the question:

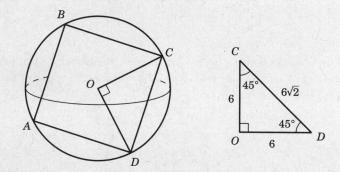

Radii OC and OD have lengths 6, and they form a right angle, $\angle COD$. They also form $\triangle OCD$, a 45–45–90 triangle, with a hypotenuse CD. You can find that the length of CD is $6\sqrt{2}$ by using the properties of a 45–45–90 triangle. Since CD is also the side of the square, you can now find the square's area. The area of a square is the square of the length of its side: $(6\sqrt{2})^2 = 72$.

17. **(B)** *Statistics: Arithmetic Mean*

The average of a set of values is equal to the sum of the values divided by the number of the values. The question tells you that the average of 5 numbers is 75. You can find the sum of these numbers by multiplying their average by 5: $75 \times 5 = 375$. The question also tells you that when one of the numbers is removed, the average is 60. You can find the sum of these 4 numbers by multiplying $60 \times 4 = 240$. The difference between these two sums is the value of the number that was removed.

$$\text{Number Removed} = 375 - 240$$
$$= 135$$

18. **(D)** *Functions: Graphing Functions*

The easiest way to solve this problem is to graph the two functions on your calculator, adjusting the window to fit the domain provided by the question: $-360° \le x \le 360°$. Make sure you set your calculator to degrees because you'll get the wrong answer if you use radians. You can see in the figure below that the graphs intersect three times within the specified domain:

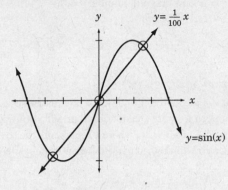

19. **(A)** *Statistics: Factorials*

You need to know the definition of a factorial for the Math IIC: $n! = n \cdot (n-1) \cdot (n-2)...(2) \cdot (1)$. For example, $4! = 4 \cdot 3 \cdot 2 \cdot 1$. To solve this problem, simplify the left side of the equation first:

$$\frac{n!}{(n-1)!} = \frac{n \cdot (n-1) \cdot (n-2)...(2)(1)}{(n-1) \cdot (n-2)...(2) \cdot (1)} = n$$

Then do the right side:

$$\frac{n!}{(n-2)!} = \frac{n(n-1)(n-2)...(2) \cdot (1)}{(n-2)...(2) \cdot (1)}$$

$$= n(n-1)$$

Now set the two sides equal to each other:

$$n = n(n-1)$$
$$n = n^2 - n$$
$$0 = n^2 - 2n$$
$$0 = n(n-2)$$

Thus $n = 0$ or $n = 2$.

20. **(C)** *Statistics: Probability*

The phrase "at least" means that you need to calculate the probability of rolling one, two, or three odd numbers in three rolls. The probability of at least one specific outcome occurring is equal to 1 minus the probability of that outcome not occurring:

$$P(\text{at least one}) = 1 - P(\text{none})$$

In one roll of a six-sided die, the probability of not rolling an odd number is $\frac{1}{2}$, since half of the numbers are even. You can calculate the probability of not rolling 3 odd numbers in a row by multiplying $\frac{1}{2} \cdot \frac{1}{2} \cdot \frac{1}{2} = \frac{1}{8}$. Subtract this number from 1 to find the probability of rolling at least one odd number:

$$P(\text{at least one odd number}) = 1 - \frac{1}{8}$$

$$= \frac{7}{8}$$

21. **(B)** *Algebra: Equation Solving*

Of the 120 students in the class, 40 take neither biology nor chemistry, so you know that 80 students take one or both of the courses. You need to write an equation that will allow you to solve for the number of students who take both courses: $75 + 60 - x = 80$, where x represents the overlap in students. You need to subtract x in the equation because you don't want to double count the students who take both biology and chemistry.

$$135 - x = 80$$
$$x = 55$$

Now you can find the percentage of students in the entire class who take both biology and chemistry: $\frac{55}{120} = 0.458$, or 45.8%.

22. **(C)** *Miscellaneous Math: Sequences and Series*

In a geometric sequence, the ratio between any term and the next term is constant. The mathematical definition of a geometric sequence is $a_n = a_1 \cdot r^{n-1}$, where a_n is the nth term in the sequence, a_1 is the first term, and r is the ratio. The question tells you that 2 is the first term ($n = 1$) in the sequence and that $\frac{1}{4}$ is the fourth term ($n = 4$). You can plug these values into the definition of a geometric sequence to find the ratio:

$$\frac{1}{4} = a_1 \cdot r^{4-1}$$

$$= a_1 \cdot r^3$$

$$= 2 \cdot r^3$$

$$\frac{1}{8} = r^3$$

$$\frac{1}{2} = r$$

Now that you have the ratio, you can find the sixth term:

$$a_6 = 2 \cdot \left(\frac{1}{2}\right)^{6-1}$$

$$= \frac{1}{16}$$

23. (A) *Functions: Domain and Range*

The domain of this function is the set of all x values that produce real values of $f(x)$. Since the square root of a negative number is complex (thus not real), you know the value under the square root sign needs to be a non-negative number. Finding the domain for this function is equivalent to solving $9 - x^2 \geq 0$.

$$9 - x^2 \geq 0$$
$$(9) \geq x^2$$
$$\sqrt{9} \geq \pm x$$
$$(3) \geq \pm x$$
$$(3) \geq x \text{ and } -3 \leq x$$

The domain of the function is $-3 \leq x \leq 3$.

24. (E) *Trigonometry: Solving Non-Right Triangles*

The question says that the ratio of the triangle's sides is $2:3:4$. To simplify the solution, you can assume that the sides have lengths 2, 3, and 4. The only information you have about this triangle is the lengths of the sides, and you're looking for the measure of the smallest angle. The law of cosines, which you should definitely memorize for the Math IIC, allows you to solve for an angle given the three sides of the triangle. It states that in any $\triangle ABC$ (like the one shown below): $c^2 = a^2 + b^2 - 2ab\cos(C)$.

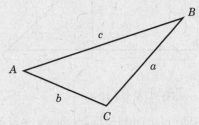

For this question, you can make $c = 2$, $a = 3$, and $b = 4$. Since the smallest angle in a triangle is opposite the shortest side of the triangle, you want to solve for $\angle C$. Plug the lengths of the sides into the formula for the law of cosines:

$$2^2 = 3^2 + 4^2 - (2 \cdot 3 \cdot 4)\cos(C)$$

$$-21 = -24\cos(C)$$

$$\frac{7}{8} = \cos(C)$$

$$C = \cos^{-1}\left(\frac{7}{8}\right)$$

$$C \approx 29°$$

25. **(D)** *Algebra: Polynomials*

The question tells you that the quadratic polynomial $2x^2 + kx + 1$ has no real roots, and asks you about k, one of the polynomial's coefficients. The relationship between the coefficients of a polynomial such as $ax^2 + bx + c$ and the polynomial's roots is summed up by something called the discriminant. The discriminant of a polynomial is defined as $b^2 - 4ac$, and it describes the nature of the polynomial's roots. When a polynomial has no real roots, $b^2 - 4ac < 0$. To solve this problem, plug the coefficients of the polynomial into $b^2 - 4ac < 0$:

$$k^2 - 8 < 0$$
$$k^2 < 8$$
$$\pm k < 2\sqrt{2}$$
$$-2\sqrt{2} < k < 2\sqrt{2}$$

26. **(B)** *Plane Geometry: Polygons*

If you rotate the shaded region in Figure 4, you can see that it is a trapezoid.

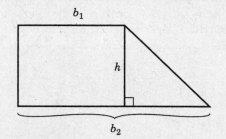

The formula for the area of a trapezoid is: $\frac{1}{2}(b_1 + b_2) \cdot h$.

The bases are the left and right sides of the shaded figure shown in the question. The lengths of the bases are given by the y-values:

$$y_1 = 3(1) + 1$$
$$= 4$$

and:

$$y_2 = 3(3) + 1$$
$$= 10$$

The height h is equal to the bottom side of the figure, so $h = 2$. Plug the bases and the height into the area formula: area of shaded region $= \frac{1}{2}(4 + 10) \cdot 2 = 14$.

27. **(B)** *Functions: Domain and Range*

The range of a function $f(x)$ is the set of all possible values of $f(x)$. An easy way to solve for the range of a function is to replace $f(x)$ with y in the equation and then solve for x.

$$y = \frac{7}{x} - 3$$
$$\frac{7}{x} = y + 3$$
$$\frac{7}{y + 3} = x$$

You can see from this equation that y cannot be equal to -3, since x is undefined when $y = -3$ (because the denominator of the expression is equal to 0). Thus the range of $f(x)$ is all real numbers except -3.

28. **(C)** *Solid Geometry: Solids that Aren't Prisms*

The volume of a cone with radius r and height h is $\frac{1}{3}\pi r^2 h$. This formula is provided at the beginning of the test booklet, but you'll save time by memorizing it before the test. The question tells you that the volume of the cone is 10 and that the height of the cone is equal to its radius ($h = r$), and you're asked to find the diameter of the cone's base. The diameter of the base is twice the radius, so you should use the volume formula to solve for the cone's radius.

$$\frac{1}{3}\pi r^2 \cdot h = \frac{1}{3}\pi r^2 \cdot r$$

$$\frac{1}{3}\pi r^3 = 10$$

$$r^3 = \frac{30}{\pi}$$

$$r \approx 2.12$$

Multiply the radius by 2 to find the diameter: 4.24.

29. **(C)** *Functions: Compound Functions*

The question tells you that $f(g(x)) = -x$, which means that plugging $g(x)$ into $f(x)$ gets the value $-x$. You can simplify the solution to this problem by making $g(x) = y$ so that $f(g(x)) = f(y)$. You're given $f(x) = 2x + 1$; plug y into $f(x)$:

$$f(y) = 2y + 1$$
$$2y + 1 = -x$$

Now solve for y:

$$2y = -1 - x$$

$$y = \frac{-1 - x}{2}$$

Since $g(x) = y$, you can substitute $g(x)$ for y:

$$y = \frac{-1 - x}{2}$$
$$g(x) = \frac{-1 - x}{2}$$
$$= -\frac{1}{2}(1 + x)$$

30. **(B)** *Coordinate Geometry: Parametric Equations, Lines and Distance*

A simple way to solve this problem is to find two (x, y) points on the line and then use these points to determine the slope. You can find two points by plugging two values for t into the parametric equations for x and y. If $t = 0$, then $x = 1$, and $y = -3$, giving you the point $(1, -3)$. If $t = 1$, then $x = 3$, and $y = -2$, giving you the point $(3, -2)$. Find the slope of the line by dividing the change in the y-value by the change in the x-value:

$$\frac{\Delta y}{\Delta x} = \frac{-3 - (-2)}{1 - 3} = \frac{1}{2}.$$

31. **(E)** *Algebra: Equation Solving, Exponential Growth & Decay*

The solution to this problem is simply a matter of plugging numbers into the provided formula. The tricky part of the problem is remembering to convert the elapsed time of 3 hours and 20 minutes (from 12:00 noon to 3:20 P.M.) into hours, since t is in hours: 3 hours and 20 minutes is equal to $3\frac{1}{3}$ hours.

$$P\left(3\frac{1}{3}\right) = 1,000(1.45)^{3\frac{1}{3}}$$
$$= 3450.59$$

Round this number to 3450, which is given by choice (E).

32. **(E)** *Algebra: Systems of Equations*

You have two unknown variables—x and y—in two equations. Since you want to solve for x in the end, you want to end up with an equation in which x is the only unknown. To do this, you should solve for y in terms of x in the first equation. Then plug the expression for y into the second equation, so you'll have everything in terms of x.

$$2x - 5y = -10$$
$$5y = 2x + 10$$
$$y = \frac{2x + 10}{5}$$

Now plug this expression for y into the second equation:

$$x^2 = y$$
$$x^2 = \frac{2x + 10}{5}$$

This equation is quadratic and can be written as:

$$5x^2 - 2x - 10 = 0$$

Plug the coefficients into the quadratic formula to find the values of x:

$$x = \frac{2 \pm \sqrt{4 + 200}}{10}$$
$$\approx -1.23, 1.63$$

Since the question states that $x \le 0$, the correct answer is $x = -1.23$.

33. **(A)** *Coordinate Geometry: Ellipses*

The question tells you that the ellipse is centered on (3, 2) and that it's tangent to the x and y-axes, which means that the ellipse touches both axes but doesn't cross them. Draw a picture of the ellipse on the coordinate plane:

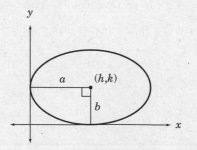

The general formula for an ellipse with its center at (h, k) and with a major axis, $2a$, and minor axis, $2b$, is given by $\frac{(x-h)^2}{a^2} + \frac{(y-k)^2}{b^2} = 1$. Since the ellipse is tangent to both the x-axis and the y-axis, you can see that $a = 3$ and $b = 2$. The values $h = 3$ and $k = 2$ are given in the question. Plug these values for h, k, a, and b into the formula for the ellipse, and you'll see that choice (A) is correct.

34. **(D)** *Functions: Inverse Functions, Logarithms*

You should follow three steps when solving for an inverse function. First, set $y = f(x)$. Then switch the places of x and y in the equation, and solve for y.

$$y = 2^{x-1}$$
$$x = 2^{y-1}$$

In order to get y out of the exponent, you should take the logarithm of both sides, using base 2:

$$\log_2 x = \log_2 2^{y-1}$$

According to the law of logarithms, $\log_2 2^x = x$ for all x, so you end up with:

$$\log_2 x = y - 1$$
$$\log_2 x + 1 = y$$
$$\log_2 x + 1 = f^{-1}(x)$$

35. **(C)** *Trigonometry: Basic Functions*

The area of $\triangle ABC$ is equal to $\frac{1}{2}bh$. Since the question asks you to find the area in terms of θ, you should use trig to find the base and height of the triangle:

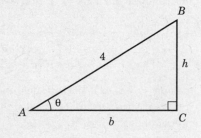

First find the height of the triangle:

$$\sin\theta = \frac{h}{4}$$
$$h = 4\sin\theta$$

Now find the base:

$$\cos\theta = \frac{b}{4}$$
$$b = 4\cos\theta$$

Plug these values for the base and height into the area formula:

$$\text{area} = \frac{1}{2}bh$$
$$= \frac{1}{2}(4\sin\theta)(4\cos\theta)$$
$$= 8\sin\theta\cos\theta$$

36. **(D)** *Miscellaneous Math: Sequences and Series*

The question defines the sequence as $x_{n+1} = \dfrac{x_n}{x_n + 1}$, which means that the next term in the sequence depends on the previous term. For example, the second term in the sequence is: $x_2 = \dfrac{x_1}{x_1 + 1}$. The simplest way to find the fourth term, x_4, is to plug x_3 into the equation. You can find x_3 using x_2, and you can find x_2 by plugging $x_1 = 1$ into the equation.

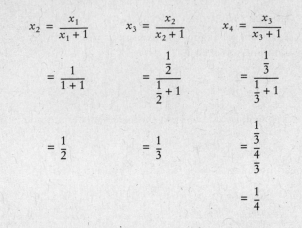

$$x_2 = \frac{x_1}{x_1 + 1} \qquad x_3 = \frac{x_2}{x_2 + 1} \qquad x_4 = \frac{x_3}{x_3 + 1}$$

$$= \frac{1}{1 + 1} \qquad\qquad = \frac{\frac{1}{2}}{\frac{1}{2} + 1} \qquad\qquad = \frac{\frac{1}{3}}{\frac{1}{3} + 1}$$

$$= \frac{1}{2} \qquad\qquad = \frac{1}{3} \qquad\qquad = \frac{\frac{1}{3}}{\frac{4}{3}}$$

$$= \frac{1}{4}$$

You can skip some of these last steps if you recognize the developing pattern, $x_n = \dfrac{1}{n}$.

37. **(C)** *Miscellaneous Math: Complex Numbers*

When a question gives you an equation in factored form, you should almost always multiply out the equation. In this case, multiply the complex numbers $(a + bi)(c + di)$ and collect any like terms, remembering that $i^2 = -1$:

$$(a + bi)(c + di) = ac + adi + bci + bdi^2$$
$$= ac + i(ad + bc) - bd$$
$$= ac - bd + i(ad + bc)$$

The question tells you that this expression is equal to 1. Since the definition of complex numbers says that a, b, c, and d are real numbers, the only way the expression can equal the real number 1 is if $ad + bc = 0$, canceling out the term with the complex i, and if $ac - bd = 1$.

38. (B) *Statistics: Probability*

The question asks you to find the probability of withdrawing a red card *or* a Queen. A standard deck of cards has 26 red cards and 4 Queens, but 2 of the 4 Queens are red. Since you don't want to double count the red Queens, you want to add the 2 black Queens to the 26 red cards to figure out how many of the 52 cards will satisfy the question: $26 + 2 = 28$. Since 28 cards are either red cards or Queens, the probability of withdrawing a red card or a Queen is $\frac{28}{52} = \frac{7}{13}$.

You can also answer this question if you remember that the probability of A or B happening is: $P(A \text{ or } B) = P(A) + P(B) - P(A \text{ and } B)$:

$$P(\text{Queens or red}) = P(\text{Queen}) + P(\text{red}) - P(\text{red Queen})$$

$$= \frac{4}{52} + \frac{26}{52} - \frac{2}{52}$$

$$= \frac{28}{52}$$

$$= \frac{7}{13}$$

39. (E) *Algebra: Equation Solving, Exponents*

The easiest way to solve this problem is to rewrite 4^n as 2^{2n}:

$$2^{2n} = 2^{n^2 + n - 6}$$

According to the law of exponents, since the bases are equal on both sides of the equation, the exponents are equal as well:

$$2n = n^2 + n - 6$$
$$0 = n^2 - n - 6$$
$$= (n - 3)(n + 2)$$
$$n = 3 \text{ or } n = -2$$

Choice (E), which says $n = 3$, is the correct answer.

40. (D) *Coordinate Geometry: Vectors*

Vectors seldom appear on the Math IIC, but you need to be prepared when they do. A vector has both magnitude and direction. The magnitude of a vector is its length, and the direction is the counterclockwise angle the vector makes with the positive x-axis. Below, the figure on the left shows a vector defined by its magnitude and direction. The figure on the right shows the same vector broken into its x- and y-components:

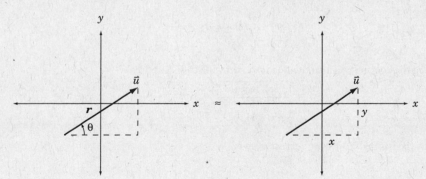

As you can see from this figure, a vector can be defined either by its length r and direction θ or by its x- and y-components. Usually, questions involving vectors will ask you to do simple calculations, such as multiplication by scalars (nonvector numbers) or vector addition. These questions are easy to answer using the x- and y-components. When multiplying a vector $\bar{u}$ by the scalar a, simply multiply the x- and y-compents of $\bar{u}$ by a: $a(x, y) = (ax, ay)$. When adding two vectors, simply add together their x-components, and then add together their y-components: $(x_1, y_1) + (x_2, y_2) = ((x_1 + x_2), (y_1 + y_2))$.

For this question, you first need to multiply the vector $\vec{v}$ by the scalar 2: if $\bar{v} = (1, 3)$, $2\bar{v} = (2, 6)$. Then you need to multiply $\overline{w}$ by 3: if $\overline{w} = (2, -7)$, $3\overline{w} = (6, -21)$. Now you can subtract $3\overline{w}$ from $2\overline{v}$ by finding the differences between the two x-values and the two y-values:

$$
\begin{aligned}
2\vec{v} - 3\vec{w} &= (2, 6) - (6, -21) \\
&= (2 - 6, 6 - (-21)) \\
&= (-4, 27)
\end{aligned}
$$

41. **(A)** *Trigonometry: Inverse Trigonometric Functions*

In order to get rid of the inverse sine function in $\sin^{-1}(\cos\theta) = \frac{\pi}{6}$, you should take the sine of both sides:

$$
\begin{aligned}
\sin(\sin^{-1}(\cos\theta)) &= \sin\left(\frac{\pi}{6}\right) \\
\cos\theta &= \sin\frac{\pi}{6} \\
\cos\theta &= \frac{1}{2}
\end{aligned}
$$

Now take the inverse cosine of both sides:

$$
\cos^{-1}(\cos\theta) = \cos^{-1}\left(\frac{1}{2}\right)
$$

$$
\theta = \frac{\pi}{3}, \text{ since } 0 \le \theta \le \frac{\pi}{2}
$$

42. **(B)** *Miscellaneous Math: Sequences and Series*

In a geometric sequence, the ratio of successive terms is constant. For example, the ratio of a_1 to a_2 is equal to the ratio of a_2 to a_3. In this question, $a_1 = 3x$, $a_2 = 2x + 1$, and $a_3 = 4x - 3$. You can write the following equation with the ratios of these terms:

$$
\frac{a_1}{a_2} = \frac{a_2}{a_3}
$$

$$
\frac{3x}{2x + 1} = \frac{2x + 1}{4x - 3}
$$

Cross multiply to get:

$$
12x^2 - 9x = 4x^2 + 4x + 1
$$
$$
8x^2 - 13x - 1 = 0
$$

You can plug the coefficients into the quadratic formula to solve for x:

$$
x = \frac{13 \pm \sqrt{169 + 32}}{16}
$$

$$
\approx -0.07, 1.70
$$

Since choice (B) is $x = 1.70$, it's the correct answer.

43. **(E)** *Solid Geometry: Prisms, Solids that Aren't Prisms*

The following illustrations show how the intersection of a cube and a cone can form a point, a line segment, a circle, and a rectangle.

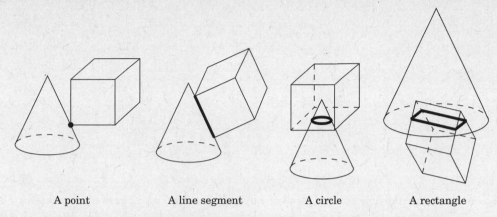

| A point | A line segment | A circle | A rectangle |

Of the answer choices, a cylinder is the only form that can't result from the intersection.

44. **(D)** *Miscellaneous Math: Limits*

The question asks you to find the limit of the function as x approaches infinity—in other words, to determine the value of the function as the value of x gets close to infinity.

When finding the limit at infinity, you should first find the terms with the highest degrees (or exponents) in the numerator and denominator of the function. In this case, $2x^2$ is the term with the highest degree in the numerator, and $5x^2$ is the term with the highest degree in the denominator. At infinity, the function essentially reduces to these highest terms, $\frac{2x^2}{5x^2}$, since the lower degree terms become insignificantly small compared to the highest degree terms as x grows infinitely large. The x^2 terms in the numerator and denominator of $\frac{2x^2}{5x^2}$ cancel out, leaving you with $\frac{2}{5}$, which is the value of the limit at infinity.

45. **(B)** *Trigonometry: Pythagorean Identities*

The Pythagorean trigonometric identities are tested on every Math IIC, so you should know them well. One of the most frequently tested of these identities is $\sin^2\theta + \cos^2\theta = 1$, which is true for all values of θ. For this question, you need to use a version of this identity: $\sin^2\theta = 1 - \cos^2\theta$. The trick is to substitute $1 - \cos^2\theta$ for $\sin^2\theta$, which results in a quadratic equation in terms of $\cos\theta$.

$$
\begin{aligned}
0 &= 2\sin^2\theta - \cos\theta + 1 \\
&= 2(1 - \cos^2\theta) - \cos\theta + 1 \\
&= 2 - 2\cos^2\theta - \cos\theta + 1 \\
&= -2\cos^2\theta - \cos\theta + 3 \\
&= (1 - \cos\theta)(2\cos\theta + 3)
\end{aligned}
$$

You end up with $\cos\theta = 1$ or $\cos\theta = \frac{3}{2}$. However, $\cos\theta = \frac{3}{2}$ cannot be correct because it suggests that a leg of a right triangle is longer than its hypotenuse. The cosine of an angle must be less than or equal to 1. $\cos\theta = 1$ is a correct statement, and it tells you that $\theta = 0$.

46. **(D)** *Statistics: Permutations and Combinations*

The question tells you that there are 10 chairs and 5 people to sit in them. In order to figure out how many ways the 5 people can sit in the chairs, you need to do a permutation. The general formula for permutations is $_nP_r = \dfrac{n!}{(n-r)!}$, where n is the total number of elements (10 chairs) and r is the size of the subgroup (5 people). The permutation tells you the number of possible arrangements of the subgroup within the set.

For this question, you have:

$$_{10}P_5 = \frac{10!}{(10-5)!}$$
$$= \frac{10 \times 9 \times 8 \times 7 \times 6 \times 5 \times 4 \times 3 \times 2 \times 1}{5 \times 4 \times 3 \times 2 \times 1}$$
$$= 10 \times 9 \times 8 \times 7 \times 6$$
$$= 30240$$

You can solve this problem in another (and slightly more intuitive) way. The first person can sit in any of the 10 chairs and thus has 10 options. The second person can sit in any of the remaining 9 chairs and thus has 9 options. The third person can sit in any of the remaining 8 chairs and thus has 8 options. Go on this way until you reach the fifth person. You can use this information to set up the following calculation:

$$\text{number of seating arrangements} = 10 \cdot 9 \cdot 8 \cdot 7 \cdot 6$$
$$= 30240$$

This method is essentially the same as the one described initially, but, instead of writing out and canceling the like terms in the factorials, you do the cancellation in your head.

47. **(B)** *Miscellaneous Math: Logic*

The writers of the Math IIC usually test only one rule of logic: a statement in the form of "If p, then q" is logically equivalent to the statement "If not q, then not p," which is called the contrapositive of the original statement. You derive the contrapositive of an "If p, then q" statement by switching the places of p and q and negating them. The original statement in this question has the p phrase "the trees are green" and the q phrase "it is not December." Now switch the two phrases and negate them, remembering that the double negative "not not" cancels out, leaving behind "it is December." You end up with the contrapositive statement: "If it is December, then the trees are not green."

48. **(C)** *Functions: Inverse Functions*

Your first step should be to find the inverse function, $f^{-1}(x)$. There are three steps for finding an inverse function, and you should definitely learn them for the Math IIC: replace $f(x)$ with y; switch the places of x and y; solve for y.

$$f(x) = \sqrt[7]{5x^3 - 3}$$

$$y = \sqrt[7]{5x^3 - 3}$$

$$x = \sqrt[7]{5y^3 - 3}$$

$$x^7 + 3 = 5y^3$$

$$\sqrt[3]{\frac{x^7 + 3}{5}} = y = f^{-1}(x)$$

Now you can evaluate $f^{-1}(x)$ at $x = 1$.

$$\sqrt[3]{\frac{(1)^7 + 3}{5}} \approx 0.93$$

49. **(C)** *Algebra: Equation Solving*

On the Math IIC, whenever you see a quadratic polynomial in unfactored form, you should try to factor it. In this case, the quadratic in the denominator factors: $\frac{1}{(x + 3)(x - 2)}$. You can see from the factored form of the quadratic that when $x = -3$ and $x = 2$, the denominator equals 0 and the expression is undefined. Thus $x = -3$ and $x = 2$ can't be included in the answer set. Now you need to figure out which values make the expression less than 0. Plug in a number that's smaller than -3, such as -4. The result is a positive fraction, which is greater than 0, so you know $x < -3$ doesn't satisfy the inequality. Plug in a number between -3 and 2, such as 1. The result is a negative fraction, so you know $-3 < x < 2$ does satisfy the inequality. Finally, plug in a number that's greater than 2, such as 3. The result is a positive fraction, so you know $x > 2$ doesn't work. $-3 < x < 2$ is the set that satisfies the inequality.

50. **(A)** *Coordinate Geometry: Hyperbolas*

Hyperbolas seldom show up on the Math IIC, but you need to be able to recognize them when they do. The equation of a hyperbola looks similar to the equation of an ellipse, except the coefficient of either x^2 or y^2 (but not both) is negative in a hyperbola, while both coefficients are positive in an ellipse. In the equation given in the question, the coefficient of x^2 is positive and the coefficient of y^2 is negative; you should be able to tell from this that you're dealing with a hyperbola. To find the center of the hyperbola, you should rewrite the equation in the question as $\frac{(x - h)^2}{a^2} - \frac{(y - k)^2}{b^2} = 1$, where (h, k) is the center.

$$0 = 9x^2 - y^2 - 18x + 4y - 31$$
$$31 = 9(x^2 - 2x) - (y^2 - 4y)$$

Since you want quadratics that factor as $(x - h)^2$ and $(y - k)^2$, you need to complete the squares for x and y. For $x^2 - 2x$, you complete the square by halving the coefficient of x, which is 2, and then by squaring the result. You end up with 1. Because the quadratic is multiplied by 9, you're really adding 9 to the right side of the equation. In order to keep the sides of the equation equal, you need to add 9 to the left side as well. Go through the same process with $y^2 - 4y$: take half of 4 to get 2; square 2 to get 4. Since this quadratic is multiplied by -1, you should subtract 4 from both sides of the equation. You end up with:

$$31 + 9 - 4 = 9(x^2 - 2x + 1) - (y^2 - 4y + 4)$$

Now you can factor the quadratics:

$$36 = 9(x - 1)^2 - (y - 2)^2$$

Divide both sides by 36 to get the standard equation of a hyperbola.

$$1 = \frac{(x - 1)^2}{4} - \frac{(y - 2)^2}{36}$$

From this equation, you can see that the point $(1, 2)$ is the center of the hyperbola.

SAT II Math IIC
Practice Test 3

MATH IIC TEST 3 ANSWER SHEET

1. Ⓐ Ⓑ Ⓒ Ⓓ Ⓔ	18. Ⓐ Ⓑ Ⓒ Ⓓ Ⓔ	35. Ⓐ Ⓑ Ⓒ Ⓓ Ⓔ
2. Ⓐ Ⓑ Ⓒ Ⓓ Ⓔ	19. Ⓐ Ⓑ Ⓒ Ⓓ Ⓔ	36. Ⓐ Ⓑ Ⓒ Ⓓ Ⓔ
3. Ⓐ Ⓑ Ⓒ Ⓓ Ⓔ	20. Ⓐ Ⓑ Ⓒ Ⓓ Ⓔ	37. Ⓐ Ⓑ Ⓒ Ⓓ Ⓔ
4. Ⓐ Ⓑ Ⓒ Ⓓ Ⓔ	21. Ⓐ Ⓑ Ⓒ Ⓓ Ⓔ	38. Ⓐ Ⓑ Ⓒ Ⓓ Ⓔ
5. Ⓐ Ⓑ Ⓒ Ⓓ Ⓔ	22. Ⓐ Ⓑ Ⓒ Ⓓ Ⓔ	39. Ⓐ Ⓑ Ⓒ Ⓓ Ⓔ
6. Ⓐ Ⓑ Ⓒ Ⓓ Ⓔ	23. Ⓐ Ⓑ Ⓒ Ⓓ Ⓔ	40. Ⓐ Ⓑ Ⓒ Ⓓ Ⓔ
7. Ⓐ Ⓑ Ⓒ Ⓓ Ⓔ	24. Ⓐ Ⓑ Ⓒ Ⓓ Ⓔ	41. Ⓐ Ⓑ Ⓒ Ⓓ Ⓔ
8. Ⓐ Ⓑ Ⓒ Ⓓ Ⓔ	25. Ⓐ Ⓑ Ⓒ Ⓓ Ⓔ	42. Ⓐ Ⓑ Ⓒ Ⓓ Ⓔ
9. Ⓐ Ⓑ Ⓒ Ⓓ Ⓔ	26. Ⓐ Ⓑ Ⓒ Ⓓ Ⓔ	43. Ⓐ Ⓑ Ⓒ Ⓓ Ⓔ
10. Ⓐ Ⓑ Ⓒ Ⓓ Ⓔ	27. Ⓐ Ⓑ Ⓒ Ⓓ Ⓔ	44. Ⓐ Ⓑ Ⓒ Ⓓ Ⓔ
11. Ⓐ Ⓑ Ⓒ Ⓓ Ⓔ	28. Ⓐ Ⓑ Ⓒ Ⓓ Ⓔ	45. Ⓐ Ⓑ Ⓒ Ⓓ Ⓔ
12. Ⓐ Ⓑ Ⓒ Ⓓ Ⓔ	29. Ⓐ Ⓑ Ⓒ Ⓓ Ⓔ	46. Ⓐ Ⓑ Ⓒ Ⓓ Ⓔ
13. Ⓐ Ⓑ Ⓒ Ⓓ Ⓔ	30. Ⓐ Ⓑ Ⓒ Ⓓ Ⓔ	47. Ⓐ Ⓑ Ⓒ Ⓓ Ⓔ
14. Ⓐ Ⓑ Ⓒ Ⓓ Ⓔ	31. Ⓐ Ⓑ Ⓒ Ⓓ Ⓔ	48. Ⓐ Ⓑ Ⓒ Ⓓ Ⓔ
15. Ⓐ Ⓑ Ⓒ Ⓓ Ⓔ	32. Ⓐ Ⓑ Ⓒ Ⓓ Ⓔ	49. Ⓐ Ⓑ Ⓒ Ⓓ Ⓔ
16. Ⓐ Ⓑ Ⓒ Ⓓ Ⓔ	33. Ⓐ Ⓑ Ⓒ Ⓓ Ⓔ	50. Ⓐ Ⓑ Ⓒ Ⓓ Ⓔ
17. Ⓐ Ⓑ Ⓒ Ⓓ Ⓔ	34. Ⓐ Ⓑ Ⓒ Ⓓ Ⓔ	

REFERENCE INFORMATION

THE FOLLOWING INFORMATION IS FOR YOUR REFERENCE IN ANSWERING SOME OF THE QUESTIONS IN THIS TEST:

Volume of a right circular cone with radius r and height h: $V = \frac{1}{3}\pi r^2 h$

Lateral area of a right circular cone with circumference of the base c and slaight height ℓ: $S = \frac{1}{2}c\ell$

Volume of a sphere with radius r: $V = \frac{4}{3}\pi r^3$

Surface area of a sphere with radius r: $S = 4\pi r^2$

Volume of a pyramid with base area B and height h: $V = \frac{1}{3}Bh$

MATHEMATICS LEVEL IIC TEST

For each of the following problems, decide which is the BEST of the choices given. If the exact numerical value is not one of the choices, select the choice that best approximates this value. Then fill in the corresponding oval on the answer sheet.

Notes: (1) A calculator will be necessary for answering some (but not all) of the questions in this test. For each question you will have to decide whether or not you should use a calcuator. The calculator you use must be at least a scientific calculator; programmable calculators and calculators that can display graphs are permitted.

(2) For some questions in this test you may need to decide whether your calculator should be in radian or degree mode.

(3) Figures that accompany problems in this test are intended to provide information useful in solving the problems. They are drawn as accurately as possible EXCEPT when it is stated in a specific problem that its figure is not drawn to scale. All figures lie in a plane unless otherwise indicated.

(4) Unless otherwise specified, the domain of any function f is assumed to be the set of all real numbers x for which $f(x)$ is a real number.

(5) Reference information that may be useful in answering the questions in this test can be found on the page preceding Question 1.

USE THIS SPACE FOR SCRATCHWORK.

. If $a < b$ and $c < 0$, which of the following must be true?

(A) $a - c > b - c$
(B) $ab > c$
(C) $ac < bc$
(D) $ac > bc$
(E) $\dfrac{a}{b} > c$

If y varies inversely with x, and $y = 45$ when $x = \dfrac{1}{3}$, what is the value of x when $y = 30$?

(A) $\dfrac{1}{8}$

(B) $\dfrac{1}{4}$

(C) $\dfrac{1}{2}$

(D) $\dfrac{2}{3}$

(E) $\dfrac{3}{4}$

$\dfrac{8!}{2!3!3!} =$

(A) 280
(B) 560
(C) 1120
(D) 2240
(E) 6720

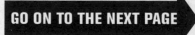
GO ON TO THE NEXT PAGE

4. The line $3x - 5y = 7$ is parallel to which of the following lines?

    (A) $y = 7 - \dfrac{5}{3}x$

    (B) $y = 7 + \dfrac{5}{3}x$

    (C) $y = 7 - \dfrac{3}{5}x$

    (D) $y = 7 + \dfrac{3}{5}x$

    (E) $y = 5 - \dfrac{7}{3}x$

5. If $f(x) = \dfrac{1}{1 + x^3}$ and $g(x) = \sqrt{x^2 - 4}$, then what is the value of $f(g(18))$?

    (A) 0.98
    (B) 1.002
    (C) 0.02
    (D) 0.002
    (E) 0.0002

6. If n is divisible by 3, 4, 7, and 11, then which of the following could <u>not</u> be the value of n?

    (A) 924
    (B) 1848
    (C) 2227
    (D) 2772
    (E) 4620

7. In Figure 1, what is the slope of the line l?

    (A) $\cot\theta$

    (B) $\tan\theta$

    (C) $2\sin\theta$

    (D) $2\cos\theta$

    (E) $\dfrac{1}{2}$

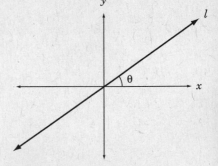

Note: Figure not drawn to scale.

Figure 1

GO ON TO THE NEXT PAGE

8. For $x \neq 0$ or $x \neq 1$, $\dfrac{1-x}{x - \dfrac{1}{x}} =$

(A) $-\dfrac{x}{x+1}$

(B) 0

(C) $\dfrac{1}{x+1}$

(D) x

(E) $\dfrac{x^2 - 1}{x}$

. If $\cos\theta = \dfrac{3}{5}$, then $1 - \sin^2\theta =$

(A) 2

(B) $\dfrac{26}{25}$

(C) 1

(D) $\dfrac{16}{25}$

(E) $\dfrac{9}{25}$

0. If $x^5 + 125 = 72$, then $x =$

(A) −3.21

(B) −2.21

(C) −1.16

(D) 2.21

(E) x is not a real number

1. If the point $(-2, -3)$ is on the graph $y = g(x)$, then which of the following points <u>must</u> be on the graph of $y = |g(x)|$?

(A) $(-2, -3)$

(B) $(-2, 3)$

(C) $(2, 3)$

(D) $(3, 2)$

(E) $(3, 3)$

2. If $\cos\theta = 0.23$, then $\cos(\pi - \theta) =$

(A) −0.46

(B) −0.23

(C) 0

(D) 0.23

(E) 0.46

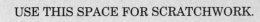

GO ON TO THE NEXT PAGE

13. A triangle has sides whose lengths are integers. If two of the sides have lengths 5 and 15, then how many possibilities are there for the length of the remaining side?

 (A) 13
 (B) 12
 (C) 11
 (D) 10
 (E) 9

14. If the zeros of a quadratic polynomial $p(x)$ add up to 1 and multiply to 4, which of the following could be the polynomial $p(x)$?

 (A) $x^2 - x + 4$
 (B) $x^2 - x - 4$
 (C) $2x^2 - 2x + 6$
 (D) $x^2 + x - 6$
 (E) $x^2 + x - 4$

15. If $f(x) = \dfrac{1}{x+3}$ and $f(g(2)) = 5$, then $g(x)$ could be which of the following?

 (A) $g(x) = x - \dfrac{24}{5}$

 (B) $g(x) = \dfrac{24}{5} - x$

 (C) $g(x) = \dfrac{x+1}{3}$

 (D) $g(x) = \dfrac{1-x}{3}$

 (E) $g(x) = \dfrac{x}{x-5}$

GO ON TO THE NEXT PAGE

16. In Figure 2, right triangle $\triangle ABC$ is inscribed in square $\square FDEG$. If $DB = BE$, $FA = AG$ and $DF = 2$, what is the area of $\triangle ABC$?

(A) $\frac{1}{3}$

(B) $\frac{1}{2}$

(C) $\frac{3}{4}$

(D) 1

(E) Not enough information to tell

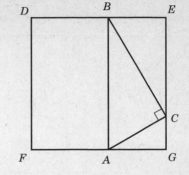

Note: Figure not drawn to scale.

Figure 2

17. If a line has the equation $x = 7$, then the slope of this line is equal to

(A) –7
(B) 0
(C) 1
(D) 7
(E) An undefined quantity

18. John's average on his quizzes is 80. If he gets 100's on the next 3 quizzes his average will be raised to 90. How many quizzes has John taken so far?

(A) 2
(B) 3
(C) 4
(D) 5
(E) 6

19. What is the area of an equilateral triangle with sides of length 5.5?

(A) 10.9
(B) 12.7
(C) 13.1
(D) 13.9
(E) 14.0

20. If $f(x) = x^2 + 1$ and $g(x) = x - 5$ and $g(f(x)) = 0$, then x could be

 (A) –3
 (B) –2
 (C) 0
 (D) 4
 (E) 6

21. The first term in a geometric sequence is 9, and the second term is 3. What is the sum of the first 4 terms?

 (A) 6

 (B) $\dfrac{20}{3}$

 (C) $\dfrac{40}{6}$

 (D) $\dfrac{40}{3}$

 (E) 40

22. If $p(x) = ax^3 + bx^2 + cx + d$ such that $p(0) = 1$, $p(1) = 3$, and $p(-1) = 5$, then the value of b is

 (A) 3
 (B) 2
 (C) 1
 (D) 0
 (E) Not enough information to tell

23. What is the domain of $f(x) = \dfrac{1}{\sqrt[4]{9 - x^2}}$?
 (A) All real numbers
 (B) $-\sqrt{3} \le x \le \sqrt{3}$
 (C) $-9 < x < 9$
 (D) $-3 \le x \le 3$
 (E) $-3 < x < 3$

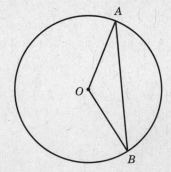

24. In Figure 3, the area of the circle is 9π and the length of AB is 5. What is the value of $\angle AOB$?

 (A) 60°
 (B) 78.2°
 (C) 112.9°
 (D) 114.6°
 (E) 120.7°

Note: Figure not drawn to scale.
Figure 3

GO ON TO THE NEXT PAGE

25. If $\sec^2\theta = 0$, then $\dfrac{1}{\sec^2\theta} + \sin^2\theta =$

    (A) -1
    (B) 0
    (C) 1
    (D) $2\sin^2\theta$
    (E) $2\sin\theta\cos\theta$

26. If $f(x) = \sqrt[3]{x-1}$ and $f(g(x)) = -x$, which of the following could be $g(x)$?

    (A) $1 - x^3$
    (B) $1 - x^2$
    (C) $1 + x^3$
    (D) $(1-x)^3$
    (E) $(1+x)^3$

27. What are the x-coordinates of the points of intersection of the line $y = -6$ and a circle of radius 10 centered at $(-1, -1)$?

    (A) $\{-10, -8\}$
    (B) $\{-9.66, 7.66\}$
    (C) $\{-8.67, 6.67\}$
    (D) $\{-4, 3\}$
    (E) $\{-3, 4\}$

28. Which of the following could be the vertical asymptote(s) of the graph of the function $f(x) = \dfrac{x^2 - 7x + 12}{x^2 - 16}$?

    (A) $x = 3$
    (B) $x = 4$
    (C) $x = -4$ and $x = 4$
    (D) $x = -4$
    (E) $y = 1$

29. A car worth \$27,000 today depreciates at a rate of 13% annually. How much will the car be worth in 7 years?

    (A) \$10,185.90
    (B) \$12,127.82
    (C) \$13,001.12
    (D) \$14,144.83
    (E) \$14,145.67

GO ON TO THE NEXT PAGE

30. What is the area of the shaded region in Figure 4?

    (A) 60
    (B) 36
    (C) 15
    (D) 14
    (E) 12

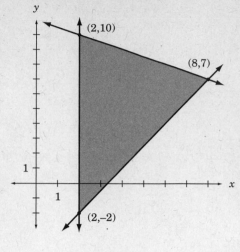

Figure 4

31. If $x_0 = 1$ and $x_{n+1} = (x_n - 1)^2$, what is the value of x_3?

    (A) −3
    (B) −2
    (C) −1
    (D) 0
    (E) 1

32. If $f(x) = 3^x$ and $f(g(x)) = x$, then $g(x) =$

    (A) $\sqrt[3]{x}$

    (B) $\dfrac{1}{3^x}$

    (C) $\log_3 x$

    (D) $\ln x$

    (E) $\log_x 3$

33. If $x^2 - y^2 = 77$ and $2x - 3y = 5$, then x could be equal to which of the following?

    (A) −13.7
    (B) −12.5
    (C) −3.7
    (D) 1.2
    (E) 10.7

 GO ON TO THE NEXT PAGE

34. The graph in Figure 5 could be the graph of which of the following functions?

(A) $f(x) = \begin{cases} 1 - x & x < 3 \\ x + 1 & x \geq 3 \end{cases}$

(B) $f(x) = \begin{cases} x + 1 & x < 3 \\ x - 1 & x \geq 3 \end{cases}$

(C) $f(x) = \begin{cases} \dfrac{3 - x}{3} & x \leq 3 \\ x & x > 3 \end{cases}$

(D) $f(x) = \begin{cases} \dfrac{3 - x}{3} & x < 3 \\ x & x \geq 3 \end{cases}$

(E) $f(x) = \begin{cases} x & x < 3 \\ \dfrac{3 - x}{3} & x \geq 3 \end{cases}$

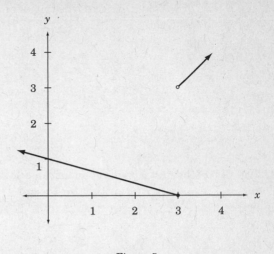

Figure 5

35. In Figure 6, what is the area of $\triangle ABC$?

(A) 21.65
(B) 20.21
(C) 20.19
(D) 20.17
(E) 18.01

36. A bag contains only red and blue marbles. The probability that a blue marble is first drawn from the bag is $\dfrac{1}{5}$ and the probability that the second marble drawn is also blue (if the first marble is not replaced) is $\dfrac{3}{19}$. How many red marbles are there in the bag?

(A) 4
(B) 11
(C) 12
(D) 15
(E) 16

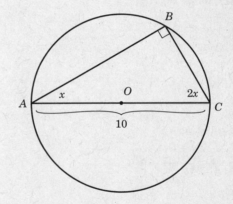

Note: Figure not drawn to scale.
Figure 6

37. For all $x > 0$, $\dfrac{\log_4 x^{15}}{\log_4 x^{12}} =$

(A) x^3

(B) $\dfrac{5}{4}$

(C) $\log_4 x^3$

(D) $\ln 4x$

(E) Not enough information to tell

GO ON TO THE NEXT PAGE

38. If vector $\vec{v}$ has a magnitude of 11.1 and vector $\vec{w}$ has a magnitude of 9.9, then which of the following could <u>not</u> be the magnitude of $3\vec{v} + 5\vec{w}$?

   (A) 82.9
   (B) 82.7
   (C) 80.5
   (D) 16.8
   (E) 16.3

39. The sum of the first 5 terms of an arithmetic sequence is 65 and the first term is 3. What is the third term?

   (A) 18
   (B) 13
   (C) 8
   (D) 5
   (E) 4

40. If $0 < x < \dfrac{\pi}{2}$ and $2\sec^2 x - 3\tan x - 5 = 0$, then x could be which of the following?

   (A) 1.0
   (B) 0.98
   (C) 0.96
   (D) 0.12
   (E) 0.11

41. $\dfrac{n!}{(n-1)!} - \dfrac{(n-1)!}{(n-2)!} =$

   (A) $n(n-1)$
   (B) $n(n+1)$
   (C) $2n-1$
   (D) 1
   (E) -1

42. A circle is to be drawn on the surface of a sphere of volume 288π. What is the maximum possible circumference for this circle?

   (A) 14π
   (B) 12π
   (C) 10π
   (D) 6π
   (E) Not enough information to tell

GO ON TO THE NEXT PAGE

43. An indirect proof of the statement "If x is an even number, then x is divisible by 2" could begin with the assumption that

(A) x is not divisible by 2
(B) $x = 3$
(C) x is divisible by 2
(D) $x = 2$
(E) x is not an even number

44. What is the area of the parallelogram $ABCD$ in Figure 7, in terms of $x, y,$ and θ ?

(A) $\frac{1}{2}xy$

(B) xy
(C) $xy\cos\theta$
(D) $xy\sin\theta$
(E) $xy\tan\theta$

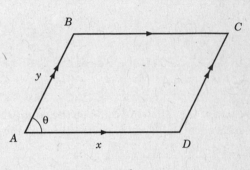

Figure 7

45. If a right circular cone is inscribed within a hemisphere of radius r, what is the ratio of the volume of the cone to the volume of S, where S is the volume of the hemisphere minus the volume of the cone?

(A) $\frac{2}{3}$

(B) 1

(C) $\frac{3}{2}$

(D) $r^{3/2}$

(E) $1 + r$

46. How many different arrangements are there of 2 red marbles, 3 green marbles, and 3 blue marbles, if marbles of the same color are considered identical?

(A) 40320
(B) 3604
(C) 2400
(D) 1120
(E) 560

47. If the graph of $f(x) = x^3 + 1$ is translated 5 units to the right and then 7 units down, what would be the value of the transformed graph at the point $x = 2.7$?

(A) 12.167
(B) 5.167
(C) –17.281
(D) –18.167
(E) –20.315

GO ON TO THE NEXT PAGE

USE THIS SPACE FOR SCRATCHWORK.

48. If $\dfrac{1}{R} = \dfrac{1}{x} + \dfrac{1}{y} + \dfrac{1}{z}$, for $x, y, z, R \neq 0$, then $R =$

    (A) $x^2 + y^2 + z^2$

    (B) $x + y + z$

    (C) $\dfrac{xyz}{xy + yz + xz}$

    (D) $\dfrac{xy + yz + xz}{xyz}$

    (E) $\dfrac{1}{x \cdot y \cdot z}$

49. Which of the following could be the equation of a hyperbola centered at $(1, 3)$, which passes through the point $(2, 4)$?

    (A) $\dfrac{(x-3)^2}{\frac{1}{2}} - \dfrac{(y-1)^2}{1} = 1$

    (B) $\dfrac{(x-1)^2}{\frac{1}{2}} - \dfrac{(y-3)^2}{1} = 1$

    (C) $\dfrac{(x+1)^2}{\frac{1}{2}} - \dfrac{(y-3)^2}{1} = 1$

    (D) $\dfrac{(x+1)^2}{2} - \dfrac{(y-3)^2}{1} = 1$

    (E) $\dfrac{(x-1)^2}{2} - \dfrac{(y-3)^2}{1} = 1$

50. Which of following sets has a Least Element?

    I. The positive prime numbers
    II. The positive rational numbers
    III. The integers

    (A) I only
    (B) II only
    (C) III only
    (D) I and III only
    (E) I, II, and III

S T O P

IF YOU FINISH BEFORE TIME IS CALLED, YOU MAY CHECK YOUR WORK ON THIS TEST ONLY.
DO NOT TURN TO ANY OTHER TEST IN THIS BOOK.

SAT II Math IIC
Practice Test 3
Explanations

Calculating Your Score

Question Number	Correct Answer	Right	Wrong	Question Number	Correct Answer	Right	Wrong	Question Number	Correct Answer	Right	Wrong
1.	D	___	___	18.	B	___	___	35.	A	___	___
2.	C	___	___	19.	C	___	___	36.	E	___	___
3.	B	___	___	20.	B	___	___	37.	B	___	___
4.	D	___	___	21.	D	___	___	38.	A	___	___
5.	E	___	___	22.	A	___	___	39.	B	___	___
6.	C	___	___	23.	E	___	___	40.	B	___	___
7.	B	___	___	24.	C	___	___	41.	D	___	___
8.	A	___	___	25.	C	___	___	42.	B	___	___
9.	E	___	___	26.	A	___	___	43.	A	___	___
10.	B	___	___	27.	B	___	___	44.	D	___	___
11.	C	___	___	28.	D	___	___	45.	B	___	___
12.	B	___	___	29.	A	___	___	46.	E	___	___
13.	E	___	___	30.	B	___	___	47.	D	___	___
14.	A	___	___	31.	D	___	___	48.	C	___	___
15.	A	___	___	32.	C	___	___	49.	B	___	___
16.	D	___	___	33.	A	___	___	50.	A	___	___
17.	E	___	___	34.	C						

Your raw score for the SAT II Math IIC test is calculated from the number of questions you answer correctly and incorrectly. Once you have determined your composite score, use the conversion table on page 18 of this book to calculate your scaled score. To calculate your raw score, count the number of questions you answered correctly: _____
A

Count the number of questions you answered incorrectly, and multiply that number by $\frac{1}{4}$:

$$\underline{\hspace{3cm}} \times \frac{1}{4} = \underline{\hspace{3cm}}$$
B   C

Subtract the value in field C from value in field A: _____
D

Round the number in field D to the nearest whole number. This is your raw score: _____
E

Test 3 Explanations

Math IIC Test 3 Explanations

1. **(D)** *Algebra: Inequalities*

The best way to approach this problem is to go through each answer choice until you find the expression that must be true. Choice (D) multiplies both sides of the inequality $a < b$ by c, resulting in $ac > bc$. The question tells you that $c < 0$, so (D) must be true because multiplication (or division) by a negative number reverses the direction of the inequality sign.

2. **(C)** *Algebra: Writing Equations, Variation*

The statement "y varies inversely with x" means that y decreases as x increases and that y increases as x decreases. You can express this relationship as $y = \dfrac{k}{x}$ (or $yx = k$), where the constant k indicates that y isn't necessarily equal to $\dfrac{1}{x}$. You can find k by plugging $y = 45$ and $x = \dfrac{1}{3}$ into the expression:

$$k = 45 \cdot \frac{1}{3}$$

$$= 15$$

The question asks you to solve for x when $y = 30$:

$$k = yx$$

$$15 = 30 \cdot x$$

$$x = \frac{1}{2}$$

3. **(B)** *Statistics: Factorials*

The Math IIC will almost always test you on multiplying out factorials. The definition of a factorial is: $n! = n(n-1)(n-2)...(3)(2)(1)$.

$$\frac{8!}{2!3!3!} = \frac{8 \cdot 7 \cdot 5 \cdot 4 \cdot 3 \cdot 2 \cdot 1}{(2 \cdot 1)(3 \cdot 2 \cdot 1)(3 \cdot 2 \cdot 1)}$$

Cancel out terms in the numerator and denominator:

$$= 8 \cdot 7 \cdot 5 \cdot 2$$
$$= 560$$

4. **(D)** *Coordinate Geometry: Lines and Distance*

Lines that are parallel to each other have the same slope. Find the slope of $3x - 5y = 7$ by rearranging the equation as $y = mx + b$, where m is the slope of the line.

$$3x - 5y = 7$$

$$5y = 3x - 7$$

$$y = \frac{3}{5}x - \frac{7}{5}$$

The line in choice (D) is parallel to $3x - 5y = 7$ because it has a slope of $\dfrac{3}{5}$.

5. **(E)** *Functions: Compound Functions*

To solve the compound function $f(g(18))$, first find the value of $g(18)$, and then plug that value into $f(x)$.

$$g(18) = \sqrt{18^2 - 4}$$

$$= \sqrt{320}$$

$$f(\sqrt{320}) = \frac{1}{1 + (\sqrt{320})^3}$$

$$\approx 0.0002$$

6. **(C)** *Fundamentals: Integers*

If a number is divisible by 3, 4, 7, and 11, then it is divisible by 924 because $3 \cdot 4 \cdot 7 \cdot 11 = 924$. Divide each of the answer choices by 924. All of the answer choices except for 2227, choice (C), are multiples of 924.

7. **(B)** *Coordinate Geometry: Lines; Trigonometry: Basic Functions*

The slope of a line is equal to the change in the y-coordinate divided by the change in the x-coordinate. The graph of this line passes through the origin, so you know that $(0, 0)$ is one point on the line. You can draw an arbitrary point on the line and call it (x, y):

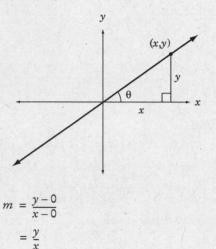

The slope of the line is:

$$m = \frac{y - 0}{x - 0}$$

$$= \frac{y}{x}$$

Four of the five answer choices are given in terms of the angle θ, which is the angle between the line and the x-axis. In the figure above, you can see the right triangle formed by the x and y coordinates of the line. Since the triangle is right, you know that $\frac{y}{x} = \tan\theta$, which is choice (B).

8. **(A)** *Algebra: Algebraic Manipulation*

Be careful as you simplify this algebraic expression.

$$\frac{1 - x}{x - \frac{1}{x}} = \frac{1 - x}{\frac{x^2 - 1}{x}}$$

$$= \frac{x(1 - x)}{(x + 1)(x - 1)}$$

Since $\dfrac{1-x}{x-1} = -1$, you can rewrite the expression as:

$$= \dfrac{-x}{x+1}$$

9. **(E)** *Trigonometry: Pythagorean Identities*

You should memorize the Pythagorean trigonometric identities, particularly $\sin^2\theta + \cos^2\theta = 1$. This identity can help you solve seemingly complicated trig problems on the Math IIC. If you rewrite the identity as $\cos^2\theta = 1 - \sin^2\theta$, you can substitute $\dfrac{3}{5}$ for $\cos\theta$:

$$1 - \sin^2\theta = \left(\dfrac{3}{5}\right)^2$$
$$= \dfrac{9}{25}$$

10. **(B)** *Algebra: Equation Solving*

This question asks you to solve for x in a straightforward equation.

$$x^5 + 125 = 72$$
$$x^5 = -53$$
$$x = (-53)^{1/5}$$
$$= -2.21$$

11. **(C)** *Functions: Transformations and Symmetry*

Answer this question in parts: first find the point that must be on $g(-x)$, then find the point that must be on $|g(-x)|$. The graph of $g(-x)$ is the graph of $g(x)$ reflected across the y-axis; you should definitely know this transformation for the Math IIC. (If you don't see why this is true, choose an expression for $g(x)$, such as $g(x) = 3x + 1$. Then solve $g(-x) = 3(-x) + 1 = -3x + 1$. Graph the two functions on your calculator to see how the two graphs relate to each other.) Since $(-2, -3)$ is on the graph of $y = g(x)$, $(2, -3)$ is on the graph of $y = g(-x)$. The question asks for the point that must be on the graph of $y = |g(-x)|$. When you take the absolute value of a function, you make all negative values of $g(-x)$ positive, so $(2, 3)$ is a point on $y = |g(-x)|$.

12. **(B)** *Trigonometry: Sum and Distance Formulas*

The angle subtraction formula for cosine says that $\cos(\theta - \varphi) = \cos\theta\cos\varphi + \sin\theta\sin\varphi$. The question asks you to find $\cos(\pi - \theta)$, so substitute these angles into the formula:

$$\cos(\pi - \theta) = \cos\pi\cos\theta + \sin\pi\sin\varphi$$
$$= -1 \cdot \cos\theta + 0 \cdot \sin\varphi$$
$$= -\cos\theta$$

Since $\cos(\theta) = 0.23$, you know $\cos(\pi - \theta) = -0.23$.

13. **(E)** *Plane Geometry: Triangles*

If a triangle has two sides of lengths a and b, then the length of its third side, c, must obey the following inequality:

$$|a - b| < c < a + b$$

For this question, you have a triangle with two sides of lengths 5 and 15. Plug these lengths into the inequality as a and b:

$$|15 - 5| < c < 15 + 5$$
$$10 < c < 20$$

The possible integer values for the length of side c are: 11, 12, 13, 14, 15, 16, 17, 18, and 19—a total of 9 values.

14. **(A)** *Algebra: Polynomials*

For a polynomial $p(x) = ax^2 + bx + c$, the sum of the zeros (also known as the roots of $ax^2 + bx + c = 0$) is equal to $-\dfrac{b}{a}$ and the product of the zeros is equal to $\dfrac{c}{a}$. The question tells you that:

$$-\frac{b}{a} = 1 \text{ and } \frac{c}{a} = 4$$

The coefficients of choice (A) satisfy these sum and product equations:

$$-\frac{(-1)}{1} = 1 \text{ and } \frac{4}{1} = 4$$

15. **(A)** *Functions: Compound Functions*

The simplest way to solve this problem is to make $g(2) = y$. If $f(g(2)) = 5$, then $f(y) = 5$. Since the question gives you $f(x)$, you can solve for y.

$$f(x) = \frac{1}{x + 3}$$

$$f(y) = \frac{1}{y + 3}$$

$$5 = \frac{1}{y + 3}$$

$$y = -2.8$$

If $y = -2.8$, then $g(2) = -2.8$. Plug 2 into the answer choices to see which function produces -2.8. Choice (A) is the correct answer since $g(2) = 2 - \dfrac{24}{5} = -2.8$.

16. **(D)** *Plane Geometry: Triangles*

You need to use the information given about the square to figure out the base and height of this triangle. The square has sides of length 2. The line AB, which is equal in length to the sides of the square, also has length 2. If you rotate the figure such that AB becomes the base of the triangle, you can see how to find the triangle's height:

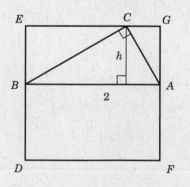

The height of the triangle is equal to EB. The question tells you that EB is equal to BD, which means that EB and BD are each half the length of the square's side, so you can figure out that $EB = 1$. You can plug the values for AB and EB into the area formula for a triangle:

$$\text{Area } \triangle ABC = \frac{1}{2}bh$$

$$= \frac{1}{2}AB \cdot EB$$

$$= \frac{1}{2} \cdot 2 \cdot 1$$

$$= 1$$

17. **(E)** *Coordinate Geometry: Lines and Distance*

You calculate the slope of a line by dividing the change in y by the change in x, or $\frac{\Delta y}{\Delta x}$. $x = 7$ is a vertical line. A vertical line has an undefined slope since the change in y over the change in x is $\frac{\infty}{0}$.

18. **(B)** *Statistics: Arithmetic Mean*

You calculate the mean of a set of values by dividing the total sum of the values by the number of values in the set. You don't know how many quizzes John has already taken, but you do know that his average score on these quizzes is 80. If you have T represent the total sum of his scores to date and x represent the number of quizzes to date, you have:

$$\frac{T}{x} = 80$$

$$T = 80x$$

If John scores 100 on each of his next three tests, he'll raise the total sum of his scores by 300 points, and he'll raise his average score to 90. You can write this as:

$$\frac{T + 300}{x + 3} = 90$$

Substitute $T = 80x$ into this equation:

$$\frac{80x + 300}{x + 3} = 90$$
$$80x + 300 = 90x + 270$$
$$10x = 30$$
$$x = 3$$

John has taken 3 tests.

19. **(C)** *Plane Geometry: Triangles*

Draw a picture of the triangle:

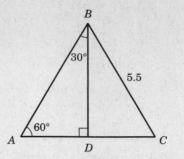

$\triangle ABC$ actually consists of two 30-60-90 triangles: $\triangle ABD$ and $\triangle CBD$. You can use the properties of a 30-60-90 triangle to find the height h of $\triangle ABC$, or you can calculate the height using the Pythagorean theorem, where the hypotenuse of the triangle is 5.5 and the other leg is $5.5 / 2 = 2.75$:

$$h^2 + (2.75)^2 = (5.5)^2$$
$$h = 4.76$$

Now you can solve for the area of $\triangle ABC$:

$$\text{Area } \triangle ABC = \frac{1}{2}(5.5)(4.76)$$
$$= 13.1$$

20. **(B)** *Functions: Compound Functions*

Since $f(x) = x^2 + 1$, plug $x^2 + 1$ into $g(x)$ to find $g(f(x))$:

$$g(x^2 + 1) = x^2 + 1 - 5$$
$$g(x^2 + 1) = x^2 - 4$$

The question tells you that $g(f(x)) = 0$, so you can write:

$$x^2 - 4 = 0$$
$$x^2 = 4$$
$$x = \pm 2$$

The correct answer is choice (B), –2.

21. **(D)** *Miscellaneous Math: Sequences and Series*

The formula for the sum of terms in a geometric sequence is $s_n = \dfrac{t_1(1-r^n)}{1-r}$, where s_n is the sum of the first n terms, t_1 is the first term, and r is the ratio between the terms. In a geometric sequence, the ratio between terms is constant. You can find the ratio by dividing a term by the term that precedes it; in this case, if you divide the second term in the sequence by the first term, you get: $r = \dfrac{3}{9} = \dfrac{1}{3}$. Since you know the values of the first term and the ratio, you can calculate the sum of the first 4 terms in the sequence:

$$s_4 = \frac{9\left(1-\left(\frac{1}{3}\right)^4\right)}{1-\frac{1}{3}}$$

$$= \frac{9\left(1-\frac{1}{81}\right)}{\frac{2}{3}}$$

$$= \frac{40}{3}$$

22. **(A)** *Algebra: Polynomials*

Plug $x = 0$, $x = 1$, and $x = -1$ into $p(x)$:

$$p(0) = a(0)^3 + b(0)^2 + c(0) + d$$
$$p(0) = d$$

Because $p(0) = 1$, you know that $d = 1$.

$$p(1) = a(1)^3 + b(1)^2 + c(1) + 1$$

Because $p(1) = 3$, you know that $a + b + c = 2$.

$$p(-1) = a(-1)^3 + b(-1)^2 + c(-1) + 1$$

Because $p(-1) = 5$, you know that $-a + b - c = 4$. Add $a + b + c = 2$ to $-a + b - c = 4$, and you get:

$$2b = 6$$
$$b = 3$$

23. **(E)** *Functions: Domain and Range*

The domain of a function is all values of x that give $f(x)$ a real value. In this function, x is under a fourth root sign. You can't take the fourth root of a negative number, so you know x has to have a value such that $9 - x^2$ is not negative. You also know that $9 - x^2$ can't be equal to zero, since a fraction has no real value if the denominator is zero. Answering this question boils down to solving the inequality $9 - x^2 > 0$ or $9 > x^2$.

$$9 > x^2$$
$$3 > \pm x$$
$$3 > x \text{ and } 3 > -x$$
$$3 > x \text{ and } -3 < x$$
$$-3 < x < 3$$

24. (C) *Trigonometry: Solving Non-Right Triangles; Plane Geometry: Circles*

If the area of the circle is 9π, then the radius is 3. Since OA and OB are two radii of the circle, you know that they have lengths of 3 and that $\triangle OAB$ has sides 3, 3, and 5. The law of cosines allows you to find an angle in a triangle if you know the lengths of the three sides but none of the angles. It states that: $c^2 = a^2 + b^2 - 2ab\cos(C)$, where a, b, and c are the sides of the triangle, and C is the angle you want to find. For this question, you want to find the angle $\angle AOB$, which is opposite the side of length 5:

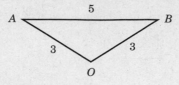

Plug the sides of the triangle into the law of cosines:

$$5^2 = 3^2 + 3^2 - 2 \cdot 3 \cdot 3\cos(\angle AOB)$$
$$7 = -18\cos(\angle AOB)$$
$$-\frac{7}{18} = \cos(\angle AOB)$$

Take $\cos^{-1} x$ of both sides:

$$\cos^{-1}\left(-\frac{7}{18}\right) = \angle AOB$$
$$112.9° = \angle AOB$$

25. (C) *Trigonometry: Pythagorean Identities*

In general, manipulating trig expressions in terms of sine, cosine, and tangent is easier than manipulating expressions in terms of cosecant, secant, and cotangent. Since the definition of $\sec\theta$ is $\frac{1}{\cos\theta}$, you can rewrite $\frac{1}{\sec^2\theta}$ as $\cos^2\theta$. After this rewriting, you end up with the expression: $\cos^2\theta + \sin^2\theta$. If you recognize that this is the Pythagorean identity $\sin^2\theta + \cos^2\theta = 1$, you'll see that the answer to this question is 1.

26. (A) *Functions: Compound Functions .*

The best way to solve for $g(x)$ in $f(g(x)) = -x$ is to make $g(x) = y$. You end up with $f(y) = -x$, or $\sqrt[3]{y-1} = -x$. Solve for y:

$$\sqrt[3]{y-1} = -x$$
$$y - 1 = (-x)^3$$
$$y = (-x)^3 + 1$$
$$= -x^3 + 1$$

Since $y = g(x)$, you have:

$$g(x) = 1 - x^3$$

27. **(B)** *Coordinate Geometry: Circles*

The circle and the line intersect where their x and y coordinates are equal; in this case, since the line is equal to $y = -6$, the circle and the line intersect where $y = -6$. You can find this intersection by plugging $y = -6$ into the equation of the circle. The general equation of a circle is $(x - h)^2 + (y - k)^2 = r^2$, where (h, k) is the center of the circle and r is its radius. The circle in the question has a radius 10 and a center $(-1, -1)$. You can use this information to write the equation of the circle: $(x + 1)^2 + (y + 1)^2 = 100$. Plug $y = -6$ into this equation to find x where the circle and line intersect.

$$(x + 1)^2 + (-6 + 1)^2 = 100$$
$$(x + 1)^2 + 25 = 100$$
$$(x + 1)^2 = 75$$
$$x + 1 = \pm 5\sqrt{3}$$
$$x = -1 \pm 5\sqrt{3}$$
$$\approx -9.66, 7.66$$

The circle and the line intersect twice at the points $(-9.66, -6)$ and $(7.66, -6)$.

28. **(D)** *Functions: Graphing Functions*

You can use your graphing calculator to find the vertical asymptotes, or you can calculate the asymptotes by hand. If you decide to find the asymptotes by hand, start by factoring the function $f(x) = \dfrac{x^2 - 7x + 12}{x^2 - 16}$, since factoring almost always reveals a solution to the problem:

$$f(x) = \frac{(x - 3)(x - 4)}{(x + 4)(x - 4)}$$
$$= \frac{x - 3}{x + 4}$$

If x equals -4, the denominator equals zero, and the function is undefined. As a result, there is a vertical asymptote at $x = -4$. The function is also undefined at $x = 4$, but this value produces a hole instead of an asymptote:

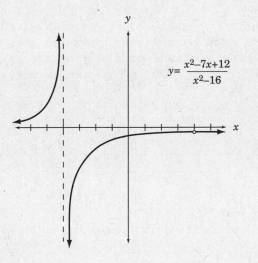

$$y = \frac{x^2 - 7x + 12}{x^2 - 16}$$

29. **(A)** *Algebra: Equation Solving, Exponential Growth and Decay*

The formula for growth or depreciation is $A(t) = A_o(1 \pm r)^t$, where A_o is the initial amount, $A(t)$ is the amount after a period of time t, r is the rate of growth or depreciation (written as a decimal), and t is the elapsed time. When you're calculating exponential decay, use the minus sign in the formula, rather than the plus sign. Plug the information from the question into this formula:

$$
\begin{aligned}
A(7) &= 27,000(1 - 0.13)^7 \\
&= 27,000(0.87)^7 \\
&= 27,000(0.377255) \\
&= 10185.9
\end{aligned}
$$

30. **(B)** *Plane Geometry and Coordinate Geometry: Triangles*

The shaded region in Figure 4 is a triangle:

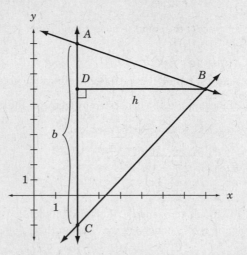

The easiest way to solve for the area of this triangle is to make AC the base of the triangle and BD the height. You can determine the length of AC by subtracting the y-coordinate of point C from the y-coordinate of point A: $10 - -2 = 12$. You can find the length of BD by subtracting the x-coordinate of D from the x-coordinate of point B. Since point D is in same vertical line as points A and C, you know that D shares the same x-coordinate as A and C: $x = 2$. The length of BD is $8 - 2 = 6$. Plug the base and height into the formula for the area of a triangle:

$$
\begin{aligned}
\text{Area } \triangle ABC &= \frac{1}{2}bh \\
&= \frac{1}{2}(12)(6) \\
&= 36
\end{aligned}
$$

31. **(D)** *Functions: Evaluating Functions*

An easy way to find the value of x_3 is to find first the values of x_1 and x_2. You can use $x_0 = 1$ to find the value of x_1:

$$
\begin{aligned}
x_{0+1} &= (x_0 - 1)^2 \\
x_1 &= (1 - 1)^2 \\
&= 0
\end{aligned}
$$

Now use $x_1 = 0$ to find x_2:

$$x_2 = (x_1 - 1)^2$$
$$= (0 - 1)^2$$
$$= 1$$

Now you can solve for x_3 since you have x_2:

$$x_3 = (x_2 - 1)^2$$
$$= (1 - 1)^2$$
$$= 0$$

32. **(C)** *Functions: Compound Functions, Logarithms*

When you see $f(g(x)) = x$, you've got an inverse function on your hands. $f(g(x)) = x$ means the same thing as $g(x) = f^{-1}(x)$. There are three main steps to solving an inverse function: first, replace $f(x)$ with y; second, switch the places of x and y; third, solve for y. Apply these steps to $f(x) = 3^x$:

$$y = 3^x$$
$$x = 3^y$$

Use a logarithm to get y out of the exponent.

$$\log_3 x = \log_3 3^y$$

Since $\log_A A^x = x$, you have:

$$\log_3 x = y$$

Finally, since $y = f^{-1}(x) = g(x)$, you end up with: $\log_3 x = g(x)$.

33. **(A)** *Algebra: Systems of Equations*

You have two variables and two equations. Since you ultimately want to solve for x, you should first solve for y in terms of x in one equation. Then you can plug that value for y into the other equation to find x.

$$2x - 3y = 5$$

$$3y = 2x - 5$$

$$y = \frac{2x - 5}{3}$$

Now plug this value for y into the second equation:

$$x^2 - \left(\frac{2x - 5}{3}\right)^2 = 77$$

$$x^2 - \frac{4x^2 - 20x + 25}{9} = 77$$

$$\frac{9x^2 - 4x^2 - 20x + 25}{9} = 77$$

$$5x^2 + 20x - 668 = 0$$

Use the quadratic formula to find x:

$$x = \frac{-20 \pm \sqrt{400 + 13360}}{10}$$

$$x \approx 9.7, -13.7$$

34. (C) *Functions: Graphing Functions*

The graph in the question splits at $x = 3$, and it behaves differently on either side of this division. Before and up to $x = 3$, the graph is the line $y = -\dfrac{x}{3} + 1$ or $y = \dfrac{3-x}{3}$. You can figure this equation out from the y-intercept ($y = 1$) and the slope (y decreases by 1 as x increases by 3). After (but not including) $x = 3$, the graph is the line $y = x$. The domain for $y = \dfrac{3-x}{3}$ is $x \leq 3$, and the domain for $y = x$ is $x > 3$. Choice (C) gives these functions and their domains.

35. (A) *Plane Geometry: Triangles; Trigonometry: Basic Functions*

The triangle in the figure is a right triangle with a hypotenuse of 10. You can find the two sides of the triangle by doing right triangle trig. The angles of a triangle add up to $180°$, so you can write: $x + 2x + 90 = 180$ or $3x = 90$. From this equation, you know that $x = 30$, and you have a 30-60-90 triangle:

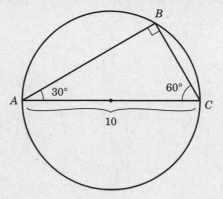

You can use either the properties of a 30-60-90 triangle or basic trig to find the lengths of the two sides:

$$\frac{BC}{10} = \sin 30°$$
$$BC = 10 \sin 30°$$

And:

$$\frac{AB}{10} = \cos 30°$$
$$AB = 10 \cos 30°$$

Now you can plug these values into the formula for the area of a triangle:

$$\text{Area } \Delta ABC = \frac{1}{2} b \cdot h$$
$$= \frac{1}{2} 10 \sin 30° (10 \cos 30°)$$
$$= 50 \sin 30° \cos 30°$$
$$\approx 21.65$$

36. **(E)** *Statistics: Probability*

The probability of drawing a blue marble is $\frac{1}{5}$, which means that, for every five marbles, one is blue. You can set b equal to the number of blue marbles and T equal to the total number of marbles in the bag. Since the proportion of b to T is the same as 1 to 5, you can write:

$$\frac{b}{T} = \frac{1}{5}$$
$$5b = T$$

The question states that $\frac{3}{19}$ is the probability that the second marble drawn is blue, if the first marble is not replaced in the bag. Since you've depleted both the total number of marbles and the number of blue marbles by one, you can set up the following equation:

$$\frac{b-1}{T-1} = \frac{3}{19}$$
$$19b - 19 = 3T - 3$$

Since $5b = T$, you have:

$$19b - 19 = 15b - 3$$
$$4b = 16$$
$$b = 4$$

$T = 5(4) = 20$. The number of red marbles is $20 - 4 = 16$.

37. **(B)** *Algebra: Equation Solving, Logarithms*

One of the laws of logarithms states that $\log_b x^N = N\log_b x$. Use this law to rewrite the problem:

$$\frac{\log_4 x^{15}}{\log_4 x^{12}} = \frac{15\log_4 x}{12\log_4 x}$$

$$= \frac{15}{12} \cdot \frac{\log_4 x}{\log_4 x}$$

$$= \frac{15}{12} \cdot 1$$

$$= \frac{5}{4}$$

38. **(A)** *Coordinate Geometry: Vectors*

Vector questions on the Math IIC ask you to do pretty basic operations. A vector has both magnitude and direction. The magnitude of a vector is its length r, and its direction is the counterclockwise angle θ that the vector makes with respect to the horizontal. Take a look at the vector $\bar{u}$ in the figure below:

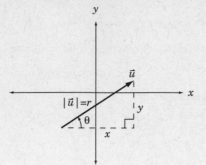

The question tells you the magnitudes of vectors $\bar{v}$ and $\bar{w}$. You should memorize the following inequality involving the magnitudes of vectors: $|\bar{v} + \bar{w}| \leq |\bar{v}| + |\bar{w}|$, where $|\bar{v}|$ is the magnitude of $\bar{v}$ and $|\bar{w}|$ is the magnitude of $\bar{w}$. (This inequality is simply the triangle inequality applied to vectors.) Since the question asks you what could NOT be the magnitude of $3\bar{v} + 5\bar{w}$, you can set up the following inequality and plug in the given magnitudes:

$$\left|3\vec{v} + 5\vec{w}\right| \leq 3\left|\vec{v}\right| + 5\left|\vec{w}\right|$$
$$\left|3\vec{v} + 5\vec{w}\right| \leq 3(11.1) + 5(9.9)$$
$$\left|3\vec{v} + 5\vec{w}\right| \leq 82.8$$

Choice (A) cannot be the magnitude of $3\vec{v} + 5\vec{w}$ because 82.9 is greater than 82.8.

39. **(B)** *Miscellaneous Math: Sequences and Series*

The formula for the nth term in an arithmetic sequence is $a_n = a_1 + (n-1)d$, where a_n is the nth term in the sequence, a_1 is the first term, and d is the difference between consecutive terms. Since you're looking for the third term in the sequence, you end up with the equation $a_3 = 3 + (3-1)d$ or $a_3 = 3 + 2d$. Because you don't know d, you can't find the third term.

The question tells you that the sum of the first five terms in the sequence is equal to 65. The formula for the sum of the first n terms of an arithmetic series is given by $S_n = \dfrac{(a_1 + a_n)}{2} \cdot n$. Plugging in the information you know, you get $65 = \dfrac{3 + a_5}{2} \cdot 5$. Replace a_5 with $a_1 + (5-1)d$:

$$65 = \frac{3 + (3 + 4d)}{2} \cdot 5$$

$$13 = \frac{3 + (3 + 4d)}{2}$$

$$26 = 6 + 4d$$
$$20 = 4d$$
$$d = 5$$

Plug this value for d into $a_3 = 3 + 2d$, and you get $a_3 = 13$.

40. **(B)** *Trigonometry: Pythagorean Identities*

In order to solve this problem, you need to use the Pythagorean trigonometric identity: $\tan^2 x + 1 = \sec^2 x$.

$$2\sec^2 x - 3\tan x - 5 = 0$$
$$2(\tan^2 x + 1) - 3\tan x - 5 = 0$$
$$2\tan^2 x - \tan x - 3 = 0$$

This is a quadratic equation in terms of $\tan x$, and you should factor it:

$$(2\tan x - 3)(\tan x + 1) = 0$$
$$2\tan x = 3 \text{ or } \tan x = -1$$

If $\tan x = \dfrac{3}{2}$, then $x = \tan^{-1}\left(\dfrac{3}{2}\right)$ and $x \approx 0.98$. Or if $\tan x = -1$, then $x = \tan^{-1}(-1)$ and $x = -\dfrac{\pi}{4}$. Choice (B) is 0.98, so it is the correct answer.

41. **(D)** *Statistics: Factorials*

You need to memorize the definition of a factorial for the Math IIC. In this question you have

$\dfrac{n!}{(n-1)!} = \dfrac{n(n-1)\ldots(2)(1)}{(n-1)\ldots(2)(1)} = n$, since everything except for n cancels out, and you have

$\dfrac{(n-1)!}{(n-2)!} = \dfrac{(n-1)(n-2)\ldots(2)(1)}{(n-2)\ldots(2)(1)} = n-1$, since everything except for $n-1$ cancels out. You end up with:

$$n - (n-1) = n - n + 1$$
$$= 1$$

42. **(B)** *Solid Geometry: Solids that Aren't Prisms; Plane Geometry: Circles*

Draw a sphere with circles on the surface:

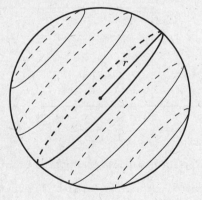

The largest circle that can be drawn on a sphere is equivalent to the sphere's "equator." If you cut along this equator, the sphere divides evenly in half. The circle at the equator of the sphere shares the same radius as the sphere. Since the volume of a sphere is given by $\frac{4}{3}\pi r^3$, you can solve for the radius of both the sphere and the circle by setting up the equation:

$$288\pi = \frac{4}{3}\pi r^3$$
$$216 = r^3$$
$$6 = r$$

Now you can find the circumference of the circle:

$$C = 2\pi r$$
$$= 12\pi$$

43. **(A)** *Miscellaneous Math: Logic*

While Math IIC logic problems will usually ask you to find the contrapositive of a statement "if p, then q," they will occasionally ask you for the assumption made by the indirect proof of the statement. All you need to know is how to find the assumption of an indirect proof; you don't need to know how to find the indirect proof itself. In an indirect proof of "if p, then q," you assume the negative of the conclusion q; in other words, you start out the proof with the assumption that you have "*not q*." In this case, you have the statement "if x is an even number, then x is divisible by 2." The assumption the indirect proof makes is the negative of "x is divisible by 2." So choice (A), which says "x is *not* divisible by 2," is correct.

44. **(D)** *Plane Geometry: Polygons*

You can redraw the parallelogram in the question as:

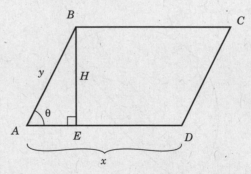

The area of a parallelogram $ABCD$ is equal to the base multiplied by the height; in this case, the area equals xH. You can find H by using right triangle trig. Since $\triangle ABE$ is a right triangle with y as the hypotenuse, you can write $\sin\theta = \frac{H}{y}$ or $H = y\sin\theta$. The question asks you to find the area in terms of x, y, and θ, so you have $\text{Area}_{ABCD} = xy\sin\theta$.

45. **(B)** *Solid Geometry: Solids that Aren't Prisms*

Draw a picture of the cone inside the hemisphere.

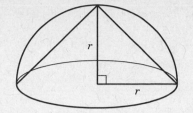

Start out by finding the volume of the cone. The formula for the volume of a cone is $\frac{1}{3}\pi r^2 h$. Both the radius

and height of the cone are equal to the radius r of the sphere. You can plug r into the volume formula to get:

$$= \frac{1}{3}\pi r^3$$

Next find the volume of the hemisphere. Because a hemisphere is half the size of a full sphere, you can find

the volume of a hemisphere by dividing the volume of a sphere in half. The formula for the volume of a

sphere is $\frac{4}{3}\pi r^3$, so the volume of a hemisphere is $\frac{2}{3}\pi r^2$. Now you can find S by subtracting the volume of

the cone from the volume of the sphere:

$$S = \text{volume hemisphere} - \text{volume cone}$$
$$= \frac{2}{3}\pi r^3 - \frac{1}{3}\pi r^3$$
$$= \frac{1}{3}\pi r^3$$

The ratio of the cone's volume to S is: $\dfrac{\text{volume cone}}{S} = \dfrac{\frac{1}{3}\pi r^3}{\frac{1}{3}\pi r^3} = 1$.

46. **(E)** *Statistics: Permutations and Combinations*

Because marbles of the same color are identical, the order the same-colored marbles come in doesn't
matter, so you're solving a combination problem. In this problem, you have 8 total marbles. $8! = 40320$
is the total number of possible arrangements. You can rearrange the two red marbles in 2! ways, the three
green marbles in 3! ways, and the three blue marbles in 3! ways. Divide 40320 by $2! \cdot 3! \cdot 3!$ to find the
number of arrangements.

$$\frac{8!}{2!3!3!} = \frac{40372}{72}$$
$$= 560$$

47. **(D)** *Functions: Evaluating Functions, Graphing Functions*

The question says that the graph is "translated" 5 units to the right and 7 units down. "Translated" simply
means that the graph shifts over; the shape of the graph doesn't change. If $y = f(x)$ is the graph of $f(x)$, then
$y = f(x - 5)$ is the graph of $f(x)$ translated five units to the right. When you translate a graph a units to the
right, you need to subtract a from x. When you translate a graph a units to the left, you need to add a to x.
(This rule may seem counterintuitive, but you're moving the coordinate plane, not the graph.) The
translation of the graph 7 units down is pretty straightforward: the translated graph is $y = f(x) - 7$. Put
these two functions together to get $y = f(x - 5) - 7$. Plug $(x - 5)$ into the function $f(x) = x^3 + 1$:

$$y = (x - 5)^3 + 1 - 7$$

Test 3 Explanations

Now plug in $x = 2.7$:

$$f(2.7) = (2.7 - 5)^3 - 6$$
$$= (-2.3)^3 - 6$$
$$= -18.167$$

48. **(C)** *Algebra: Equation Solving*

This problem is a tricky algebraic manipulation. From $\frac{1}{R} = \frac{1}{x} + \frac{1}{y} + \frac{1}{z}$ you can get $R = \dfrac{1}{\frac{1}{x} + \frac{1}{y} + \frac{1}{z}}$. The common denominator of these fractions is xyz.

$$R = \frac{1}{\frac{1(yz)}{x(yz)} + \frac{1(xz)}{y(xz)} + \frac{1(xy)}{z(xy)}}$$

$$= \frac{1}{\frac{yz + xz + xy}{xyz}}$$

$$= \frac{xyz}{yz + xz + xy}$$

49. **(B)** *Coordinate Geometry: Hyperbolas*

You should memorize the general equation for a hyperbola centered at (h, k): $\frac{(x - h)^2}{a^2} - \frac{(y - k)^2}{b^2} = 1$. (You may also see an equation for a hyperbola in the form $\frac{(y - k)^2}{b^2} - \frac{(x - h)^2}{a^2} = 1$.) For this question, you're told that the center of the hyperbola is at $(1, 3)$ and a point on the hyperbola is $(2, 4)$. Plug the coordinates of the hyperbola's center into the equation:

$$\frac{(x - 1)^2}{a^2} - \frac{(y - 3)^2}{b^2} = 1$$

You can rule out choices (A), (C), and (D) because their values for h and k are wrong. Now you need to figure out the values of a^2 and b^2. You can do so by plugging in the point $(2, 4)$, giving you an equation for a and b:

$$\frac{(2 - 1)^2}{a^2} - \frac{(4 - 3)^2}{b^2} = 1$$

$$\frac{1^2}{a^2} - \frac{1^2}{b^2} = 1$$

$$b^2 - a^2 = a^2 b^2$$

In choice (B), $a^2 = \frac{1}{2}$ and $b^2 = 1$. In choice (E), $a^2 = 2$ and $b^2 = 1$. Choice (B) is the correct equation for the hyperbola because:

$$1 - \frac{1}{2} = \frac{1}{2} \cdot 1$$

$$\frac{1}{2} = \frac{1}{2}$$

50. **(A)** *Fundamentals: Numbers*

The least element in a set is exactly what its name implies: the smallest element in a set. For example, −1 is the least element in the set $\{-1, 0, 1, 2\}$. Of the answer choices, only the positive prime numbers have a least element, which is 2. The two other sets extend infinitely, so they do not have least elements. The set of integers extends infinitely in both the negative and positive directions. The set of positive rational numbers is also infinite because no matter how small a rational number you choose, there will always be a rational number that is closer to zero.

SAT II Math IIC
Practice Test 4

MATH IIC TEST 4 ANSWER SHEET

1. Ⓐ Ⓑ Ⓒ Ⓓ Ⓔ	18. Ⓐ Ⓑ Ⓒ Ⓓ Ⓔ	35. Ⓐ Ⓑ Ⓒ Ⓓ Ⓔ
2. Ⓐ Ⓑ Ⓒ Ⓓ Ⓔ	19. Ⓐ Ⓑ Ⓒ Ⓓ Ⓔ	36. Ⓐ Ⓑ Ⓒ Ⓓ Ⓔ
3. Ⓐ Ⓑ Ⓒ Ⓓ Ⓔ	20. Ⓐ Ⓑ Ⓒ Ⓓ Ⓔ	37. Ⓐ Ⓑ Ⓒ Ⓓ Ⓔ
4. Ⓐ Ⓑ Ⓒ Ⓓ Ⓔ	21. Ⓐ Ⓑ Ⓒ Ⓓ Ⓔ	38. Ⓐ Ⓑ Ⓒ Ⓓ Ⓔ
5. Ⓐ Ⓑ Ⓒ Ⓓ Ⓔ	22. Ⓐ Ⓑ Ⓒ Ⓓ Ⓔ	39. Ⓐ Ⓑ Ⓒ Ⓓ Ⓔ
6. Ⓐ Ⓑ Ⓒ Ⓓ Ⓔ	23. Ⓐ Ⓑ Ⓒ Ⓓ Ⓔ	40. Ⓐ Ⓑ Ⓒ Ⓓ Ⓔ
7. Ⓐ Ⓑ Ⓒ Ⓓ Ⓔ	24. Ⓐ Ⓑ Ⓒ Ⓓ Ⓔ	41. Ⓐ Ⓑ Ⓒ Ⓓ Ⓔ
8. Ⓐ Ⓑ Ⓒ Ⓓ Ⓔ	25. Ⓐ Ⓑ Ⓒ Ⓓ Ⓔ	42. Ⓐ Ⓑ Ⓒ Ⓓ Ⓔ
9. Ⓐ Ⓑ Ⓒ Ⓓ Ⓔ	26. Ⓐ Ⓑ Ⓒ Ⓓ Ⓔ	43. Ⓐ Ⓑ Ⓒ Ⓓ Ⓔ
10. Ⓐ Ⓑ Ⓒ Ⓓ Ⓔ	27. Ⓐ Ⓑ Ⓒ Ⓓ Ⓔ	44. Ⓐ Ⓑ Ⓒ Ⓓ Ⓔ
11. Ⓐ Ⓑ Ⓒ Ⓓ Ⓔ	28. Ⓐ Ⓑ Ⓒ Ⓓ Ⓔ	45. Ⓐ Ⓑ Ⓒ Ⓓ Ⓔ
12. Ⓐ Ⓑ Ⓒ Ⓓ Ⓔ	29. Ⓐ Ⓑ Ⓒ Ⓓ Ⓔ	46. Ⓐ Ⓑ Ⓒ Ⓓ Ⓔ
13. Ⓐ Ⓑ Ⓒ Ⓓ Ⓔ	30. Ⓐ Ⓑ Ⓒ Ⓓ Ⓔ	47. Ⓐ Ⓑ Ⓒ Ⓓ Ⓔ
14. Ⓐ Ⓑ Ⓒ Ⓓ Ⓔ	31. Ⓐ Ⓑ Ⓒ Ⓓ Ⓔ	48. Ⓐ Ⓑ Ⓒ Ⓓ Ⓔ
15. Ⓐ Ⓑ Ⓒ Ⓓ Ⓔ	32. Ⓐ Ⓑ Ⓒ Ⓓ Ⓔ	49. Ⓐ Ⓑ Ⓒ Ⓓ Ⓔ
16. Ⓐ Ⓑ Ⓒ Ⓓ Ⓔ	33. Ⓐ Ⓑ Ⓒ Ⓓ Ⓔ	50. Ⓐ Ⓑ Ⓒ Ⓓ Ⓔ
17. Ⓐ Ⓑ Ⓒ Ⓓ Ⓔ	34. Ⓐ Ⓑ Ⓒ Ⓓ Ⓔ	

REFERENCE INFORMATION

THE FOLLOWING INFORMATION IS FOR YOUR REFERENCE IN ANSWERING SOME OF THE QUESTIONS IN THIS TEST:

Volume of a right circular cone with radius r and height h: $V = \frac{1}{3}\pi r^2 h$

Lateral area of a right circular cone with circumference of the base c and slaight height ℓ: $S = \frac{1}{2}c\ell$

Volume of a sphere with radius r: $V = \frac{4}{3}\pi r^3$

Surface area of a sphere with radius r: $S = 4\pi r^2$

Volume of a pyramid with base area B and height h: $V = \frac{1}{3}Bh$

MATHEMATICS LEVEL IIC TEST

For each of the following problems, decide which is the BEST of the choices given. If the exact numerical value is not one of the choices, select the choice that best approximates this value. Then fill in the corresponding oval on the answer sheet.

<u>Notes:</u> (1) A calculator will be necessary for answering some (but not all) of the questions in this test. For each question you will have to decide whether or not you should use a calcuator. The calculator you use must be at least a scientific calculator; programmable calculators and calculators that can display graphs are permitted.

(2) For some questions in this test you may need to decide whether your calculator should be in radian or degree mode.

(3) Figures that accompany problems in this test are intended to provide information useful in solving the problems. They are drawn as accurately as possible EXCEPT when it is stated in a specific problem that its figure is not drawn to scale. All figures lie in a plane unless otherwise indicated.

(4) Unless otherwise specified, the domain of any function f is assumed to be the set of all real numbers x for which (x) is a real number.

(5) Reference information that may be useful in answering the questions in this test can be found on the page preceding Question 1.

USE THIS SPACE FOR SCRATCHWORK.

. If x is an integer, then which of the following is the least value of x that satisfies $3^x > 240$?

(A) 3
(B) 4
(C) 5
(D) 6
(E) 7

If $\dfrac{1}{z} = \dfrac{x+y}{2}$, what is x in terms of y and z?

(A) $\dfrac{2}{z} + y$

(B) $\dfrac{2}{z} - y$

(C) $\dfrac{2-y}{z}$

(D) $\dfrac{2+y}{z}$

(E) $\dfrac{2}{z-y}$

GO ON TO THE NEXT PAGE

USE THIS SPACE FOR SCRATCHWORK.

3. Figure 1 shows the graph of which of the following equations?

(A) $y = \frac{4}{3}x + 2$

(B) $y = \frac{4}{3}x + \frac{9}{4}$

(C) $y = \frac{3}{4}x + 2$

(D) $y = \frac{3}{4}x + \frac{9}{4}$

(E) $y = \frac{3}{4}x + 3$

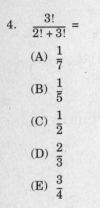

Figure 1

4. $\frac{3!}{2! + 3!} =$

(A) $\frac{1}{7}$

(B) $\frac{1}{5}$

(C) $\frac{1}{2}$

(D) $\frac{2}{3}$

(E) $\frac{3}{4}$

5. If $h(x) = \frac{x^2 + x + 1}{2}$ and $f(x) = x \cdot h(x)$, what is $f(2)$?

(A) $\frac{7}{2}$

(B) 7

(C) 8

(D) $\frac{17}{2}$

(E) 20

6. Let f be a function defined on pairs of positive integers as $f(a, b) = a^b$. For which of the following does $f(a, b) = f(b, a)$?

(A) $a = 1, b = 2$
(B) $a = 2, b = 4$
(C) $a = 2, b = 3$
(D) $a = 3, b = 4$
(E) $a = 3, b = 5$

GO ON TO THE NEXT PAGE

7. How many vertical asymptotes does the graph of

$f(x) = \dfrac{x-3}{(x+2)(x^2-9)}$ have?

(A) None
(B) One
(C) Two
(D) Three
(E) Four

8. $\dfrac{\sin^2\theta}{\cos^2\theta} - \dfrac{1}{\cos^2\theta} =$

(A) −1

(B) 0

(C) $\dfrac{1}{2}$

(D) 1

(E) $\sec^2\theta$

In Figure 2, if $\cos(\theta) = \dfrac{2}{7}$, then $\tan(\tau) =$

(A) 0.8
(B) 0.6
(C) 0.5
(D) 0.4
(E) 0.3

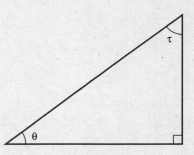

Note: Figure not drawn to scale.
Figure 2

If $f(x) = \dfrac{3}{\sqrt{x^3+8}}$ and $f(a) = 3$, then $a =$

(A) 2.73
(B) 1.91
(C) −1.85
(D) −1.91
(E) −2.13

Line l intersects plane P perpendicularly at point p. How many lines in plane P pass through p <u>and</u> are perpendicular to l ?

(A) None
(B) One
(C) Two
(D) Infinitely many
(E) Not enough information to tell

GO ON TO THE NEXT PAGE

12. In a certain game the probability that John wins is $\frac{2}{7}$ and, independently, the probability that Robert wins is $\frac{1}{3}$. What is the probability that Robert wins and John loses?

(A) $\frac{2}{21}$

(B) $\frac{5}{21}$

(C) $\frac{2}{7}$

(D) $\frac{1}{3}$

(E) $\frac{13}{21}$

13. If the surface area of a cube is 1, what is its volume?

(A) $\frac{1}{2}$

(B) $\frac{\sqrt{6}}{6}$

(C) $\frac{\sqrt{6}}{36}$

(D) $\frac{\sqrt{6}}{216}$

(E) $\frac{1}{216}$

14. If $f(x) = x^2 - 6x + k$ has exactly one real root, then $k =$

(A) 9
(B) 8
(C) 7
(D) 6
(E) 0

15. If $5^x = 72$, then $x =$

(A) 0.38
(B) 1.78
(C) 2.51
(D) 2.66
(E) 2.75

GO ON TO THE NEXT PAGE

16. If $(x, h(x))$ is a point on the graph of $h(x) = x^2 + 1$, what is the slope of the line between the points $(-1, h(-1))$ and $(4, h(4))$?

   (A) −4
   (B) −3
   (C) 1
   (D) 2
   (E) 3

17. Given the triangles in Figure 3, what is the value of $\sin(a + b)$?

   (A) $\dfrac{57}{65}$

   (B) $\dfrac{56}{65}$

   (C) $\dfrac{55}{65}$

   (D) $\dfrac{54}{65}$

   (E) $\dfrac{12}{39}$

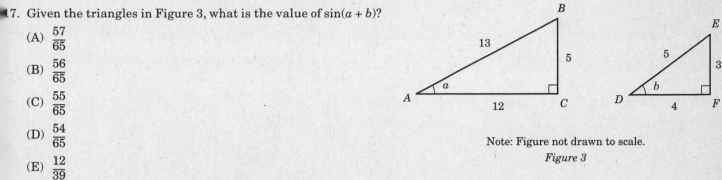

Note: Figure not drawn to scale.

Figure 3

18. How many even integers between 100 and 200 are divisible by 3?

   (A) 17
   (B) 16
   (C) 15
   (D) 14
   (E) 13

19. In 1957, Peter deposited $1,900.00 in a bank account with an annual interest rate of 7%. Assuming he never removed any money, how much would be in the account in 2003?

   (A) $37,111.12
   (B) $39,881.97
   (C) $40,881.97
   (D) $41,697.98
   (E) $42,697.98

GO ON TO THE NEXT PAGE

20. The cost of shipping a package in terms of its weight is given by the formula $C = 3.00 + 0.76\lceil x - 1 \rceil$ where C is the cost (in dollars), x is the weight (in lbs.) and $\lceil x \rceil$ is the greatest integer less than or equal to x. What is the cost of shipping a $25\frac{1}{2}$ lb. package?

   (A) $19.76
   (B) $20.76
   (C) $21.24
   (D) $22.00
   (E) $22.24

21. If $x + 3$ is a factor of $x^3 + x^2 - 4cx + 1$, what is the value of c?

   (A) 5

   (B) $\dfrac{17}{4}$

   (C) $\dfrac{17}{15}$

   (D) $\dfrac{17}{12}$

   (E) $\dfrac{17}{13}$

22. What is the distance between the points $(1, 2, 3)$ and $(7, -9, 12)$?

   (A) 14.78
   (B) 15.13
   (C) 15.43
   (D) 16.97
   (E) 17.06

23. Which of the following is the polar coordinate representation for the point $(2\sqrt{3}, 2)$ in the (x, y) plane?

   (A) $(4, 60°)$
   (B) $(4, 30°)$
   (C) $(4, 25°)$
   (D) $(2, 60°)$
   (E) $(2, 30°)$

GO ON TO THE NEXT PAGE

24. Which of the following equations produces an infinite set of points that are 3 units from the origin?

(A) $y^2 - x^2 = 3$
(B) $y^2 - x^2 = 9$
(C) $x^2 - y^2 = 3$
(D) $x^2 + y^2 = 3$
(E) $x^2 + y^2 = 9$

5. If $(x + y)^3 = 64$ and $\sqrt{x - y} = 4$ then $x =$

(A) 10
(B) 11
(C) 12
(D) 13
(E) Not enough information to tell

6. What is the maximum value of $f(x) = 3 - \sqrt{x - 4}$ if $x \geq 4$?

(A) 4
(B) 3
(C) 2
(D) 0
(E) −3

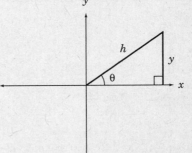

Figure 4

7. In Figure 4, which of the following expressions is equal to $\sec(\theta)$?

(A) $\dfrac{h^2 - y^2}{h}$

(B) $\dfrac{h^2 + y^2}{h}$

(C) $\sqrt{\dfrac{h}{h^2 - y^2}}$

(D) $\dfrac{h}{\sqrt{h^2 - y^2}}$

(E) $\dfrac{h}{\sqrt{h^2 + y^2}}$

. The graph of $y = \dfrac{2 - x}{x - 2}$ and $y = x - 2$ intersect when $x =$

(A) −1
(B) 0
(C) 1
(D) 2
(E) 3

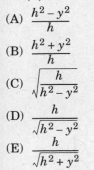

GO ON TO THE NEXT PAGE

USE THIS SPACE FOR SCRATCHWORK.

29. If $0 \leq \theta \leq 2\pi$ and the tangent of θ is equal to the sine of θ, then which of the following must be true?

(A) $\cos\theta = \dfrac{\sqrt{2}}{2}$ or $\cos\theta = \dfrac{-\sqrt{2}}{2}$

(B) $\cos\theta = \dfrac{\sqrt{3}}{2}$

(C) $\cos\theta = -1$ or $\cos\theta = 1$

(D) $\cos\theta = 1$ only

(E) $\cos\theta = \dfrac{\sqrt{2}}{2}$ only

30. A triangle has 2 vertices at the points $(2, 3)$ and $(2, 6)$. The third vertex lies somewhere on the line $x = -4$. The area of this triangle is

(A) 8
(B) 9
(C) any number less than 9
(D) any number greater than 9
(E) Not enough information to tell

31. What is the maximum number of points of intersection between the perimeter of a square and the circumference of a circle?

(A) 3
(B) 4
(C) 6
(D) 8
(E) 9

32. If $0 \leq \theta < \dfrac{\pi}{2}$ and $2\cos^2\theta + 3\cos\theta - 2 = 0$, then $\theta =$

(A) $\dfrac{\pi}{3}$
(B) $\dfrac{\pi}{4}$
(C) $\dfrac{\pi}{6}$
(D) $\dfrac{\pi}{7}$
(E) $\dfrac{\pi}{12}$

33. Figure 5 shows a plane intersecting a rectangular parallelepiped with sides of lengths 2, 4, and 8. What is the area of rectangle *ABCD*?

(A) 30.9
(B) 34.5
(C) 34.7
(D) 35.2
(E) 35.8

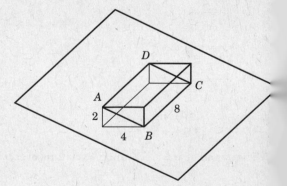

Figure 5

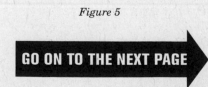
GO ON TO THE NEXT PAGE

34. Which of the following could be a portion of the graph of
$$\frac{x^2}{9} - \frac{y^2}{16} = 1\,?$$

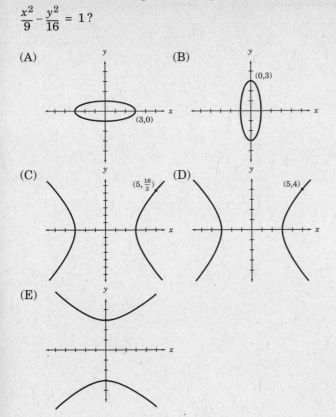

(A)

(B)

(C)

(D)

(E)

35. If $n > 0$, $m > 0$, and $\sqrt{\dfrac{n}{m}}$ is an integer, which of the following
<u>must</u> also be an integer?

(A) $\dfrac{n}{m}$

(B) n

(C) m

(D) $\dfrac{n^2}{2m}$

(E) $\dfrac{2n}{m^2}$

GO ON TO THE NEXT PAGE

USE THIS SPACE FOR SCRATCHWORK.

36. What is the limit of $f(x) = \dfrac{x^2 - 16}{4 - x}$ as x approaches 4?

   (A) −10
   (B) −8
   (C) −4
   (D) 8
   (E) ∞

37. $f(x) = ax + b$ and $f^{-1}(x) = f(x)$ for all real x. If $f(0) = 3$, then what is the value of $f^{-1}(1)$?

   (A) 2

   (B) 1

   (C) $\dfrac{1}{2}$

   (D) 0

   (E) −2

38. What is the area of the circle defined by the equation $x^2 - 4x + y^2 - 6y - 212 = 0$?

   (A) 144π
   (B) 169π
   (C) 196π
   (D) 225π
   (E) 256π

GO ON TO THE NEXT PAGE

39. Which of the following could be a portion of the graph
$y = \frac{1}{2}e^{-x^2}$?

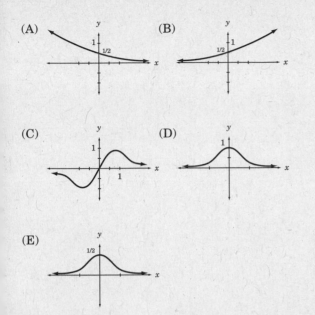

(A)

(B)

(C)

(D)

(E)

40. What is the measure of the largest angle in a triangle with sides of lengths 12, 17, and 24?

(A) 109.7°
(B) 110.5°
(C) 112.1°
(D) 112.8°
(E) 112.9°

41. The shaded area in Figure 6 could be the solution set to which of the following pairs of inequalities?

(A) $\begin{cases} y \le 1 - x^2 \\ y \le x \end{cases}$

(B) $\begin{cases} y \le 1 - x^2 \\ y < x \end{cases}$

(C) $\begin{cases} y \le 1 - x^2 \\ y \ge x \end{cases}$

(D) $\begin{cases} y \ge 1 - x^2 \\ y \le x \end{cases}$

(E) $\begin{cases} y \ge 1 - x^2 \\ y \ge x \end{cases}$

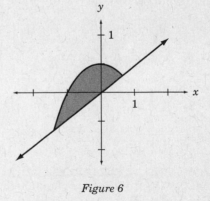

Figure 6

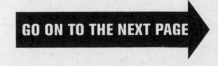
GO ON TO THE NEXT PAGE

USE THIS SPACE FOR SCRATCHWORK.

42. How many possible rearrangements can one make using all of the letters in the word COFFEE?

    (A) 960
    (B) 720
    (C) 240
    (D) 190
    (E) 180

43. If $f(x, y) = \begin{cases} x^2 & x \le y \\ 1-x & x > y \end{cases}$, what is the value of

    $f(2, 1) - f(1, 2)$?

    (A) –2
    (B) –1
    (C) 0
    (D) 2
    (E) 6

44. If the volume of a sphere is tripled, then its surface area will grow by a factor of

    (A) $\sqrt[2]{3}$
    (B) $\sqrt[2]{9}$
    (C) $\sqrt[3]{3}$
    (D) $\sqrt[3]{9}$
    (E) $\sqrt[3]{18}$

45. If the graph of $f(x) = 2(x-4)^3 - 7$ is translated 7 units up and 4 units left, what is the y-value of the transformed graph at $x = 2$?

    (A) –23
    (B) 14
    (C) 16
    (D) 18
    (E) 20

46. A function $f(x)$ is said to be <u>odd</u> if $f(-x) = -f(x)$ for all x in the domain. Which of the following functions is odd?

    (A) $f(x) = x^4 + x + 1$
    (B) $f(x) = x^4 + x^3$
    (C) $f(x) = x^4 + x^2 + 1$
    (D) $f(x) = x^3 + 3x^2$
    (E) $f(x) = x^3 - 3x$

GO ON TO THE NEXT PAGE

47. An indirect proof of the statement "if x is a member of set P, then x is a member of set Q" could begin with the assumption that

    (A) x is not a member of Q
    (B) x is a member of Q
    (C) x is a member of P
    (D) x is not a member of P
    (E) x is neither a member of P or Q

48. Figure 7 shows the intersection of a rhombus and a circle. What is the ratio of the area of the shaded region to the area of the rhombus ?

    (A) 0.81
    (B) 0.75
    (C) 0.66
    (D) 0.60
    (E) 0.51

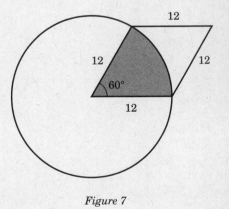

Figure 7

GO ON TO THE NEXT PAGE

49. Water is leaking out of a right circular cone of radius 7 and height 15, as shown in Figure 8. What volume of water will remain in the cone when the height of the water is 9?

(A) 167.8
(B) 166.3
(C) 156.3
(D) 151.2
(E) 140.5

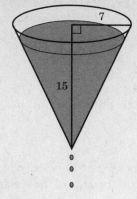

Figure 8

50. If $\left(2x - \dfrac{2}{x}\right)^2 + \left(3x - \dfrac{3}{x}\right) = 0$, then x could equal which of the following?

(A) –2
(B) –1
(C) 0
(D) 2
(E) 7.2

S T O P

IF YOU FINISH BEFORE TIME IS CALLED, YOU MAY CHECK YOUR WORK ON THIS TEST ONLY.
DO NOT TURN TO ANY OTHER TEST IN THIS BOOK.

SAT II Math IIC
Practice Test 4
Explanations

Calculating Your Score

Question Number	Correct Answer	Right	Wrong	Question Number	Correct Answer	Right	Wrong	Question Number	Correct Answer	Right	Wrong
1.	C	——	——	18.	A	——	——	35.	A	——	——
2.	B	——	——	19.	E	——	——	36.	B	——	——
3.	D	——	——	20.	C	——	——	37.	A	——	——
4.	E	——	——	21.	D	——	——	38.	D	——	——
5.	B	——	——	22.	C	——	——	39.	E	——	——
6.	B	——	——	23.	B	——	——	40.	B	——	——
7.	C	——	——	24.	E	——	——	41.	C	——	——
8.	A	——	——	25.	A	——	——	42.	E	——	——
9.	E	——	——	26.	B	——	——	43.	A	——	——
10.	D	——	——	27.	D	——	——	44.	D	——	——
11.	D	——	——	28.	C	——	——	45.	C	——	——
12.	B	——	——	29.	C	——	——	46.	E	——	——
13.	C	——	——	30.	B	——	——	47.	A	——	——
14.	A	——	——	31.	D	——	——	48.	D	——	——
15.	D	——	——	32.	A	——	——	49.	B	——	——
16.	E	——	——	33.	E	——	——	50.	B	——	——
17.	B	——	——	34.	C	——	——				

Your raw score for the SAT II Math IIC test is calculated from the number of questions you answer correctly and incorrectly. Once you have determined your composite score, use the conversion table on page 18 of this book to calculate your scaled score. To calculate your raw score, count the number of questions you answered correctly: _____
A

Count the number of questions you answered incorrectly, and multiply that number by $\frac{1}{4}$:

$$\underline{\qquad}_{B} \times \frac{1}{4} = \underline{\qquad}_{C}$$

Subtract the value in field C from value in field A: _____
D

Round the number in field D to the nearest whole number. This is your raw score: _____
E

Math IIC Test 4 Explanations

1. **(C)** *Algebra: Inequalities*

The simplest way to solve this problem is to plug the answer choices into the inequality. Since the choices are given in increasing order, you should start with choice (C). If choice (C) produces a value greater than 240, you'll know to try a smaller number for x. If choice (C) produces a value less than 240, you'll know to try a larger number. Choice (C) says that $x = 5$. Plug 5 into the inequality: $3^5 = 243$ and $243 > 240$. Now try $x = 4$: $3^4 = 81$ and $81 < 240$. Choice (C) is correct.

You can also solve this problem using logarithms. Take the log of both sides of the inequality:

$$\log 3^x > \log 240$$

$$x \log 3 > \log 240$$

$$x > \frac{\log 240}{\log 3}$$

$$x > 4.99$$

Since x is the smallest integer that's greater than 4.99, you know that x equals 5.

2. **(B)** *Algebra: Equation Solving*

This is a straightforward algebra question that asks you to solve for x. To isolate x, start by multiplying both sides by 2:

$$\frac{1}{z} = \frac{x+y}{2}$$

$$\frac{2}{z} = x + y$$

Subtract y from both sides:

$$\frac{2}{z} - y = x$$

3. **(D)** *Coordinate Geometry: Lines*

The question asks you to find the equation of the line shown in Figure 1. Since the answer choices are given in slope-intercept form ($y = mx + b$), you know you need to calculate the slope and y-intercept of the line. First use the two points shown in the figure to determine the slope:

$$m = \frac{\Delta y}{\Delta x}$$

$$= \frac{3-0}{1-(-3)}$$

$$= \frac{3}{4}$$

Now plug the slope into the slope-intercept equation:

$$y = \frac{3}{4}x + b$$

You can solve for the y-intercept, b, by plugging the point $(-3, 0)$ into the equation:

$$0 = \frac{3}{4}(-3) + b$$

$$\frac{9}{4} = b$$

You end up with the equation $y = \frac{3}{4}x + \frac{9}{4}$.

4. **(E)** *Statistics: Factorials*

For the Math IIC, you definitely need to know how to solve factorials:

$$n! = n \cdot (n-1) \cdot (n-2)...(1)$$

Apply this definition to each of the factorials in the expression:

$$\frac{3!}{2! + 3!} = \frac{3 \cdot 2 \cdot 1}{2 \cdot 1 + 3 \cdot 2 \cdot 1}$$

$$= \frac{6}{2 + 6}$$

$$= \frac{6}{8}$$

$$= \frac{3}{4}$$

5. **(B)** *Functions: Evaluating Functions*

The question tells you that $f(x) = x \cdot h(x)$ and that $h(x) = \frac{x^2 + x + 1}{2}$. Find $f(x)$ by multiplying $h(x)$ by x:

$$f(x) = x \cdot \left(\frac{x^2 + x + 1}{2}\right)$$

$$= \frac{x^3 + x^2 + x}{2}$$

Now find $f(2)$ by plugging 2 into $f(x)$:

$$f(2) = \frac{2^3 + 2^2 + 2}{2}$$

$$= 7$$

6. **(B)** *Functions: Evaluating Functions*

If $f(a, b) = a^b$, then $f(b, a) = b^a$. The question asks you for the values of a and b when $f(a, b) = f(b, a)$, which is the same as $a^b = b^a$. The easiest way to solve this problem is to go through the answer choices plugging in the possible values for a and b. Choice (B) is the correct answer since $2^4 = 4^2$.

7. **(C)** *Functions: Graphing Functions*

Vertical asymptotes and holes occur at points where $f(x)$ is undefined—in other words, whenever one of the factors in the denominator of $f(x)$ equals zero. To find the vertical asymptotes of $f(x)$, first factor the function into its simplest form:

$$f(x) = \frac{x - 3}{(x + 2)(x^2 - 9)}$$

$$= \frac{x - 3}{(x + 2)(x + 3)(x - 3)}$$

Cancel $x - 3$ from the numerator and the denominator of the function. At $x = 3$, the function has a hole. The simplified function is:

$$f(x) = \frac{1}{(x + 2)(x + 3)}$$

The function is undefined at $x = -3$ and $x = -2$ because both of those values make the denominator equal to zero. Thus $f(x)$ has two vertical asymptotes: at $x = -3$ and at $x = -2$.

8. **(A)** *Trigonometry: Pythagorean Identities*

The Pythagorean Trigonometric Identities will help you simplify seemingly complicated trig problems on the Math IIC. The most useful trig identity is $\sin^2\theta + \cos^2\theta = 1$. You can see how this identity will help you out if you rewrite the expression as a single fraction:

$$\frac{\sin^2\theta}{\cos^2\theta} - \frac{1}{\cos^2\theta} = \frac{\sin^2\theta - 1}{\cos^2\theta}$$

By rearranging the trig identity, you find that $\sin^2\theta - 1 = -\cos^2\theta$. Plug $-\cos^2\theta$ into the equation:

$$= \frac{-\cos^2\theta}{\cos^2\theta}$$
$$= -1$$

9. **(E)** *Trigonometry: Basic Functions*

The question asks you to find $\tan(\tau)$. Since you know that $\cos\theta = \frac{2}{7}$, you can label the triangle's sides like this:

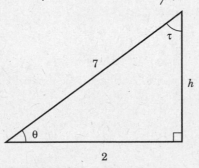

$\tan(\tau)$ is equal to the opposite side, 2, over the adjacent side, h. You can find the side h using the Pythagorean Theorem:

$$7^2 = h^2 + 2^2$$
$$45 = h^2$$
$$3\sqrt{5} = h$$

Now plug this value for h into the equation $\tan(\tau) = \frac{2}{h}$:

$$\tan(\tau) = \frac{2}{3\sqrt{5}}$$
$$= 0.3$$

You can also solve this problem by first finding the angle θ. Since $\cos(\theta) = \frac{2}{7}$, you know that $\theta = \cos^{-1}\left(\frac{2}{7}\right)$. Plug this inverse function into your calculator, and you'll find that $\theta = 73.4°$. Since the three angles in a triangle add up to $180°$, you can find the angle τ by subtracting θ and the right angle from $180°$:

$$\tau = 180 - 90 - \theta$$
$$= 180 - 90 - 73.4$$
$$= 16.6°$$

Now plug this angle into $\tan(\tau)$: $\tan(16.6°) = 0.3$

10. **(D)** *Functions: Evaluating Functions*

If $f(x) = \dfrac{3}{\sqrt{x^3 + 8}}$, then $f(a) = \dfrac{3}{\sqrt{a^3 + 8}}$. Since the question states that $f(a) = 3$, you can set up the following equation: $\dfrac{3}{\sqrt{a^3 + 8}} = 3$. Use this equation to solve for a:

$$3 = \frac{3}{\sqrt{a^3 + 8}}$$

$$1 = \frac{1}{\sqrt{a^3 + 8}}$$

$$\sqrt{a^3 + 8} = 1$$

Square each side of the equation:

$$a^3 + 8 = 1$$
$$a^3 = -7$$
$$a = \sqrt[3]{-7}$$
$$= -1.91$$

11. **(D)** *Plane Geometry: Lines and Planes*

This problem is difficult because you need to visualize a three-dimensional intersection. The perpendicular intersection of the line and the plane looks like this:

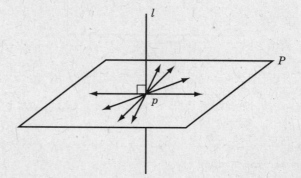

From this picture, you should see that any line in the plane P that passes through the point p is perpendicular to the line l. Plane P contains an infinite amount of lines passing through point p, so the correct answer is choice (D).

12. **(B)** *Statistics: Probability*

If you have two independent events A and B, the probability of both of them happening is the product of their independent probabilities: $P(A \text{ and } B) = P(A) \cdot P(B)$. The question tells you that the probability of Robert winning is $\frac{1}{3}$ and that the probability of John winning is $\frac{2}{7}$. In order to solve the problem, though, you need to find the probability of John *losing*. The probability of John losing is equal to 1 minus the probability of his winning:

$$P(\text{Robert wins and John loses}) = P(\text{Robert wins}) \cdot P(\text{John loses})$$

$$= P(\text{Robert wins})[1 - P(\text{John wins})]$$

$$= \frac{1}{3}\left(1 - \frac{2}{7}\right)$$

$$= \frac{1}{3}\left(\frac{5}{7}\right)$$

$$= \frac{5}{21}$$

13. **(C)** *Solid Geometry: Prisms*

In order to find the volume of a cube, you need to find the length s of the cube's sides. The question tells you that the surface area of the cube is equal to 1. Since the surface area of a cube is $6s^2$, you can solve for s by setting $6s^2 = 1$.

$$6s^2 = 1$$

$$s^2 = \frac{1}{6}$$

$$s = \frac{1}{\sqrt{6}}$$

Now plug this value for s into the volume formula, $V = s^3$:

$$V = \left(\frac{1}{\sqrt{6}}\right)^3$$

$$= \frac{1}{6\sqrt{6}}$$

$$= \frac{\sqrt{6}}{36}$$

14. **(A)** *Functions: Roots*

The question tells you that $x^2 - 6x + k$ has exactly one real root. If this root is at $x = a$, you know that $x^2 - 6x + k = (x - a)^2$ must be true. Multiply out $(x - a)^2$ to get: $x^2 - 6x + k = x^2 - 2ax + a^2$. Since the coefficients of the x term must be equal, you can set up the equation $-6x = -2ax$, which tells you that $a = 3$. Since $k = a^2$, you know that $k = 9$.

You could also have used the discriminant to solve this problem. If a function has only one real root, then its discriminant equals zero: $b^2 - 4ac = 0$. In this function, $a = 1$, $b = -6$, and $c = k$. Plug these numbers into the discriminant: $36 - 4k = 0$ so $k = 9$.

15. **(D)** *Algebra: Equation Solving, Logarithms*

When the variable in an equation is an exponent, you need to use logarithms to "pull down" the variable. Take the log of both sides of the equation:

$$5^x = 72$$
$$\log 5^x = \log 72$$

Since $\log A^x = x \log A$, you can rewrite the equation as:

$$x \log 5 = \log 72$$
$$x = \frac{\log 72}{\log 5}$$
$$= 2.66$$

16. **(E)** *Coordinate Geometry: Lines; Functions: Evaluating Functions*

Before you can find the slope between these two points, you first need to figure out what the points are by evaluating $h(x)$ at $x = -1$ and $x = 4$. If $h(x) = x^2 + 1$, then $h(-1) = (-1)^2 + 1 = 2$ and $h(4) = 4^2 + 1 = 17$. Now find the slope between $(-1, 2)$ and $(4, 17)$ by dividing the change in the y-value by the change in the x-value:

$$\frac{\Delta y}{\Delta x} = \frac{17 - 2}{4 - (-1)}$$
$$= \frac{15}{5}$$
$$= 3$$

17. **(B)** *Trigonometry: Sum and Difference Formulas*

You should memorize the angle addition formulas for $\sin \theta$ and $\cos \theta$. This question requires that you use the addition formula for $\sin \theta$: $\sin(a + b) = \sin a \cos b + \cos a \sin b$. In $\triangle ABC$, $\sin a = \frac{5}{13}$ and $\cos a = \frac{12}{13}$. In $\triangle DEF$, $\sin b = \frac{3}{5}$ and $\cos b = \frac{4}{5}$. Plug these values into the formula:

$$\sin(a + d) = \sin a \cos b + \cos a \sin b$$

$$= \frac{5}{13} \cdot \frac{4}{5} + \frac{12}{13} \cdot \frac{3}{5}$$
$$= \frac{4}{13} + \frac{36}{65}$$
$$= \frac{56}{65}$$

18. **(A)** *Fundamentals: Integers*

Even numbers are divisible by 2. If an even number is also divisible by 3, then the number must be a multiple of 6, since 6 is the least integer divisible by both 2 and 3. The smallest multiple of 6 greater than 100 is 102 (17×6) and the largest multiple of 6 less than 200 is 198 (33×6). The number of multiples of 6 between 100 and 200 is equal to the inclusive difference between 33 and 17: $33 - 17 + 1 = 17$.

19. **(E)** *Algebra: Equation Solving, Exponential Growth and Decay*

Word problems involving exponential growth and decay often appear on the Math IIC, so you should memorize the formula for exponential growth: $A(t) = A_o(1 + r)^t$, where A_o is the initial investment, r is the rate of interest written as a decimal, t is elapsed time, and $A(t)$ is the amount of money after time t. In this problem, A_o is 1900, r is 0.07 (or 7%), and t is 46 years (2003 – 1957). Plug these values into the exponential growth formula:

$$\begin{aligned} A(46) &= 1900(1 + 0.07)^{46} \\ &= 1900(1.07)^{46} \\ &= \$42697.98 \end{aligned}$$

20. **(C)** *Functions: Evaluating Functions*

This question looks complicated because of the unfamiliar operation, but answering it is mostly a matter of plugging $x = 25\frac{1}{2}$ into the provided formula:

$$\begin{aligned} C &= 3.00 + 0.76\lceil x - 1 \rceil \\ &= 3.00 + 0.76\left\lceil 25\frac{1}{2} - 1 \right\rceil \\ &= 3.00 + 0.76\left\lceil 24\frac{1}{2} \right\rceil \end{aligned}$$

Here's the tricky part. The question says that whatever is inside the operation $\lceil\ \rceil$ should be rounded down to the nearest integer. So you end up with:

$$\begin{aligned} &= 3.00 + 0.76(24)\text{ , since the greatest integer less than or equal to } 24\frac{1}{2} \text{ is 24} \\ &= 21.24 \end{aligned}$$

21. **(D)** *Algebra: Polynomials*

The question tells you that $(x + 3)$ is a factor of the polynomial $x^3 + x^2 - 4cx + 1$, practically begging you to solve the problem using polynomial long division. The polynomial version of long division says that any polynomial $P(x)$ can be written $P(x) = (x - a) \cdot Q(x) + R$, where $(x - a)$ is the divisor, $Q(x)$ is the quotient, and R is the remainder. The remainder R can be found by plugging a into $P(x)$, since $P(a) = (a - a) \cdot Q(a) + R = R$.

There are two unknown variables in this question: x and c. Since you want to solve for c, you need to make it the only unknown in an equation. You can do this by plugging in a value for x that will give you a value you've already determined for $P(x)$, such as $P(a) = R$. In this question, $a = -3$, since $(x + 3)$ is the divisor $(x - a)$. Because $(x + 3)$ is a factor of $P(x)$, it divides $P(x)$ evenly, leaving no remainder. Since $R = 0$, you know $P(a) = 0$. You can solve for c by setting $P(a) = 0$ and plugging in $a = -3$:

$$\begin{aligned} P(a) &= a^3 + a^2 - 4ca + 1 = 0 \\ P(-3) &= (-3)^3 + (-3)^2 - 4c(-3) + 1 = 0 \end{aligned}$$

Now you have an equation in which c is the only variable:

$$\begin{aligned} -27 + 9 + 12c + 1 &= 0 \\ 12c &= 17 \\ c &= \frac{17}{12} \end{aligned}$$

22. (C) Coordinate Geometry: Lines and Distance

You can calculate the distance between points (x_1, y_1, z_1) and (x_2, y_2, z_2) in three-dimensional space by using the formula: $d = \sqrt{(x_1 - x_2)^2 + (y_1 - y_2)^2 + (z_1 - z_2)^2}$. Plug the two points given in the question into this formula:

$$d = \sqrt{(1-7)^2 + (2-(-9))^2 + (3-12)^2}$$
$$= \sqrt{36 + 121 + 81}$$
$$= \sqrt{238}$$
$$= 15.43$$

23. (B) Coordinate Geometry: Polar Coordinates

Polar coordinate questions rarely appear on the Math IIC. When they do, the question will most likely ask you to convert an (x, y) point into polar coordinate form, (r, θ). You should memorize the conversion before you take the test; fortunately, it's pretty straightforward: $r = \sqrt{x^2 + y^2}$ and $\theta = \tan^{-1}\left(\frac{y}{x}\right)$.

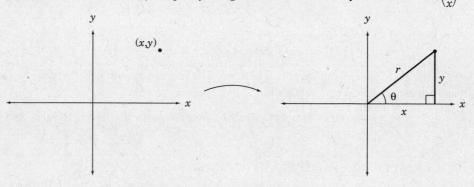

As you can see from the figure, r is the hypotenuse of a right triangle formed by the lengths x and y, so you can find r using the Pythagorean Theorem:

$$r = \sqrt{x^2 + y^2}$$
$$= \sqrt{(2\sqrt{3})^2 + 2^2}$$
$$= \sqrt{16}$$
$$= 4$$

Since the triangle is a right triangle, you can solve for θ using inverse tangent:

$$\theta = \tan^{-1}\left(\frac{y}{x}\right)$$
$$= \tan^{-1}\left(\frac{2}{2\sqrt{3}}\right)$$
$$= 30°$$

24. (E) Plane Geometry: Circles

The infinite set of points 3 units from the origin is a circle of radius 3 centered at the origin. The equation for a circle centered at the origin is $x^2 + y^2 = r^2$. Plug in $r = 3$ to solve the problem: $x^2 + y^2 = 9$.

25. **(A)** *Algebra: Systems of Equations*

You should start by getting rid of the exponent and root in these two equations. Simplify the first equation by taking the cube root of both sides:

$$(x + y)^3 = 64$$
$$x + y = 64^{1/3}$$
$$x + y = 4$$

Now simplify the second equation by squaring both sides:

$$\sqrt{x - y} = 4$$
$$x - y = 4^2$$
$$x - y = 16$$

If you add the equations $x + y = 4$ and $x - y = 16$, you can cancel out y, leaving you with:

$$2x = 20$$
$$x = 10$$

26. **(B)** *Functions: Evaluating Functions*

In order to maximize the value of $f(x)$ over the domain $x \geq 4$, you need to make $\sqrt{x - 4}$ as small as possible. If $x \geq 4$, then the smallest value of $\sqrt{x - 4}$ is zero, which you get when $x = 4$. Thus the maximum value of $f(x)$ is 3, since $3 - \sqrt{4 - 4} = 3$. If x is greater than 4, the number under the square root will be positive, so you'll end up subtracting a positive number from 3.

You could also answer this problem by graphing $f(x)$ on your calculator and finding the maximum value of y.

27. **(D)** *Trigonometry: Basic Functions*

$\sec\theta$ is equal to $\dfrac{1}{\cos\theta}$ or $\dfrac{\text{hypotenuse}}{\text{adjacent}}$. Figure 4 shows you that the triangle's hypotenuse is h and that the side opposite θ is y.

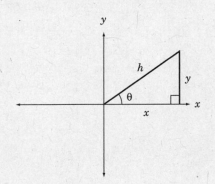

In order to find the adjacent leg, x, you need to use the Pythagorean Theorem:

$$x^2 + y^2 = h^2$$
$$x^2 = h^2 - y^2$$
$$x = \sqrt{h^2 - y^2}$$

Now you can solve for $\sec\theta$:

$$\sec\theta = \frac{1}{\cos\theta}$$

$$= \frac{h}{x}$$

$$= \frac{h}{\sqrt{h^2 - y^2}}$$

28. **(C)** *Coordinate Geometry: Lines; Algebra: Equation Solving*

The graphs of $y = \frac{2-x}{x-2}$ and $y = x-2$ intersect when the equations equal each other: when $\frac{2-x}{x-2} = x-2$. You can solve this equation quickly if you recognize that $\frac{2-x}{x-2}$ is the same as $\frac{-(x-2)}{x-2} = -1$. Now you can simplify $\frac{2-x}{x-2} = x-2$ as $-1 = x-2$, and using this equation, you can find that $x = 1$.

29. **(C)** *Trigonometry: Basic Functions*

When you see $\tan\theta$ in a trig problem, you can often spot the solution by rewriting $\tan\theta$ as $\frac{\sin\theta}{\cos\theta}$.

$$\tan\theta = \sin\theta$$

$$\frac{\sin\theta}{\cos\theta} = \sin\theta$$

$$0 = \sin\theta - \frac{\sin\theta}{\cos\theta}$$

$$0 = \sin\theta\left(1 - \frac{1}{\cos\theta}\right)$$

According to this equation, either $\sin\theta = 0$ or $1 - \frac{1}{\cos\theta} = 0$.

$$\sin\theta = 0, \text{ and } 0 \le \theta \le 2\pi$$

$$\theta = 0, \pi, 2\pi$$

If $\theta = 0, \pi, 2\pi$, then $\cos\theta = 1, -1$.

$$1 - \frac{1}{\cos\theta} = 0$$

$$\cos\theta = 1$$

Choice (C) is the correct answer because it says that $\cos\theta$ equals either 1 or -1.

30. **(B)** *Plane Geometry: Triangles; Coordinate Geometry: Coordinate Plane*

Draw a picture of the situation described in the question:

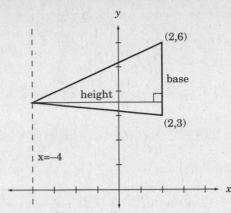

In order to find the area of the triangle, you need to know the triangle's base and height. The base of the triangle is the vertical distance between the points $(2, 6)$ and $(2, 3)$: $6 - 3 = 3$. As you can see from the picture, no matter where you draw the triangle's third vertex along the line $x = -4$, the height of $\triangle ABC$ will be 6. Plug these values for the base and height into the triangle area formula:

$$
\begin{aligned}
\text{Area } \triangle ABC &= \tfrac{1}{2}bh \\
&= \tfrac{1}{2}(3)(6) \\
&= 9
\end{aligned}
$$

31. **(D)** *Plane Geometry: Circles, Polygons*

Try intersecting a circle and a square in different ways.

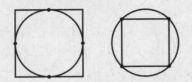

The drawing on the left shows a square inscribed within a circle, and the drawing on the right shows a circle inscribed within a square. In both of these drawings, the circle and square intersect four times. Now try drawing the circle and the square so that neither one is inscribed within the other:

In this drawing the circle and square intersect eight times—the maximum number of possible intersections.

32. **(A)** *Algebra: Equation Solving; Trigonometry: Inverse Trigonometric Functions*

The trigonometric expression in this question is actually a quadratic equation, in which $\cos\theta$ is the variable. You can solve this equation as you would $x^2 + 3x - 2 = 0$:

$$
\begin{aligned}
2\cos^2\theta + 3\cos\theta - 2 &= 0 \\
(2\cos\theta - 1)(\cos\theta + 2) &= 0
\end{aligned}
$$

The possible solutions to this equation are:

$$2\cos\theta - 1 = 0$$
$$2\cos\theta = 1$$
$$\cos\theta = \frac{1}{2}$$
$$\theta = \cos^{-1}\left(\frac{1}{2}\right)$$
$$\theta = \frac{\pi}{3}$$

and

$$\cos\theta + 2 = 0$$
$$\cos\theta = -2, \text{ which has no solution since } -1 \leq \cos\theta \leq 1$$

33. (E) *Plane Geometry: Polygons*

The area of a rectangle is equal to the product of its width and length. For the rectangle in this problem, the area is $AB \times BC$. Since Figure 5 shows you that BC is 8, all you need to do is figure out the length of AB. Redraw the figure without the plane to see how to find AB.

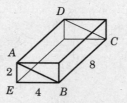

As you can see from the picture, ΔABE is a right triangle, and AB is its hypotenuse. Since you know AE and EB, you can use the Pythagorean Theorem to find AB.

$$AB^2 = AE^2 + EB^2$$
$$= 2^2 + 4^2$$
$$= 20$$
$$AB = \sqrt{20}$$

Now you can find the area of the rectangle:

$$\text{Area } ABCD = AB \times BC$$
$$= \sqrt{20} \times 8$$
$$= 35.8$$

34. (C) *Coordinate Geometry: Hyperbolas*

Although hyperbola and ellipse questions don't appear often on the Math IIC, you should know the equations for both of them, and you should be able to tell the difference between their equations. The equation of a hyperbola is $\frac{(x-h)^2}{a^2} - \frac{(y-k)^2}{b^2} = 1$ or $\frac{(y-k)^2}{b^2} - \frac{(x-h)^2}{a^2} = 1$, where (h, k) is the center of the hyperbola. The equation of an ellipse is $\frac{(x+h)^2}{a^2} + \frac{(y+k)^2}{b^2} = 1$, where (h, k) is the center of the ellipse. The equation in the question has a minus sign, so you should instantly recognize it as the equation of a hyperbola. You can rule out choices (A) and (B), since they show the graphs of ellipses. Try plugging some points from the graphs into the equation. Both choices (C) and (D) contain the point (3, 0). When you plug this point into the equation, you get $1 = 1$, so you know that point is on the graph. Because choice (E) doesn't include that point, you can rule it out as an answer. Now plug in the point $(5, \frac{16}{3})$:

$$\frac{5^2}{9} - \frac{\left(\frac{16}{3}\right)^2}{16} = \frac{25}{9} - \frac{16}{9}$$

$$= \frac{9}{9}$$

$$= 1$$

Choice (C) is correct because it contains the point $(5, \frac{16}{3})$.

35. **(A)** *Fundamentals: Integers*

If you try plugging in values for n and m, you'll get yourself into a mess. Instead, you should remember that the square of an integer always equals another integer. So if $\sqrt{\frac{n}{m}}$ is an integer, then $\left(\sqrt{\frac{n}{m}}\right)^2 = \frac{n}{m}$ must also be an integer.

36. **(B)** *Miscellaneous Math: Limits*

This question asks you to find the limit of $f(x)$ as x approaches 4. You can answer this question by graphing $f(x)$ on your calculator and seeing what value y approaches as x gets closer to 4.

You can also answer this question by factoring the function into its simplest form:

$$f(x) = \frac{x^2 - 16}{4 - x}$$

$$= \frac{(x + 4)(x - 4)}{4 - x}$$

$$= \frac{(x + 4)(x - 4)}{-(x - 4)}$$

$$= -(x + 4)$$

Now plug $x = 4$ into this simplified form of $f(x)$:

$$f(4) = -(4 + 4)$$

$$= -8$$

As x approaches 4, $f(x)$ approaches -8.

37. (A)   Functions: Inverse Functions

You need to solve for the three unknowns: a, b, and x. The question tells you that $f(0) = 3$, so you know that $a(0) + b = 3$, or $b = 3$. Now you have two unknowns left. In order to solve for them, you need to write another equation. Your next step should be to find $f^{-1}(x)$. Finding an inverse function requires three steps. First, replace $f(x)$ with y, so that $y = ax + 3$. Second, switch x and y, so that $x = ay + 3$. Third, solve for y:

$$x = ay + 3$$
$$x - 3 = ay$$
$$y = \frac{x-3}{a}$$
$$f^{-1}(x) = \frac{x-3}{a}$$

Because $f(x) = f^{-1}(x)$, you know that $f^{-1}(0) = 3$. Plug $x = 0$ into $f^{-1}(x)$:

$$f^{-1}(0) = \frac{0-3}{a} = 3$$
$$-3 = 3a$$
$$a = -1$$

Now you have the inverse function $f^{-1}(x) = -\frac{x-3}{1}$. Plug $x = 1$ into this function to solve the problem:

$$f^{-1}(1) = -\frac{1-3}{1} = 2.$$

38. (D)   Coordinate Geometry and Plane Geometry: Circles

In order to find the area of the circle, you need to know the circle's radius. To find the radius, rewrite the given equation in the standard form for a circle: $(x - h)^2 + (y - k)^2 = r^2$, where (h, k) is the center and r is the radius. Complete the squares of x and y:

$$x^2 - 4x + y^2 - 6y - 212 = 0$$
$$x^2 - 4x + y^2 - 6y = 212$$
$$(x^2 - 4x + 4) + (y^2 - 6y + 9) = 212 + 9 + 4$$
$$(x - 2)^2 + (y - 3)^2 = 225$$

According to the standard form of a circle's equation, $225 = r^2$. Since the area of a circle is πr^2, you don't need to solve for r.

$$\text{Area}_{circle} = \pi r^2$$
$$= 225\pi$$

39. (E)   Functions: Graphing Functions

The best way to answer this problem is to graph the function on your calculator. The graph of $y = \frac{1}{2}e^{-x^2}$ should look like this:

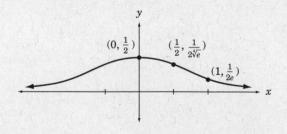

Choices (D) and (E) both resemble the graph above, but choice (E) has the correct y-intercept: $(0, \frac{1}{2})$. You can double check that (E) is correct by plugging $x = 0$ into $y = \frac{1}{2}e^{-x^2}$:

$$y = \frac{1}{2}e^{-(0)^2}$$

$$= \frac{1}{2}(1)$$

$$= \frac{1}{2}$$

40. **(B)** *Trigonometry: Solving Non-Right Triangles*

When you're given the three sides of a non-right triangle, you can use the law of cosines to determine the angles in the triangle. According to the law of cosines, $c^2 = a^2 + b^2 - 2ab\cos C$ in $\triangle ABC$:

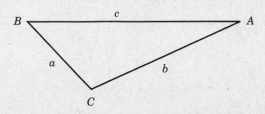

As you can see from the picture, the largest angle of a triangle is opposite the largest side. Since you're looking for the largest angle in a triangle with sides 12, 17, and 24, you should make $c = 24$. Plug the triangle's sides into the law of cosines:

$$24^2 = 12^2 + 17^2 - 2(12)(17)\cos C$$

$$24^2 - 12^2 - 17^2 = -408\cos C$$

$$-\frac{143}{408} = \cos C$$

$$C = \cos^{-1}\left(-\frac{143}{408}\right)$$

$$= 110.5°$$

41. **(C)** *Coordinate Geometry: Graphing Linear Inequalities*

Since the answer choices give the same equations for the two lines, all you need to do is figure out the correct inequality signs. Since the lines in Figure 6 are solid, the inequalities must be inclusive; in other words, they must look like ≤ or ≥. To figure out the direction of the inequality signs, start by graphing the curve $y = 1 - x^2$ and the line $y = x$ on your calculator:

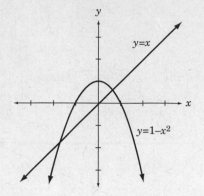

The shaded area is above $y = x$ and below $y = 1 - x^2$, and you can represent the area as the intersection of the inequalities $y \geq x$ and $y \leq 1 - x^2$.

42. **(E)** *Statistics: Combinations and Permutations*

There are six letters in COFFEE, but two of the letters—F and E—are duplicated. When figuring out the number of possible rearrangements, you need to take these duplicated letters into account so you don't double count any arrangements. Divide the number of possible arrangements of six letters by the number of arrangements of EE and FF:

$$\frac{(\text{total number of letters})!}{(\text{number of Es})!(\text{number of Fs})!} = \frac{6!}{2!2!}$$
$$= 180$$

43. **(A)** *Functions: Piecewise Functions*

Piecewise functions have different definitions for different intervals in their domains. The function in this question is a piecewise function with two input values: x and y. The question asks you to find the difference between two points on the function. Your first step should be to figure out the values of $f(2, 1)$ and $f(1, 2)$. At the point $f(2, 1)$, $x = 2$ and $y = 1$. Since $2 > 1$, you need to plug the points into $f(x, y) = 1 - x$, which is true when $x > y$:

$$f(2, 1) = 1 - 2 = -1$$

At the point $f(1, 2)$, $x = 1$ and $y = 2$. Since $1 < 2$, you need to plug the point into $f(x, y) = x^2$, which is true when $x \leq y$:

$$f(1, 2) = (1)^2 = 1$$

Now that you know the values of the two points, you can find the difference between them:

$$f(2, 1) - f(1, 2) = -1 - 1$$
$$= -2$$

44. **(D)** *Solid Geometry: Solids that Aren't Prisms*

The question asks you what happens to the surface area of a sphere when its volume is tripled. Since a sphere's volume and surface area depend on its radius, you should first figure out what happens to the radius when the volume triples. Call the original radius r and the new radius R. The original volume of the sphere is:

$$V = \frac{4}{3}\pi r^3$$

The new volume of the sphere is:

$$3V = \frac{4}{3}\pi(R)^3$$
$$3\left(\frac{4}{3}\pi r^3\right) = \frac{4}{3}\pi R^3$$
$$3r^3 = R^3$$

Take the cube root of both sides:

$$\sqrt[3]{3}\,r = R$$

This equation tells you that the sphere's radius increases by $\sqrt[3]{3}$ when the volume triples. The sphere's original surface area is $4\pi r^2$, and the new surface area is $4\pi R^2$. Replace R with $\sqrt[3]{3}\,r$ to see how the surface area changes:

$$4\pi R^2 = 4\pi(\sqrt[3]{3}\,r)^2$$
$$= 4\pi\sqrt[3]{9}\,r^2$$
$$= \sqrt[3]{9}(4\pi r^2)$$
$$= \sqrt[3]{9}(SA)$$

The new surface area is $\sqrt[3]{9}$ times as large as the original surface area.

45. **(C)** *Functions: Graphing Functions*

A "translated" graph moves to a different position in the coordinate plane, but doesn't change its shape. Call the graph of the function in the question $y = f(x)$. When you move the graph vertically, you're changing its y-value. To move the function in the question up by 7 units, add 7 to $f(x)$: $y = f(x) + 7$. When you move the graph horizontally, you're changing its x-value. To move the function 4 units to the left, you need to add 4 to x: $y = f(x + 4)$. Now combine these translations:

$$y = f(x + 4) + 7$$
$$= 2((x + 4) - 4)^3 - 7 + 7$$
$$= 2x^3$$

Your new function is $h(x) = 2x^3$. The question asks you for the y-value of the transformed graph at $x = 2$. To find this value, simply plug $x = 2$ into $h(x)$.

$$h(2) = 2(2)^3$$
$$= 2(8)$$
$$= 16$$

46. **(E)** *Functions: Transformations and Symmetry*

If a function is odd, then $f(-x) = -f(x)$. This definition means that the graph of the function contains the points (x, y) and $(-x, -y)$. The easiest way to answer this question is to plug $-x$ into each of the functions in the answer choices. You'll see that $f(-x) = -f(x)$ is true only for choice (E):

$$
\begin{aligned}
f(x) &= x^3 - 3x \\
f(-x) &= (-x)^3 - 3(-x) \\
&= x^3 + 3x \\
&= -(x^3 - 3x) \\
f(-x) &= -f(x)
\end{aligned}
$$

47. **(A)** *Miscellaneous Math: Logic*

Occasionally, Math IIC questions will ask what assumption is made by the indirect proof of a statement. These questions sound more complicated than they are. All you need to know is how to find the assumption of an indirect proof; you don't need to know how to find the indirect proof itself. In an indirect proof of "if p, then q," you assume the negative of the conclusion q; in other words, you start out the proof with the assumption that you have "*not q*." In this case, you have the statement "if x is a member of set P, then x is a member of set Q." The assumption the indirect proof makes is the negative of "x is a member of set Q." So choice (A), which states that "x is *not* a member of set Q," is correct.

48. **(D)** *Plane Geometry: Polygons, Sectors; Fundamentals: Ratios*

In order to solve this problem, you need to find the area of the rhombus and the area of the shaded region. The area of a rhombus is the product of its base and height.

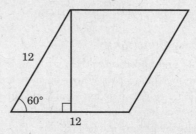

The base of the rhombus is 12. Its height h is equal to $12\sin 60°$. Plug the base and height into the area formula: $\text{Area}_{rhombus} = 12 \times 12\sin 60° = 72\sqrt{3}$. Now you need to find the area of the shaded region. As you can see from this picture, the shaded region is a sector:

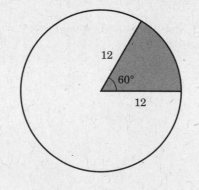

The formula for the area of a sector is: $\text{Area}_{sector} = \dfrac{n}{360} \times \pi r^2$, where n is the central angle of the sector and r is the radius of the circle. The central angle of the sector is the same as the angle of the rhombus: $60°$. The radius of the circle is the same as the side of the rhombus: 12. Plug these values into the formula to find the sector's area:

$$\text{Area}_{sector} = \frac{60}{360} \times \pi(12)^2$$
$$= 24\pi$$

Now you can find the ratio of the area of the sector to the area of the rhombus:

$$\frac{\text{Area}_{sector}}{\text{Area}_{rhombus}} = \frac{24\pi}{72\sqrt{3}}$$
$$= 0.60$$

49. **(B)** *Solid Geometry: Solids that Aren't Prisms*

The volume of a cone depends on its radius, so you need to figure out the radius of the cone that's formed when the water is at a height of 9. Redraw Figure 8 to show the sunken water level:

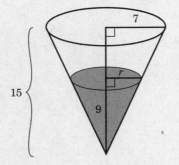

As you can see from this picture, you have two similar right triangles: one with base 7 and height 15, and the other with base r and height 9. Because these triangles are similar, you can find r using the following ratio of height to base:

$$\frac{15}{7} = \frac{9}{r}$$
$$r = \frac{7(9)}{15}$$
$$= \frac{21}{5}$$

Now you can plug r into the formula for the volume of a cone:

$$\text{Volume}_{cone} = \frac{1}{3}\pi r^2 h$$
$$= \frac{1}{3}\pi\left(\frac{21}{5}\right)^2(9)$$
$$= \frac{1323}{25}\pi$$
$$= 166.3$$

50. **(B)** *Algebra: Equation Solving*

You may be tempted to multiply out this equation, but if you do, you'll end up with some really messy math. The trick to answering this question is to factor a constant out of each of the expressions, so you end up with a constant number multiplied by $\left(x - \frac{1}{x}\right)$:

$$\left(2x - \frac{2}{x}\right)^2 + \left(3x - \frac{3}{x}\right) = 0$$

$$2^2\left(x - \frac{1}{x}\right)^2 + 3\left(x - \frac{1}{x}\right) = 0$$

Since both of the expressions contain $\left(x - \frac{1}{x}\right)$, you can factor again:

$$\left(x - \frac{1}{x}\right)\left[4\left(x - \frac{1}{x}\right) + 3\right] = 0$$

The solution to this equation is either $x - \frac{1}{x} = 0$ or $x - \frac{1}{x} = -\frac{3}{4}$. If $x - \frac{1}{x} = 0$, then $x^2 - 1 = 0$ and $x = \pm 1$. You don't need to solve $x - \frac{1}{x} = -\frac{3}{4}$ since choice (B) says that x can equal -1.

SAT II Math IIC
Practice Test 5

MATH IIC TEST 5 ANSWER SHEET

1. Ⓐ Ⓑ Ⓒ Ⓓ Ⓔ	18. Ⓐ Ⓑ Ⓒ Ⓓ Ⓔ	35. Ⓐ Ⓑ Ⓒ Ⓓ Ⓔ
2. Ⓐ Ⓑ Ⓒ Ⓓ Ⓔ	19. Ⓐ Ⓑ Ⓒ Ⓓ Ⓔ	36. Ⓐ Ⓑ Ⓒ Ⓓ Ⓔ
3. Ⓐ Ⓑ Ⓒ Ⓓ Ⓔ	20. Ⓐ Ⓑ Ⓒ Ⓓ Ⓔ	37. Ⓐ Ⓑ Ⓒ Ⓓ Ⓔ
4. Ⓐ Ⓑ Ⓒ Ⓓ Ⓔ	21. Ⓐ Ⓑ Ⓒ Ⓓ Ⓔ	38. Ⓐ Ⓑ Ⓒ Ⓓ Ⓔ
5. Ⓐ Ⓑ Ⓒ Ⓓ Ⓔ	22. Ⓐ Ⓑ Ⓒ Ⓓ Ⓔ	39. Ⓐ Ⓑ Ⓒ Ⓓ Ⓔ
6. Ⓐ Ⓑ Ⓒ Ⓓ Ⓔ	23. Ⓐ Ⓑ Ⓒ Ⓓ Ⓔ	40. Ⓐ Ⓑ Ⓒ Ⓓ Ⓔ
7. Ⓐ Ⓑ Ⓒ Ⓓ Ⓔ	24. Ⓐ Ⓑ Ⓒ Ⓓ Ⓔ	41. Ⓐ Ⓑ Ⓒ Ⓓ Ⓔ
8. Ⓐ Ⓑ Ⓒ Ⓓ Ⓔ	25. Ⓐ Ⓑ Ⓒ Ⓓ Ⓔ	42. Ⓐ Ⓑ Ⓒ Ⓓ Ⓔ
9. Ⓐ Ⓑ Ⓒ Ⓓ Ⓔ	26. Ⓐ Ⓑ Ⓒ Ⓓ Ⓔ	43. Ⓐ Ⓑ Ⓒ Ⓓ Ⓔ
10. Ⓐ Ⓑ Ⓒ Ⓓ Ⓔ	27. Ⓐ Ⓑ Ⓒ Ⓓ Ⓔ	44. Ⓐ Ⓑ Ⓒ Ⓓ Ⓔ
11. Ⓐ Ⓑ Ⓒ Ⓓ Ⓔ	28. Ⓐ Ⓑ Ⓒ Ⓓ Ⓔ	45. Ⓐ Ⓑ Ⓒ Ⓓ Ⓔ
12. Ⓐ Ⓑ Ⓒ Ⓓ Ⓔ	29. Ⓐ Ⓑ Ⓒ Ⓓ Ⓔ	46. Ⓐ Ⓑ Ⓒ Ⓓ Ⓔ
13. Ⓐ Ⓑ Ⓒ Ⓓ Ⓔ	30. Ⓐ Ⓑ Ⓒ Ⓓ Ⓔ	47. Ⓐ Ⓑ Ⓒ Ⓓ Ⓔ
14. Ⓐ Ⓑ Ⓒ Ⓓ Ⓔ	31. Ⓐ Ⓑ Ⓒ Ⓓ Ⓔ	48. Ⓐ Ⓑ Ⓒ Ⓓ Ⓔ
15. Ⓐ Ⓑ Ⓒ Ⓓ Ⓔ	32. Ⓐ Ⓑ Ⓒ Ⓓ Ⓔ	49. Ⓐ Ⓑ Ⓒ Ⓓ Ⓔ
16. Ⓐ Ⓑ Ⓒ Ⓓ Ⓔ	33. Ⓐ Ⓑ Ⓒ Ⓓ Ⓔ	50. Ⓐ Ⓑ Ⓒ Ⓓ Ⓔ
17. Ⓐ Ⓑ Ⓒ Ⓓ Ⓔ	34. Ⓐ Ⓑ Ⓒ Ⓓ Ⓔ	

REFERENCE INFORMATION

THE FOLLOWING INFORMATION IS FOR YOUR REFERENCE IN ANSWERING SOME OF THE QUESTIONS IN THIS TEST:

Volume of a right circular cone with radius r and height h: $V = \frac{1}{3}\pi r^2 h$

Lateral area of a right circular cone with circumference of the base c and slaight height ℓ: $S = \frac{1}{2}c\ell$

Volume of a sphere with radius r: $V = \frac{4}{3}\pi r^3$

Surface area of a sphere with radius r: $S = 4\pi r^2$

Volume of a pyramid with base area B and height h: $V = \frac{1}{3}Bh$

MATHEMATICS LEVEL IIC TEST

For each of the following problems, decide which is the BEST of the choices given. If the exact numerical value is not one of the choices, select the choice that best approximates this value. Then fill in the corresponding oval on the answer sheet.

Notes: (1) A calculator will be necessary for answering some (but not all) of the questions in this test. For each question you will have to decide whether or not you should use a calcuator. The calculator you use must be at least a scientific calculator; programmable calculators and calculators that can display graphs are permitted.

(2) For some questions in this test you may need to decide whether your calculator should be in radian or degree mode.

(3) Figures that accompany problems in this test are intended to provide information useful in solving the problems. They are drawn as accurately as possible EXCEPT when it is stated in a specific problem that its figure is not drawn to scale. All figures lie in a plane unless otherwise indicated.

(4) Unless otherwise specified, the domain of any function f is assumed to be the set of all real numbers x for which $f(x)$ is a real number.

(5) Reference information that may be useful in answering the questions in this test can be found on the page preceding Question 1.

USE THIS SPACE FOR SCRATCHWORK.

If $x \le y$ and $y \le x$, then which of the following must be true?

(A) $x = 0$
(B) $y = 0$
(C) $x = y$
(D) $x = -y$
(E) $x = 1 - y$

If x is a nonzero integer, then which of the following must be a positive integer?

(A) $(-x)^3$
(B) $-x^2$
(C) $2 + (-x)^3$
(D) $2 + (-x)^2$
(E) $2 + (-x)$

If $f(x) = -x^3 + 3x^2 + kx + 2$, and $f(1) = 0$, then $k =$

(A) -5
(B) -4
(C) -2
(D) 1
(E) 2

GO ON TO THE NEXT PAGE

4. n has a remainder of 7 when it is divided by 9. What is the remainder when $2n + 5$ is divided by 9?

(A) 1
(B) 2
(C) 3
(D) 4
(E) 5

5. If $f(x) = x^2 + x$, then $f(t + 1) =$

(A) $t^2 + 2t$
(B) $t^2 + 2t + 1$
(C) $t^2 + 2t + 2$
(D) $t^2 + 3t + 1$
(E) $t^2 + 3t + 2$

6. John made an average of d dollars per day for the first 3 days of the week. If he made \$1200 total for the 5 days of work he did that week, what were his average earnings per day for the last 2 days of the week?

(A) $600 - \dfrac{3}{2}d$

(B) $600 - \dfrac{2}{3}d$

(C) $600 - \dfrac{1}{2}d$

(D) $600 + \dfrac{1}{2}d$

(E) $600 + \dfrac{3}{2}d$

7. If $f(x) = x^2$, $g(x) = x + 1$, and $h(x) = 3x - 1$, then $f(g(h(3))) =$

(A) 61
(B) 72
(C) 81
(D) 85
(E) 121

GO ON TO THE NEXT PAGE

8. If the average of a and b is equal to the average of c, d, and e, then which of the following <u>must</u> be true?

I. $2a + 2b = 3c + 3d + 3e$
II. $3a + 3b = 2c + 2d + 2e$
III. $a + b = c + d + e$

(A) I only
(B) II only
(C) III only
(D) I and II only
(E) I, II, and III

The midpoint of the line segment joining the points $(1.2, 2.6)$ and $(7.8, -11)$ is

(A) $(3.3, 6.8)$
(B) $(-4.2, -4.5)$
(C) $(4.2, 4.5)$
(D) $(4.5, -4.2)$
(E) $(4.5, 4.2)$

. If $2^x = 7$, then $2 \cdot x =$

(A) 2.81
(B) 3.15
(C) 4.03
(D) 5.61
(E) 8.97

. If $x \neq -\dfrac{4}{3}$ and $\dfrac{2x - 1}{3x + 4} = y$, then $x =$

(A) $\dfrac{2y - 1}{3y + 4}$

(B) $\dfrac{y + 1}{3y + 4}$

(C) $\dfrac{2 + 3y}{4 - y}$

(D) $\dfrac{2 - 3y}{1 + 4y}$

(E) $\dfrac{1 + 4y}{2 - 3y}$

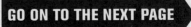

GO ON TO THE NEXT PAGE

USE THIS SPACE FOR SCRATCHWORK.

12. A right triangle is rotated $360°$ around one of its legs. What kind of solid does this revolution generate?

(A) A cylinder
(B) A sphere
(C) A cone
(D) A cube
(E) A pyramid

13. The chart in Figure 1 shows the breakdown of all of the students in a high school. What is the probability of selecting at random a male sophomore from the student body?

(A) 18/160
(B) 19/160
(C) 37/160
(D) 19/78
(E) 19/37

	Male	Female	Total
Freshmen	200	250	450
Sophomores	190	180	370
Juniors	195	200	395
Seniors	195	190	385
Total	780	820	1600

Figure 1

14. If $\log_3 x = 4$, then $x =$

(A) 81
(B) 80
(C) 27
(D) 26
(E) 9

15. In Figure 2, which of the points lies on the circle $x^2 + y^2 = 100$?

(A) A
(B) B
(C) C
(D) D
(E) E

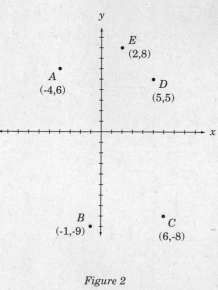

Figure 2

GO ON TO THE NEXT PAGE

16. How many times does the graph of the function
$p(x) = -2x^2 + 3x - 7$ cross the x-axis?

(A) Zero
(B) One
(C) Two
(D) Three
(E) Not enough information to tell

17. What is the range of $f(x) = 2\cos x$?

(A) $0 < f(x) < 2$
(B) $0 \le f(x) \le 2$
(C) $-1 \le f(x) \le 1$
(D) $-2 \le f(x) \le 2$
(E) $-2 < f(x) < 2$

18. If the first term in a geometric sequence is 3 and the fourth term
is $\dfrac{3}{8}$, then the twentieth term is

(A) 6^{-17}
(B) 6^{-18}
(C) 6^{-19}
(D) 3×2^{-18}
(E) 3×2^{-19}

. If $f(x) = \dfrac{x-2}{(x+2)(x^2+9)}$, then for what value of x is $f(x)$
undefined?

(A) $x = 3$
(B) $x = 2$
(C) $x = 0$
(D) $x = -2$
(E) $x = -3$

A large cube with a volume of 216 is cut up into 27 identical
smaller cubes. What is the ratio of the surface area of the larger
cube to the surface area of one of the smaller cubes?

(A) 27:1
(B) 9:1
(C) 8:1
(D) 3:1
(E) 2:1

GO ON TO THE NEXT PAGE

21. Where defined $\dfrac{\csc x}{\sec x} =$

    (A) $\sin x \cos x$
    (B) $\dfrac{1}{\sin x \cos x}$
    (C) 1
    (D) $\cot x$
    (E) $\tan x$

22. If $f(x) = e^x$, then where does $f^{-1}(x)$ cross the x-axis?

    (A) -1
    (B) 0
    (C) 1
    (D) 2
    (E) $f^{-1}(x)$ never crosses the x-axis.

23. If $f(x) = \dfrac{1}{x}$, which of the following could be the graph of
$y = f(x^2)$?

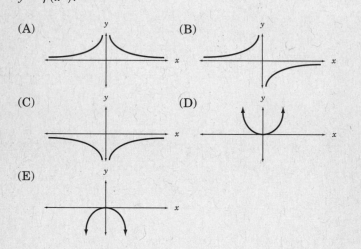

(A)   (B)

(C)   (D)

(E)

GO ON TO THE NEXT PAGE

24. If $\tan\dfrac{\pi}{6} = \cos\left(\dfrac{\pi}{3} + \theta\right)$ and $-\dfrac{\pi}{2} < \theta < \dfrac{\pi}{2}$, then $\theta =$

   (A) 24.7
   (B) 0.09
   (C) 0
   (D) −0.01
   (E) −0.09

25. The area of an ellipse is given by the formula $A = \pi ab$, where a and b come from the general equation of an ellipse, $\dfrac{(x-h)^2}{a^2} + \dfrac{(y-b)^2}{b^2} = 1$. What is the area of the ellipse represented by the equation $\dfrac{(x-2)^2}{48} + \dfrac{(y-3)^2}{27} = 1$?

   (A) 24π
   (B) 36π
   (C) 38π
   (D) 42π
   (E) 1296π

26. What is the area of the triangle in Figure 3?

   (A) 19.12
   (B) 23.83
   (C) 37.19
   (D) 41.80
   (E) 43.65

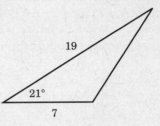

Note: Figure not drawn to scale.

Figure 3

GO ON TO THE NEXT PAGE

USE THIS SPACE FOR SCRATCHWORK.

27. What is the limit of $f(x) = \dfrac{x^2 + 5x - 14}{x - 2}$ as x approaches 2 ?

   (A) −7
   (B) −2
   (C) 7
   (D) 9
   (E) The limit does not exist.

28. If $x + 2$ is a factor of $x^3 - cx^2 - 4x + 3$, then $c =$

   (A) $-\dfrac{3}{4}$

   (B) $\dfrac{3}{7}$

   (C) $\dfrac{3}{4}$

   (D) $\dfrac{4}{3}$

   (E) $\dfrac{8}{3}$

29. From an applicant pool of 10 people, 5 must be chosen for Committee A, and then 2 must be chosen for Committee B. If a person can be chosen for only one committee, how many possible committees could be formed?

   (A) 2520
   (B) 2490
   (C) 2180
   (D) 2000
   (E) 1900

30. A line is represented by the parametric equations $x = 5 - 3t$ and $y = 2 + 3t$, where t is the parameter. Which of the following is the slope of the line?

   (A) $\dfrac{2 + 3t}{5 - 3t}$

   (B) $\dfrac{5 - 3t}{2 + 3t}$

   (C) −3

   (D) −1

   (E) 1

GO ON TO THE NEXT PAGE

31. $(-i)^k$ is a negative integer if $k =$

(A) 1021
(B) 1022
(C) 1023
(D) 1024
(E) 1025

2. If $f(x) = b^x$ and $f(x + 2) = 2.25 \cdot f(x)$, then $b =$

(A) 0.15
(B) 0.7
(C) 1.5
(D) 1.7
(E) 1.9

3. If $\sin x = 3 \cos x$ and $0 \le x \le \pi$, then $x =$

(A) 0.77
(B) 0.98
(C) 1.00
(D) 1.03
(E) 1.25

4. The statement "If the car costs less than $10,000, then Nick will purchase it" is true. Which of the following can be logically concluded based upon this statement?

I. If the car costs $20,000, then Nick will not purchase it.
II. If Nick did not purchase the car, then it did not cost less than $10,000.
III. If Nick purchased the car, then it cost less than $10,000.

(A) I only
(B) II only
(C) III only
(D) I and II only
(E) I, II, and III

GO ON TO THE NEXT PAGE

35. $\dfrac{(n+1)!}{n!} - \dfrac{(n-1)!}{n!} =$

   (A) $\dfrac{n^2 - 1}{n}$

   (B) $\dfrac{n + 1}{n}$

   (C) $\dfrac{n}{n^2 + n - 1}$

   (D) $\dfrac{n^2 + n - 1}{n}$

   (E) $\dfrac{n^2 + n + 1}{n}$

36. What is the range of the functioned defined by $f(x) = \dfrac{3}{x} + 3$?

   (A) All real numbers
   (B) All real numbers except –3
   (C) All real numbers except 0
   (D) All real numbers except 1
   (E) All real numbers except 3

37. If $\cos x = 0.78$ and $0 \le x \le \dfrac{\pi}{2}$, then $2\sin 2x =$

   (A) 0.78
   (B) 0.93
   (C) 1.52
   (D) 1.95
   (E) 2.01

38. If $\displaystyle\sum_{i=1}^{20} i = 210$, then what is the value of $\displaystyle\sum_{i=1}^{20} (2i + 1) =$

   (A) 440
   (B) 375
   (C) 352
   (D) 270
   (E) 210

39. S is the infinite collection of points located 2 units below the line $y = 3$. Any line containing the set S must be

   (A) perpendicular to $y = 3$
   (B) parallel to $y = 3$
   (C) transverse to $y = 3$
   (D) the same line as $y = 3$
   (E) none of the above

GO ON TO THE NEXT PAGE

40. If $f(x) = \dfrac{3x-1}{4}$ and $f(g(x)) = -2x$, then $g(x) =$

(A) $\dfrac{8x-1}{3}$

(B) $\dfrac{1+8x}{3}$

(C) $\dfrac{1-8x}{3}$

(D) $\dfrac{3-x}{8}$

(E) $\dfrac{3+x}{8}$

1. 2 and $\dfrac{2}{7}$ are the first and second terms, respectively, of a geometric sequence. What is the sum of the first 7 terms in the sequence?

(A) 4.00
(B) 3.17
(C) 3.00
(D) 2.67
(E) 2.33

. As x gets very large, which of the following functions will have the largest value?

(A) $f(x) = 2^x$

(B) $f(x) = x^2$

(C) $f(x) = 2x$

(D) $f(x) = x$

(E) $f(x) = \dfrac{1}{x}$

GO ON TO THE NEXT PAGE

43. In the parallelogram in Figure 4, what is the length of the diagonal AC?

(A) 7.77
(B) 9.85
(C) 12.01
(D) 15.34
(E) 16.97

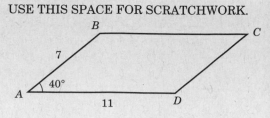

Figure 4

44. Company Q has estimated that the profits generated by the sales of its product Z can be modeled by the equation $p(x) = -x^2 + 3800x + 800000$ where $p(x)$ is the profit (in dollars), and x is the number of units manufactured. What is the maximum profit for Company Q (in millions of dollars)?

(A) 5.25
(B) 4.41
(C) 3.82
(D) 1.225
(E) 0.80

45. If $f(x) = \sqrt[5]{x^3 + 3}$, what is $f^{-1}(5)$?

(A) 8.5
(B) 10.7
(C) 12.2
(D) 14.6
(E) 16.8

46. If matrix $A = \begin{bmatrix} 1 & 0 \\ 0 & 1 \end{bmatrix}$ and matrix $B = \begin{bmatrix} 1 & 2 \\ 3 & 1 \end{bmatrix}$, which of the following is the matrix $2A + B$?

(A) $\begin{bmatrix} 2 & 2 \\ 3 & 2 \end{bmatrix}$

(B) $\begin{bmatrix} 3 & 2 \\ 2 & 3 \end{bmatrix}$

(C) $\begin{bmatrix} 3 & 2 \\ 3 & 3 \end{bmatrix}$

(D) $\begin{bmatrix} 3 & 3 \\ 3 & 3 \end{bmatrix}$

(E) $\begin{bmatrix} 3 & 4 \\ 5 & 6 \end{bmatrix}$

GO ON TO THE NEXT PAGE

47. $\triangle ABC$ has coordinates $A = (2, 5)$, $B = (5, 9)$, and $C = (1, 6)$. If each of these coordinates is doubled to create $\triangle DEF$, what is the ratio of the area of $\triangle DEF$ to the area of $\triangle ABC$?

(A) 8:1
(B) 4:1
(C) $2\sqrt{3}$:1
(D) $2\sqrt{2}$:1
(E) 2:1

48. The object in Figure 5 is a tetrahedron. If all of the edges of this tetrahedron are equal to 1, what is the total surface area of the tetrahedron?

(A) $4\sqrt{6}$
(B) $4\sqrt{3}$
(C) $3\sqrt{3}$
(D) $2\sqrt{3}$
(E) $\sqrt{3}$

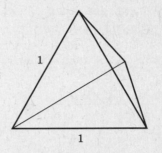

1

1

Figure 5

49. Given a set with 15 distinct elements, how many possible subsets are there containing either 2 or 3 elements?

(A) 560
(B) 620
(C) 720
(D) 810
(E) 990

GO ON TO THE NEXT PAGE

50. Which of the following graphs represents the solution set to
$|x| + |y| = 1$?

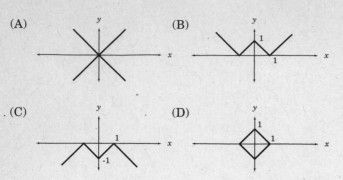

(A)   (B)

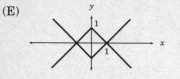

.(C)   (D)

(E)

S T O P

IF YOU FINISH BEFORE TIME IS CALLED, YOU MAY CHECK YOUR WORK ON THIS TEST ONLY.
DO NOT TURN TO ANY OTHER TEST IN THIS BOOK.

SAT II Math IIC
Practice Test 5
Explanations

Calculating Your Score

Question Number	Correct Answer	Right	Wrong	Question Number	Correct Answer	Right	Wrong	Question Number	Correct Answer	Right	Wrong
1.	C	—	—	18.	E	—	—	35.	D	—	—
2.	D	—	—	19.	D	—	—	36.	E	—	—
3.	B	—	—	20.	B	—	—	37.	D	—	—
4.	A	—	—	21.	D	—	—	38.	A	—	—
5.	E	—	—	22.	C	—	—	39.	B	—	—
6.	A	—	—	23.	A	—	—	40.	C	—	—
7.	C	—	—	24.	E	—	—	41.	E	—	—
8.	B	—	—	25.	B	—	—	42.	A	—	—
9.	D	—	—	26.	B	—	—	43.	E	—	—
10.	D	—	—	27.	D	—	—	44.	B	—	—
11.	E	—	—	28.	C	—	—	45.	D	—	—
12.	C	—	—	29.	A	—	—	46.	C	—	—
13.	B	—	—	30.	D	—	—	47.	B	—	—
14.	A	—	—	31.	B	—	—	48.	E	—	—
15.	C	—	—	32.	C	—	—	49.	A	—	—
16.	A	—	—	33.	E	—	—	50.	D	—	—
17.	D	—	—	34.	B	—	—				

Your raw score for the SAT II Math IIC test is calculated from the number of questions you answer correctly and incorrectly. Once you have determined your composite score, use the conversion table on page 18 of this book to calculate your scaled score. To calculate your raw score, count the number of questions you answered correctly: _____
A

Count the number of questions you answered incorrectly, and multiply that number by $\frac{1}{4}$:

_____ $\times \frac{1}{4}$ = _____
B   C

Subtract the value in field C from value in field A: _____
D

Round the number in field D to the nearest whole number. This is your raw score: _____
E

Test 5 Explanations

Math IIC Test 5 Explanations

1. (C) Algebra: Inequalities
This question tests your understanding of inequalities. If $x \le y$ and $y \le x$, then $x = y$ must be true.

2. (D) Fundamentals: Integers
The question says that x can be any negative or positive integer other than zero, and it asks you to find an expression that is positive for all values of x. When a nonzero integer is raised to an even exponent, the result is a positive integer. When a nonzero integer is raised to an odd exponent, the result is a negative integer. Choice (D) adds a positive integer, 2, to another positive integer, x^2; the sum of these positive integers must be positive too.

3. (B) Functions: Evaluating Functions
To find k, evaluate $f(1)$ and set the function equal to 0:

$$f(1) = -(1)^3 + 3(1)^2 + k(1) + 2$$
$$0 = -1 + 3 + k + 2$$
$$0 = 4 + k$$
$$-4 = k$$

4. (A) Fundamentals: Integers
Choose a value for n that leaves a remainder of 7 when divided by 9. For example, both 16 and 25 leave remainders of 7 when divided by 9. Set $n = 16$, and plug this value into $2n + 5$:

$$2n + 5 = 2(16) + 5$$
$$= 32 + 5$$
$$= 37$$

If you divide 37 by 9, you get a remainder of 1.

5. (E) Functions: Evaluating Functions
To find $f(t + 1)$, plug $x = (t + 1)$ into $f(x) = x^2 + x$:

$$f(t + 1) = (t + 1)^2 + (t + 1)$$
$$= t^2 + 2t + 1 + t + 1$$
$$= t^2 + 3t + 2$$

6. (A) Algebra: Writing Equations, Arithmetic Mean
John's average earnings are equal to the total money he made divided by the number of days it took him to earn it. In order to find the average amount he made over the last two days of work, you need to figure out the total amount he earned during that two-day period. If John made an average of d dollars per day for the first 3 days, then his earnings were $3d$ for those 3 days. If he made \$1200 total over the five days, then the amount he made in the last two days was $(1200 - 3d)$ dollars. Over the last two days, John earned an average of $\frac{1200 - 3d}{2} = 600 - \frac{3}{2}d$ dollars.

7. **(C)** *Functions: Compound Functions*

In order to solve the compound function $f(g(h(3)))$, you need to work from the inside out. First find $h(3)$ by plugging $x = 3$ into $h(x)$:

$$
\begin{aligned}
h(3) &= 3 \cdot (3) - 1 \\
&= 8
\end{aligned}
$$

Now plug $x = h(3) = 8$ into $g(x)$:

$$
\begin{aligned}
g(8) &= 8 + 1 \\
&= 9
\end{aligned}
$$

Now you can solve the problem by plugging $x = g(h(x)) = 9$ into $f(x)$:

$$
\begin{aligned}
f(9) &= 9^2 \\
&= 81
\end{aligned}
$$

8. **(B)** *Statistics: Arithmetic Mean*

The average of a and b is $\frac{a+b}{2}$, and the average of c, d, and e is $\frac{c+d+e}{3}$. Since the question says that these averages are equal, you can set up the equation $\frac{a+b}{2} = \frac{c+d+e}{3}$. When you cross multiply, you get: $3a + 3b = 2c + 2d + 2e$, so you know that option II must be true. Since you can't derive the equations in options I or III from $\frac{a+b}{2} = \frac{c+d+e}{3}$, you know that those options are not necessarily true.

9. **(D)** *Coordinate Geometry: Lines*

The midpoint of a line segment joining points (a, b) and (c, d) is given by $\left(\frac{a+c}{2}, \frac{b+d}{2}\right)$. Plug the given points into the midpoint formula:

$$
\begin{aligned}
\left(\frac{1.2 + 7.8}{2}, \frac{2.6 - 11}{2}\right) &= \left(\frac{9}{2}, \frac{-8.4}{2}\right) \\
&= (4.5, -4.2)
\end{aligned}
$$

10. **(D)** *Algebra: Equation Solving, Logarithms*

When the variable in an equation is an exponent, you should use logarithms to pull it down. Take the log of both sides of $2^x = 7$:

$$
\log 2^x = \log 7
$$

Since $\log A^x = x \log A$, you can rewrite the equation as:

$$
\begin{aligned}
x \log 2 &= \log 7 \\
x &= \frac{\log 7}{\log 2} \\
&= 2.807
\end{aligned}
$$

Multiply x by 2 to solve the problem: $2x = 5.61$.

11. (E) Algebra: Equation Solving

You need to rearrange this equation to find x in terms of y.

$$\frac{2x-1}{3x+4} = y$$
$$2x - 1 = (3x+4)y$$
$$2x - 1 = 3xy + 4y$$

You want to end up with all of the x terms on one side of the equation, so subtract $3xy$ from and add 1 to both sides of the equation:

$$2x - 3xy = 1 + 4y$$
$$x(2 - 3y) = 1 + 4y$$
$$x = \frac{1 + 4y}{2 - 3y}$$

12. (C) Solid Geometry: Solids that Aren't Prisms

Draw a right triangle and imagine rotating it around one of its axes:

As you can see, the rotated triangle creates a cone.

13. (B) Statistics: Probability

Finding the probability of picking a male sophomore out of the entire student body is the same as finding the fraction of male sophomores in the student body. The chart tells you that there are 190 male sophomores and 1600 students total. Thus the probability of picking a male sophomore is $\frac{190}{1600}$, or $\frac{19}{160}$.

14. (A) Algebra: Equation Solving, Logarithms

The definition of a logarithm will help you solve this problem. It says that $\log_b x = a$ is another way of writing $b^a = x$. Therefore, $\log_3 x = 4$ is a rewriting of $3^4 = x$. The answer is $x = 81$.

15. (C) Coordinate Geometry: Circles

The equation $x^2 + y^2 = 100$ tells you two things about the circle: one, that it's centered at the origin, and two, that its radius is $\sqrt{100} = 10$. If the point (a, b) lies on the circle $x^2 + y^2 = 100$, then (a, b) must be 10 units away from the origin. Using the distance formula, $D = \sqrt{a^2 + b^2}$, you know that $\sqrt{a^2 + b^2} = 10$. Plug the coordinates given in Figure 2 into this equation. Only choice (C) works:

$$D = \sqrt{a^2 + b^2}$$
$$10 = \sqrt{6^2 + (-8)^2}$$
$$= \sqrt{36 + 64}$$
$$= 10$$

16. **(A)** *Functions: Roots*

One way to answer this question is to graph the function on your calculator and count how many times the graph crosses the x-axis. You'll see that the function has no real zeros.

Another (more elegant) way to solve the problem is to use the function's discriminant. If $p(x) = ax^2 + bx + c$, then the discriminant of $p(x)$ is $b^2 - 4ac$. The discriminant tells you what kind of roots the function has. If $b^2 - 4ac = 0$, then the graph of the function touches the x-axis once. If $b^2 - 4ac > 0$, then the function crosses the x-axis twice and has two real roots. If $b^2 - 4ac < 0$, then the function never crosses the x-axis, and it has two complex roots. To figure out how many times $p(x) = -2x^2 + 3x - 7$ crosses the x-axis, plug its coefficients into the discriminant. The coefficients of $p(x)$ are $a = -2$, $b = 3$, and $c = -7$.

$$
\begin{aligned}
b^2 - 4ac &= 3^2 - 4(-2)(-7) \\
&= 9 - 56 \\
&= -47
\end{aligned}
$$

Since the discriminant is less than zero, you know that $p(x)$ never crosses the x-axis.

17. **(D)** *Trigonometry: Graphing Trigonometric Functions*

You should definitely know the domains and ranges of common trigonometric functions for Math IIC. The domain of $\cos(x)$ includes all real numbers, and its range is $-1 \le \cos(x) \le 1$. If $f(x) = 2\cos(x)$, then the range of the function is $-2 \le 2\cos(x) \le 2$, since doubling $\cos(x)$ also doubles its range. The answer to this question is $-2 \le f(x) \le 2$. You can double check your answer by graphing $f(x)$.

18. **(E)** *Miscellaneous Math: Sequences and Series*

In a geometric sequence, the ratio between successive terms is constant. To find the n-th term in a geometric sequence, use the formula $b_n = b_1 r^{n-1}$, where b_n is the n-th term, b_1 is the first term, and r is the ratio between terms. The question tells you that $b_1 = 3$ and $b_4 = \frac{3}{8}$. Plug these terms into the formula to find the ratio r:

$$
\begin{aligned}
\frac{3}{8} &= 3 \cdot r^{4-1} \\
&= 3 \cdot r^3 \\
\frac{1}{8} &= r^3 \\
r &= \frac{1}{2}
\end{aligned}
$$

Now find the twentieth term by plugging the first term and the ratio into the formula:

$$
\begin{aligned}
b_{20} &= b_1 r^{20-1} \\
b_{20} &= 3\left(\frac{1}{2}\right)^{20-1} \\
&= 3\left(\frac{1}{2}\right)^{19} \\
&= 3(2^{-19})
\end{aligned}
$$

19. (D) *Functions: Evaluating Functions*

The function $f(x) = \dfrac{x-2}{(x+2)(x^2+9)}$ is undefined when a value of x makes the denominator equal to zero.

Set each factor in the denominator equal to zero:

$$x + 2 = 0$$
$$x = -2$$

If $x = -2$, then $f(x)$ is undefined. Now try setting $(x^2 + 9)$ equal to zero:

$$x^2 + 9 = 0$$
$$x^2 = -9$$
$$x = \sqrt{-9}$$

There is no real value of x that makes the function undefined since the square root of a negative number is imaginary. $x = -2$ is the only value at which $f(x)$ is undefined.

20. (B) *Solid Geometry: Prisms*

Both the volume and the surface area of a cube depend on the length of its sides. You can figure out the length of the sides of the large cube using the volume formula: $V = s^3$. The question says that the large cube's volume is 216:

$$s^3 = 216$$
$$s = 6$$

You can figure out the surface area of the large cube by plugging s into the surface area formula: $SA = 6s^2$:

$$SA = 6(6^2)$$
$$= 216$$

The question says that the large cube is cut into 27 identical small cubes. The volume of each of these cubes must be $\dfrac{1}{27}$-th the large cube's volume, so each of them has a volume of $\dfrac{216}{27} = 8$. To figure out the length of the small cube's sides, plug 8 into the volume formula: $8 = s^3$ and $s = 2$. Now you can determine the surface area of the small cube:

$$SA = 6(2^2)$$
$$= 24$$

The ratio of the large cube's surface area to the small cube's surface area is: $\dfrac{SA_{\text{large cube}}}{SA_{\text{small cube}}} = \dfrac{216}{24} = \dfrac{9}{1}$, or 9:1.

21. (D) *Trigonometry: Basic Functions*

When you see cosecant, secant, or cotangent in a trig problem, you should almost always rewrite the function in terms of sine or cosine. Since $\csc x = \dfrac{1}{\sin x}$ and $\sec x = \dfrac{1}{\cos x}$, you can rewrite the question as:

$$\frac{\csc x}{\sec x} = \frac{\frac{1}{\sin x}}{\frac{1}{\cos x}}$$

$$= \frac{\cos x}{\sin x}$$

$$= \cot x$$

22. **(C)** *Functions: Inverse Functions*

The inverse function of $f(x) = e^x$ is $f^{-1}(x) = \ln(x)$. You should memorize this inversion since it appears frequently in math problems. If you don't have it memorized, you can derive it using three steps:

1) Replace $f(x)$ with y:

$$y = e^x$$

2) Switch y and x:

$$x = e^y$$

3) Solve for y. In this case, take the ln of both sides of the equation:

$$\ln x = \ln e^y$$
$$\ln x = y \ln e$$

Since $\ln e = 1$, you end up with $y = \ln x$.

If you graph $g(x) = \ln x$, you'll see that the function crosses the x-axis at $x = 1$. You can also calculate the y-intercept by plugging $y = 0$ into the equation and solving for x. If $0 = \ln x$, then $e^0 = x$ and $x = 1$.

23. **(A)** *Functions: Evaluating Functions, Graphing Functions*

In order to graph $y = f(x^2)$, you first need to evaluate $f(x^2)$ by plugging x^2 into $f(x) = \dfrac{1}{x}$:

$$f(x^2) = \frac{1}{x^2}$$

Now graph $y = \dfrac{1}{x^2}$ on your calculator:

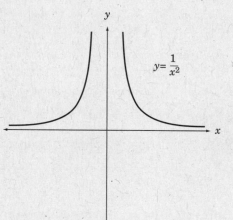

This graph matches the graph in choice (A), which is the correct answer.

24. **(E)** *Trigonometry: Inverse Trigonometric Functions*

Don't try to solve this problem by using the angle addition formula. Instead, you should use inverse trig:

$$\tan\frac{\pi}{6} = \cos\left(\frac{\pi}{3} + \theta\right)$$
$$\frac{\sqrt{3}}{3} = \cos\left(\frac{\pi}{3} + \theta\right)$$

Now take the inverse cosine of both sides of the equation:

$$\cos^{-1}\left(\frac{\sqrt{3}}{3}\right) = \frac{\pi}{3} + \theta$$

$$\cos^{-1}\left(\frac{\sqrt{3}}{3}\right) - \frac{\pi}{3} = \theta$$

$$\theta = 0.9553 - 1.0472$$

$$= -0.09$$

25. **(B)** *Coordinate Geometry: Ellipses*

The question tells you that the general equation of an ellipse is $\frac{(x-h)^2}{a^2} + \frac{(y-k)^2}{b^2} = 1$ and that the area of an ellipse is πab. According to the general equation, in the ellipse $\frac{(x-2)^2}{48} + \frac{(y-3)^2}{27} = 1$, $a^2 = 48$, and $b^2 = 27$; thus $a = 4\sqrt{3}$ and $b = 3\sqrt{3}$. Plug these values for a and b into the area formula: $A = \pi ab$.

$$A = \pi(4\sqrt{3})(3\sqrt{3})$$

$$= \pi 12(3)$$

$$= 36\pi$$

26. **(B)** *Plane Geometry: Triangles, Trigonometry: Basic Functions*

If you have a triangle with sides a, b, and an included angle θ, you can find the area of the triangle using the formula, $A = \frac{1}{2}ab\sin\theta$. This formula is the same as $A = \frac{1}{2}bh$, but h is rewritten as $b\sin\theta$:

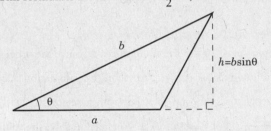

Plug the two sides, 19 and 7, and the included angle, 21°, into the area formula:

$$A = \frac{1}{2}(7)(19)\sin 21°$$

$$= 66.5 \cdot \sin 21°$$

$$= 23.83$$

27. **(D)** *Miscellaneous Math: Limits*

This question asks you to find the limit of $f(x)$ as x approaches 2. You can answer this question by graphing $f(x)$ on your calculator and seeing what value y approaches as x gets closer to 2.

You can also answer this question by factoring the function into its simplest form:

$$f(x) = \frac{x^2 + 5x - 14}{x - 2}$$

$$= \frac{(x-2)(x+7)}{x-2}$$

$$= x + 7$$

Now plug $x = 2$ into this simplified form of $f(x)$:

$$f(2) = 2 + 7$$
$$= 9$$

As x approaches 2, $f(x)$ approaches 9.

28. **(C)** *Algebra: Polynomials*

The question tells you that $(x + 2)$ is a factor of the polynomial $x^3 - cx^2 - 4x + 3$. The word "factor" should tip you off to use polynomial long division to solve this problem. The polynomial version of long division says that any polynomial $P(x)$ can be written $P(x) = (x - a) \cdot Q(x) + R$, where $(x - a)$ is the divisor, $Q(x)$ is the quotient, and R is the remainder. The remainder R can be found by plugging a into $P(x)$, since $P(a) = (a - a) \cdot Q(a) + R = R$.

There are two unknown variables in this question: x and c. Since you want to solve for c, you need to make c the only unknown in an equation. You can do this by plugging in a value for x that will give you a value you've already determined for $P(x)$, such as $P(a) = R$. In this question, $a = -2$, since $(x + 2)$ is the divisor $(x - a)$. Because $(x + 2)$ is a factor of $P(x)$, it divides $P(x)$ evenly, leaving no remainder. Since $R = 0$, you know $P(a) = 0$. You can solve for c by setting $P(a) = 0$ and plugging in $a = -2$:

$$(-2)^3 - c(-2)^2 - 4(-2) + 3 = 0$$
$$-8 - 4c + 8 + 3 = 0$$
$$-4c = -3$$
$$c = \frac{3}{4}$$

29. **(A)** *Statistics: Permutations and Combinations*

You need to choose 5 people out of 10 to form Committee A. Since the order in which you pick these 5 people doesn't matter, you should realize that you're solving a combination. A combination is represented as $\binom{n}{r}$, where r is the size of the subgroup selected from a set of size n. The formula for solving a combination is $\binom{n}{r} = \frac{n!}{r!(n - r)!}$. For Committee A, you need to solve the combination $\binom{10}{5}$:

$$\binom{10}{5} = \frac{10!}{5!(10 - 5)!}$$
$$= 252$$

There are 252 possible arrangements of Committee A.

Now you need to determine how many combinations there are of Committee B. The 2 members on Committee B are selected from the group of people *not* selected for Committee A, so you're selecting 2 out of 5 people. Solve the combination $\binom{5}{2}$:

$$\binom{5}{2} = \frac{5!}{2!(5 - 2)!}$$
$$= 10$$

There are 10 possible arrangements of Committee B.

The total number of possible arrangements is equal to the combinations of Committee A multiplied by the combinations of Committee B: $\binom{10}{5} \cdot \binom{5}{2} = 252 \cdot 10 = 2520$ possible arrangements.

30. **(D)** *Coordinate Geometry: Parametric Equations*

You need to find the slope of the line represented by the equations $y = 2 + 3t$ and $x = 5 - 3t$. The best way to find the slope is to eliminate the parameter t and write an equation in terms of $y = mx + b$, where m is the slope of the line. Your first step should be to solve the equation $x = 5 - 3t$ in terms of $3t$, since the term $3t$ also appears in $y = 2 + 3t$:

$$x - 5 = -3t$$
$$5 - x = 3t$$

Substitute this expression for $3t$ into $y = 2 + 3t$:

$$y = 2 + 3t$$
$$= 2 + (5 - x)$$
$$= 7 - x$$
$$y = -x + 7$$

This equation shows you that the slope m equals -1.

31. **(B)** *Miscellaneous Math: Complex Numbers*

For the Math IIC, you need to know what happens to the powers of i:

$$i^1 = i$$
$$i^2 = -1$$
$$i^3 = -i$$
$$i^4 = 1$$

When you raise i to an exponent larger than 4, you can figure out the value of the expression by dividing the exponent by 4 and looking at the remainder. If 4 divides the exponent evenly, leaving a remainder of 0, then the expression is equivalent to $i^4 = 1$. If the division leaves a remainder of 1, then the expression is equivalent to $i^1 = i$. If you get a remainder of 2, then the expression is equivalent to $i^2 = -1$. If the remainder is 3, then the expression is equivalent to $i^3 = -i$.

Use the law of exponents to rewrite $(-i)^k$ as $(-1)^k (i)^k$. The question tells you that $(-i)^k$ equals a negative integer, so you know that k must be an even number, since even exponents produce the integers 1 or -1. If k is even, then $(-1)^k = 1$ and $(-1)^k (i)^k = (i)^k$. In order for $(i)^k$ to equal -1, k must leave a remainder of 2 when divided by 4. Divide each of the answer choices by 4 and see what remainder each division produces. Only choice (B), 1022, leaves a remainder of 2, so it is the correct answer.

32. **(C)** *Algebra: Equation Solving, Exponents*

The question tells you that $f(x + 2) = 2.25 \cdot f(x)$, or $f(x + 2) = 2.25 \cdot b^x$. You can also find $f(x + 2)$ by plugging $(x + 2)$ into $f(x)$:

$$f(x + 2) = b^{x+2}$$
$$= b^x \cdot b^2$$

Now you can solve for b by setting these two expressions for $f(x + 2)$ equal to each other.

$$b^x \cdot b^2 = 2.25 \cdot b^x$$
$$b^2 = 2.25$$
$$b = \sqrt{2.25}$$
$$= 1.5$$

33. **(E)** *Trigonometry: Basic Functions, Inverse Trigonometric Functions*

In this trigonometric equation, $\sin x$ and $\cos x$ are on opposite sides of the equal sign. You can divide through by $\cos x$ to isolate x on one side of the equation.

$$\sin x = 3\cos x$$

$$\frac{\sin x}{\cos x} = 3$$

$$\tan x = 3$$

Now you can solve for x by taking the inverse tangent of 3. Make sure that your calculator is set to radians.

$$x = \tan^{-1}(3)$$

$$= 1.25$$

34. **(B)** *Miscellaneous Math: Logic*

Logic statements appear in the form of "If p, then q." The Math IIC primarily tests one rule of logic associated with such statements: when you have "If p, then q," its contrapositive, "If *not* q, then *not* p," is always true. You form the contrapositive of "If p, then q" by switching p and q and then negating each of them (in other words, putting "not" in front of each): "if *not* q, then *not* p." In this question, the statement "If the car costs less that \$10,000, then Nick will purchase it" is logically equivalent to the statement "If Nick *did not purchase the car*, then it *did not cost less than \$10,000*." The contrapositive is the only statement that is logically equivalent to the original, so choice (B) is correct.

35. **(D)** *Statistics: Factorials*

This problem may look complicated, but each expression simplifies because of the factorial in the denominator.

$$\frac{(n+1)!}{n!} - \frac{(n-1)!}{n!} = \frac{(n+1)(n)(n-1)\ldots(1)}{(n)(n-1)\ldots(1)} - \frac{(n-1)\ldots(1)}{(n)(n-1)\ldots(1)}$$

$$= (n+1) - \left(\frac{1}{n}\right)$$

$$= \frac{n^2 + n - 1}{n}$$

36. **(E)** *Functions: Domain and Range*

A simple way to solve this problem is to graph the function on your calculator and look for any holes or horizontal asymptotes. The main danger with this approach is that you risk missing any holes that appear outside the calculator's window.

You can avoid making this mistake by solving the range by hand. Take the function $f(x) = \frac{3}{x} + 3$ and solve for x:

$$f(x) - 3 = \frac{3}{x}$$

$$x = \frac{3}{f(x) - 3}$$

From this equation, you can see that $f(x) \neq 3$. If $f(x)$ equals 3, then the denominator becomes zero, and x is undefined.

37. **(D)** *Trigonometry: Inverse Trigonometric Functions*

Find x by taking the inverse cosine of 0.78; then plug the value of x into $2\sin 2x$. When you solve $\cos^{-1}(0.78)$ on your calculator, make sure to set the mode to radians.

$$x = \cos^{-1}(0.78)$$
$$= 0.68$$

Plug $x = 0.68$ into $2\sin 2x$:

$$2\sin(2 \cdot 0.68) = 2\sin(1.36)$$
$$= 1.95$$

38. **(A)** *Miscellaneous Math: Summation Notation*

Summation notation rarely appears on the Math IIC, but you need to be prepared in case it does. The notation $\sum_{i=1}^{20} i$ means that you add the variable i to itself 20 times and that initially $i = 1$, then $i = 2$, then $i = 3$, and so on up until $i = 20$; in other words, $\sum_{i=1}^{20} i = 1 + 2 + \ldots + 20$. Multiplying i by a constant is the same as multiplying the entire summation by that constant: $\sum_{i=1}^{20} 2i = 2\sum_{i=1}^{20} i$. The notation $\sum_{i=1}^{20} 1$ means that you add 1 to itself 20 times. Additionally, $\sum_{i=1}^{20} (2i + 1)$ splits into the two summations $2\sum_{i=1}^{20} i + \sum_{i=1}^{20} 1$:

$$\sum_{i=1}^{20} (2i + 1) = 2\sum_{i=1}^{20} i + \sum_{i=1}^{20} 1$$
$$= 2\sum_{i=1}^{20} i + 20$$
$$= 2(210) + 20$$
$$= 440$$

39. **(B)** *Plane Geometry: Geometrical Reasoning*

Draw a coordinate plane with the line $y = 3$. Next add an "infinite" set of points 2 units below the line $y = 3$:

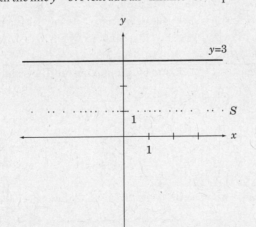

As you can see from this picture, S, the "infinite" set of points, forms a line that is parallel to the line $y = 3$. Choice (B) is correct.

40. **(C)** *Functions: Compound Functions*

You're asked to find $g(x)$ given $f(x) = \frac{3x-1}{4}$ and $f(g(x)) = -2x$. To simplify the problem, replace $g(x)$ with y, so you have $f(y) = -2x$. You can find another expression for $f(y)$ by plugging y into $f(x)$:

$$f(x) = \frac{3x-1}{4}$$
$$f(y) = \frac{3y-1}{4}$$

Set this expression for $f(y)$ equal to $-2x$, and solve for y:

$$-2x = \frac{3y-1}{4}$$
$$-8x = 3y - 1$$
$$1 - 8x = 3y$$
$$\frac{1-8x}{3} = y$$

Since $y = g(x)$, you've solved the problem: $g(x) = \frac{1-8x}{3}$.

41. **(E)** *Miscellaneous Math: Sequences and Series*

In a geometric series, the ratio between successive terms is constant. You should memorize the formula for finding the sum of the first n terms in a geometric sequence: $S_n = \frac{b_1(1-r^n)}{1-r}$, where S_n is the sum of the first n terms, b_1 is the first term in the sequence, and r is the ratio between terms. The question gives you the first and second terms of the sequence. You can determine the ratio by dividing the second term by the first: $\frac{2}{7} \div 2 = \frac{1}{7}$. Plug $b_1 = 2$, $r = \frac{1}{7}$, and $n = 7$ into the formula to find the sum of the first 7 terms:

$$S_7 = \frac{2\left(1 - \left(\frac{1}{7}\right)^7\right)}{1 - \frac{1}{7}}$$

$$= 2.33$$

42. **(A)** *Functions: Evaluating Functions*

Choose a large value for x, such as $x = 1000$, and plug it into the functions in the answer choices:

$$\text{Choice (A): } 2^{1000} \approx 1 \times 10^{301}$$
$$\text{Choice (B): } (1000)^2 = 1 \times 10^6$$
$$\text{Choice (C): } 2(1000) = 2 \times 10^3$$
$$\text{Choice (D): } 1000 = 1 \times 10^3$$
$$\text{Choice (E): } \frac{1}{1000} = 1 \times 10^{-3}$$

Choice (A) is correct because it produces the largest value of all the answer choices.

43. **(E)** *Trigonometry: Solving Non-Right Triangles*

In parallelograms, consecutive angles are supplementary; in other words, two adjacent angles in a parallelogram add up to 180°. Since $\angle A = 40°$, $\angle D = 140°$.

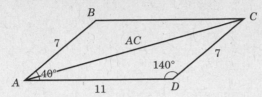

As you can see above, $\triangle ADC$ is a non-right triangle with sides 7 and 11 and an angle of 140°. When you have two sides and an angle of a non-right triangle, you can solve the triangle using the law of cosines. The law of cosines says that $c^2 = a^2 + b^2 - 2ab\cos C$, where a, b, and c are the triangle's sides, and C is the angle opposite side c. Plug the triangle in this problem into the law of cosines:

$$(AC)^2 = (AD)^2 + (DC)^2 - 2(AD)(DC)\cos D$$
$$(AC)^2 = 11^2 + 7^2 - 2(11)(7)\cos 140°$$
$$= 170 - 154\cos 140°$$

Take the square root of both sides of the equation:

$$AC = \sqrt{170 - 154\cos 140°}$$
$$= 16.97$$

44. **(B)** *Functions: Graphing Functions*

The easiest way to solve this problem is to graph $y = -x^2 + 3800x + 800000$ on your calculator. The maximum profit for the company is the y-coordinate at the vertex of the parabola. Make the window of your calculator big enough to see the vertex:

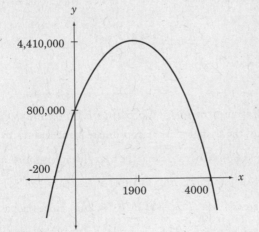

The vertex of the parabola occurs when $x = 1900$ and $y = 4,410,000$. Choice (B), which says that the maximum profit is 4.41 million, is correct.

45. **(D)** *Functions: Inverse Functions*

There are three steps for solving the inverse function of $f(x) = \sqrt[5]{x^3 + 3}$. First, replace $f(x)$ with y:

$$y = \sqrt[5]{x^3 + 3}$$

Second, switch the positions of x and y:

$$x = \sqrt[5]{y^3 + 3}$$

Third, solve for y:

$$x = \sqrt[5]{y^3 + 3}$$
$$x^5 = y^3 + 3$$
$$x^5 - 3 = y^3$$
$$\sqrt[3]{x^5 - 3} = y$$

This equation is the inverse function of $f(x)$. Plug $x = 5$ into $f^{-1}(x) = \sqrt[3]{x^5 - 3}$:

$$f^{-1}(5) = \sqrt[3]{(5)^5 - 3}$$
$$= 14.6$$

46. **(C)** *Miscellaneous Math: Matrices*

Matrix questions rarely appear on the Math IIC; when they do, they tend to be straightforward tests of operations. This question asks you to solve $2A + B$, where $A = \begin{bmatrix} 1 & 0 \\ 0 & 1 \end{bmatrix}$ and $B = \begin{bmatrix} 1 & 2 \\ 3 & 1 \end{bmatrix}$. Multiplying a matrix by a constant, such as 2, is the same as multiplying each term inside the matrix by that constant. Find $2A$:

$$2A = 2\begin{bmatrix} 1 & 0 \\ 0 & 1 \end{bmatrix}$$

$$= \begin{bmatrix} 2 & 0 \\ 0 & 2 \end{bmatrix}$$

When you add two matrices, simply add together the corresponding terms in each:

$$2A + B = \begin{bmatrix} 2 & 0 \\ 0 & 2 \end{bmatrix} + \begin{bmatrix} 1 & 2 \\ 3 & 1 \end{bmatrix}$$

$$= \begin{bmatrix} (2+1) & (0+2) \\ (0+3) & (2+1) \end{bmatrix}$$

$$= \begin{bmatrix} 3 & 2 \\ 3 & 3 \end{bmatrix}$$

47. **(B)** *Plane Geometry: Triangles; Coordinate Geometry: Coordinate Plane*

You'll waste time if you plot the triangles in the coordinate plane and try to figure out their areas. The easiest way to answer this question is to realize that the triangles are proportionally similar, since each side in $\triangle DEF$ is twice as long as each side in $\triangle ABC$. The area of $\triangle ABC$ is $\frac{1}{2}bh$, where b is the base and h is the height of the triangle. The area of $\triangle DEF$ is $\frac{1}{2}(2b)(2h) = 2bh$, since the base and height of $\triangle DEF$ are twice the length of the base and height of $\triangle ABC$. To find the ratio of the areas, divide the area of $\triangle DEF$ by the area of $\triangle ABC$: $\frac{2bh}{\frac{1}{2}bh} = \frac{4}{1}$. In other words, the area of $\triangle DEF$ is four times the area of $\triangle ABC$.

48. (E) *Solid Geometry: Solids that Aren't Prisms*

A tetrahedron has four identical faces. If all of the edges in the tetrahedron are equal to 1, then each face of the tetrahedron is an equilateral triangle with sides of length 1. To find the surface area of the tetrahedron, find the area of the equilateral triangle, and multiply the triangle's area by 4. The area of the triangle is equal to $\frac{1}{2}bh$, where b is the base and h is the height of the triangle. The base of the triangle is 1; you can figure out the height of the triangle using right triangle trig or the Pythagorean Theorem.

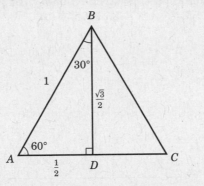

Since $\triangle ABD$ is a 30-60-90 triangle and since $AB = 1$, you know that $AD = \frac{1}{2}$ and $DB = \frac{\sqrt{3}}{2}$. You can also find DB by using the Pythagorean Theorem, since you know two sides of the triangle: AB and AD (which is half the length of AB).

Plug the base and the height into the area formula:

$$\text{Area}_{\triangle ABC} = \frac{1}{2}(1)\left(\sqrt{\frac{3}{2}}\right)$$
$$= \frac{\sqrt{3}}{4}$$

Multiply the area of the triangle by 4 to find the surface area of the tetrahedron:

$$SA_{tetrahedron} = 4\left(\frac{\sqrt{3}}{4}\right)$$
$$= \sqrt{3}$$

49. (A) *Statistics: Permutations and Combinations*

Since the ordering of the elements in the subsets doesn't matter, you want to solve a combination $\binom{n}{r}$, where r is the size of the subset made from a set of size n. The combination $\binom{n}{r}$, which is sometimes denoted $_nC_r$ on calculators, is calculated as $\frac{n!}{r!(n-r)!}$. First figure out the number of subsets with 2 elements by calculating $\binom{15}{2}$:

$$\frac{15!}{2!(15-2)!} = \frac{15 \cdot 14}{2 \cdot 1}$$
$$= 105$$

Now figure out the number of subsets with 3 elements by calculating $\binom{15}{3}$:

$$\frac{15!}{3!(15-3)!} = \frac{15 \cdot 14 \cdot 13}{3 \cdot 2 \cdot 1}$$
$$= 455$$

To find the total number of subsets containing either 2 or 3 elements, simply add the number of combinations:

$$\binom{15}{2} + \binom{15}{3} = 105 + 455$$
$$= 560$$

50. **(D)** *Functions: Graphing Functions, Absolute Value*

In order to graph $|x| + |y| = 1$, you need to break the function into pieces. Rearrange the equation as $|y| = 1 - |x|$. Since this equation involves the absolute value of y, you should realize that y can take on two different values. The absolute value of y can be broken down as:

$$y = \begin{cases} 1 - |x| & y \geq 0 \\ |x| - 1 & y < 0 \end{cases}, \text{ since } y = \begin{cases} y & y \geq 0 \\ -y & y < 0 \end{cases}$$

Graph $y = 1 - |x|$ and $y = |x| - 1$ on your calculator:

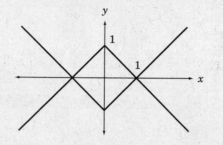

Since the original equation says that $|x| + |y| = 1$, the domain of the function is $-1 \leq x \leq 1$ and the range is $-1 \leq y \leq 1$, so choice (D) is correct.

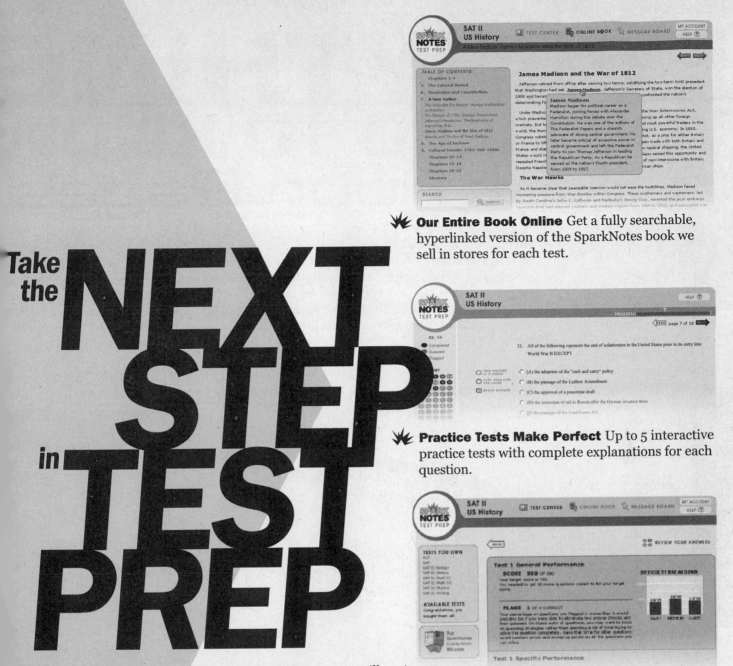

Take the NEXT STEP in TEST PREP

SparkNotes™ interactive online test preparation system will raise your scores on the SAT, ACT, and SAT II subject tests in Biology, Physics, U.S. History, Math IC and IIC, and Writing.

testprep.sparknotes.com

Our Entire Book Online Get a fully searchable, hyperlinked version of the SparkNotes book we sell in stores for each test.

Practice Tests Make Perfect Up to 5 interactive practice tests with complete explanations for each question.

Instant Diagnostic Feedback Get instant results: overall score, strengths, weaknesses, progress. Then see a personalized study plan that links back to the book.

Don't Go It Alone Message boards connect you to other students taking the same test you are.

Awesome and Affordable We've made test prep dynamic, interactive, and affordable. At $14.95 it's the best deal online or off.

SPARKCHARTS™

EVERYTHING
YOU NEED TO KNOW
in Just Four Pages

Accounting
Algebra I
Algebra II
Calculus II
Chemistry
Circulatory System
Digestive System
English Composition
English Grammar
Essays & Term Papers
Finance
French Grammar
French Vocabulary
General Anatomy
Geometry
Macroeconomics
Math Basics
Microbiology
Microeconomics
Muscular System
Mythology
Periodic Table
   with Chemistry Formulas
Philosophy
Physics
Physics Formulas
Pre-Calculus
Psychology
Reproductive System
Resumes & Cover Letters
SAT Math
SAT Verbal
SAT Vocabulary
Shakespeare
Skeletal System
Spanish Grammar
Spanish Vocabulary
Statistics
Trigonometry
U.S. Constitution
U.S. Government
U.S. History 1865–2002
Weights & Measures
Western Civilization
World History

...and more.

Imagine if the top student in your course organized the most important points from your textbook or lecture into an easy-to-read, laminated chart that could fit directly into your notebook or binder. SparkCharts are study companions and reference tools that cover a wide range of subjects, including Math, Science, History, Business, Humanities, Foreign Language, and Writing. Titles like Presentations and Public Speaking, Essays and Term Papers, and Test Prep give you what it takes to find success in high school, college, and beyond.

Outlines and summaries cover key points, while diagrams and tables make difficult conce easier to digest. All for the price of that late-night cappuccino you'll no longer need!

Time to cut standardized tests down to size.